P9-DEB-018

THE SIXTH GRADE DROPOUT
WHO ASTOUNDED THE SCIENTIFIC
EXPERTS OF THE WORLD!

Edgar Cayce was a grade school dropout, yet doctors and therapists throughout the country are now successfully treating arthritis, psoriasis, abdominal disorders and innumerable other complaints, by following the advice he prescribed in thousands of clairvoyant readings.

His deathless legacy of medical readings—containing clues to the control and cure of such diseases as cancer and rheumatism—are being studied by knowledgeable scientists today.

Here is the startling biography of America's greatest mystic, written by Jess Stearn, the only trained researcher and reporter to gain complete access to the prophet's previously unavailable case histories and medical readings. Journalist Stearn employed a geologist from Harvard, experts in medicine, and scientists in many diverse fields to examine the technical material left by Edgar Cayce. Mr. Stearn personally interviewed many of the people for whom Cayce had done readings and effected cures. The result of his incisive research adds much to the growing legend of Cayce's amazing abilities. Here is the whole fascinating story of the humble and, perhaps, most fantastically gifted prophet of all time!

DIANE KUZMESKI

"In addition to all the destruction he saw, Cayce also saw the passage of world events. He saw wars and peace, depressions, racial strife, labor wars, even the Great Society, which he saw doomed to failure. He saw things for individuals, as well as for nations, predicting that they would marry, divorce, have children, become lawyers, doctors, architects, sailors, and marines. Most of his prophetic impressions came during his sleep-readings, but he was spontaneously psychic in his waking state, and fled from a room full of young people once because he saw instantly that all would go to war, and three would not come back.

"His batting average on predictions was incredibly high, close to one hundred percent . . . So much of what he said has come so miraculously true . . ."

—Jess Stearn

Bantam Books by Jess Stearn

EDGAR CAYCE—THE SLEEPING PROPHET
SOULMATES
YOGA, YOUTH, AND REINCARNATION

D. KUZMESKI 1988

EDGAR CAYCE —
THE SLEEPING PROPHET
Jess Stearn

BANTAM BOOKS

TORONTO • NEW YORK • LONDON • SYDNEY • AUCKLAND

*This low-priced Bantam Book
has been completely reset in a type face
designed for easy reading, and was printed
from new plates. It contains the complete
text of the original hard-cover edition.*
NOT ONE WORD HAS BEEN OMITTED.

EDGAR CAYCE—THE SLEEPING PROPHET
*A Bantam Book / published by arrangement with
Doubleday & Company, Inc.*

PRINTING HISTORY
Doubleday edition published January 1967

2nd printing ... January 1967	5th printing .... March 1967
3rd printing .. February 1967	6th printing ..... April 1967
4th printing .... March 1967	7th printing ..... June 1967

*Mystic Arts Book Society edition published July 1967
Bantam edition / January 1968
29 printings through April 1986*

*All rights reserved.
Copyright © 1967 by Jess Stearn.
This book may not be reproduced in whole or in part, by
mimeograph or any other means, without permission.
For information address: Doubleday & Company, Inc.,
245 Park Avenue, New York, N.Y. 10167.*

ISBN 0-553-26085-5

Published simultaneously in the United States and Canada

*Bantam Books are published by Bantam Books, Inc. Its trade-
mark, consisting of the words "Bantam Books" and the por-
trayal of a rooster, is Registered in U.S. Patent and Trademark
Office and in other countries. Marca Registrada. Bantam
Books, Inc., 666 Fifth Avenue, New York, New York 10103.*

PRINTED IN THE UNITED STATES OF AMERICA

KR   38 37 36 35 34 33 32 31 30

WITH THANKS TO BOB AND ISABEL ADRIANCE,
WHO HELPED MORE THAN THEY KNEW.

God is our refuge and strength, a very present help in trouble. Therefore will not we fear, though the earth be removed, and though the mountains be carried into the midst of the sea.

Psalm 46

Contents

Chapter One

THE SLEEPING WONDER

It was like any other day for Edgar Cayce. He went to sleep, by merely lying down and closing his eyes, and then he started to talk in his sleep. But when he awakened a half-hour or so later, he realized from the faces of those around him that he must have said something very extraordinary. And he had. In trance, on that hot, sultry day of August 1941, in the same voice that he would have prescribed an innocent herb for somebody with the sniffles, he had predicted the destruction of most of Los Angeles, San Francisco, and New York.

The greatest mystic America had ever known reacted philosophically to his Cassandra-like prophecy. In the past, he had foreseen great wars and holocausts, and they had come to pass. From his own "readings," which had helped thousands, he had come to believe in an endless cycle of life, and though he could consciously grieve for those who knew sorrow or pain in this lifetime, he felt it was all part of God's plan. And so it was with a shake of the head and a shrug that he dismissed the forecast. "What do you make of that?" he said, scratching his head, "I hope it's wrong, but it's never been wrong before." "It" was the subconscious information, apparently the product of a Universal Mind, which had been streaming through him for forty years, and which were rather incongruously known as readings.

1

Cayce's forecast had come quite inadvertently, out of the same blue that produced his amazingly accurate diagnoses of ailing people whom he had never seen, and their consequent cures. As with other Cayce predictions, many of them already startlingly confirmed, the forecast was in response to a question that had little or nothing to do with the original request for the reading. A New York businessman, concerned not only by the continuing strain of big city life, but the threat of wartime bombing, had said to Cayce, "I have for many months felt that I should move out of New York."

"This is well, as indicated," the slumbering Cayce observed. "There is too much unrest; there will continue to be the character of vibrations that to the body will be disturbing, and eventually those destructive forces, though these will be in the next generation."

The businessman asked: "Will Los Angeles be safe?"

The answer came clearly, directly, without equivocation, "Los Angeles, San Francisco, most all of these will be among those that will be destroyed before New York even."

The mechanics of this destruction was neither asked, nor given. However, in keeping with other prognostications of Cayce's, it would appear that the destruction—if it comes—will be through the agency of Nature, and not the Bomb, unless, of course, it would be the Bomb that touched off a natural catastrophe.

The predicted destruction in this country, part of the general Cayce forecast of sweeping upheavals around the world, has been tabbed for the period beginning in 1958, and extending to the end of the century, when a new millennium will hopefully begin. Some of these preliminary changes, in the Mediterranean and the South Pacific, and in Alaska, have apparently already taken place, with Connecticut, New England, Alabama, Georgia, Japan, and northern Europe, among others still to be sharply affected. But it may be a comfort to many, as more than one geologist has noted, that the many cataclysmic events predicted by Cayce are out of harmony with the standard geological concept of uniformitarianism or gradual change. On the other hand, at least one leading geologist, erstwhile head of a college geology department, has checked out the Cayce readings, and sees as eminently possible the drastic earth changes merging out of Cayce's stated cause—the tilting of the earth's rotational axis, beginning far below the crust of the earth in 1936.

Cayce had a flair for prophecy and some even interpret a reading in 1939, shortly after the outbreak of World War II in Europe, as foreshadowing the current war in Vietnam. "Before that we find the entity [the complex of body, soul and spirit] was in the land now known as or called Indochina. . . . There we find the entity was one in authority, one in power, in that city that must be unfolded to the minds, if there is not the greater war over same." It was a disjointed excerpt from a past life reading, a Cayce specialty, and could be applied, if the French-Indochina war, which took the French out of Vietnam, was the lesser war. But one usually didn't have to look this hard for signs of Cayce predictions come true. He had foreseen, correctly, virtually every major world crisis, from before World War I, through the uneasy years of the League of Nations, and beyond through World War II, whose end he had predicted for 1945, the year of his own death. In the intervals, casually, while reading psychically for individuals, he picked off earthquakes, storms, volcanic eruptions. He not only saw far afield, but close at home, where his predictions making Norfolk-Newport News a preeminent port, greater even than New York, have rather remarkably materialized, along with his pinpointing of a local realty boom to the very year, nearly fifteen years after his own death.

Through the clear channel of his subconscious he peered down the corridors of time into the troubled international scene, describing the future of Russia, China, Japan, England, the United States. He foresaw England losing India, when nobody else did; he saw a free India unloved, because it was unloving, and he tied in the end of Communism with another and more astonishing prediction of a free God-fearing Russia. What he saw for China, eventual democratization, is certainly not being predicted, logically, anywhere else, and for an America, unconquerable, except through internal strife, he saw eventual world leadership, shared with another power, as the center of civilization gradually gravitated westward.

To me, Cayce was no new phenomenon. I had "discovered" him originally, five years before, in preparing my book, *The Door to the Future*. I had become familiar with many of his prophecies, his remarkable way of apparently traveling in time and space to treat the ill; his concept of reincarnation, with its concept of many lives for the same soul spirit. Cayce seemed gifted with a Universal Mind, which seemingly drew on a subconscious register of everything that had ever happened or was going to happen. It seemed an incredible quality, but as one studied Cayce, as he would any other individual, work or phenomenon, checking as he could with the evidence on hand, it became apparent that Cayce somehow, some way, was able to look inside of everything that fell into the realm of his unconscious—the human body and soul, the earth, the Universe itself. He was the man with the X-ray eyes.

In my current research, I soon became aware that the Cayce influence was stronger now than in his lifetime. It was almost as though a self-limiting world, softened up by flights to the moon, laser rays and television, was catching up posthumously to the sage who had sleep-talked of a forgotten civilization, technologically comparable with our own—the Lost Continent of Atlantis, a visionary experience shared with that great figure of antiquity, the philosopher Plato.

Twenty years after his death, the mystic's life work was thriving, slowly and painfully collected from thousands of readings and left as his legacy in the files of the Association for Research and Enlightenment in Virginia Beach. Scorned, generally, by the medical profession while alive, the dead Cayce, and his readings on disease, was now a magnet for the inquiring minds of distinguished medical researchers. "Cayce," one medical authority reported, "was one hundred years ahead of his time, medically, and one day we may rewrite the textbooks on physiology and anatomy to conform with his concept of health flowing out of a perfect harmony of blood, lymph, glands and nerves." Years before psychosomatic medicine, Cayce stressed that tensions and strains were responsible for stomach ulcers. In a benign Nature, he saw the remedy for any health deviation or illness man was heir to, though, at the same time, he realized that not everyone could be helped when their time was at hand. Thirty years before the revelation of a rabbit serum "cure" for cancer blazoned across the country's front pages in 1966, Cayce had prescribed such a serum for cancer cases, and described how it should be prepared. However, as he recommended it in only five cases of the seventy-eight he diagnosed as cancer, in his schemata it was obviously only helpful for certain cancers.

In the years since his death, five hundred healers of every

description—MDs, osteopaths, chiropractors, physiotherapists—have familiarized themselves with his methods, and in such diverse areas as Virginia, New York, Michigan, Arizona, Connecticut, and California, people who could get no help elsewhere are being successfully treated out of his readings. One woman was cured of a vaginal tumor by a therapist who had studied his Cayce well; again, dramatically, I learned of a man cured of incurable psoriasis, by a voice from the dead, so to speak. I sat and marveled, watching a distinguished American composer, a semi-invalid only a short time before, rolling around on the floor, doing the Cayce-inspired exercises that had magically loosened the arthritic joints of his shoulders, arms, and fingers. He was a new man, he told me gratefully, thanks to the dead Cayce.

There was little question of Cayce's healing force, for I was able to check this out with the hopelessly ill who had been helped. I spoke to therapists, principally osteopaths, whom he did not consciously know, to whom in his lifetime he directed patients. He had told one Staten Island mother, with an ailing child, "Find Dobbins," and her steps finally took her to a young osteopath, Dr. Frank Dobbins, so newly arrived to Staten Island that his name was not yet in the New York City telephone directory. And just as Cayce had not consciously known of him, so Dobbins had never heard of Cayce. The prescriptions he recommended were often as incomprehensible. Some had a dozen different ingredients, many of which the average pharmacist had never heard of, and yet Cayce himself was completely unschooled, never having gone beyond the sixth grade in his native Hopkinsville, Kentucky. Often the preparations were completely unknown. Once, for instance, he had recommended clary water for a man troubled with rheumatism. No druggist had heard of it. So the subject took an advertisement in a trade paper, asking how it might be obtained or compounded. From Paris, seeing the ad, a man wrote that his father had developed the product, but that production had been discontinued nearly fifty years before. He enclosed a copy of the original prescription. "You may have it duplicated if you wish." Meanwhile, Cayce had made a check reading, asking himself in trance how clary water could be made. His new information tallied exactly with the prescription from Paris.

How did he do it? Dr. Wesley H. Ketchum, an MD with an orthodox background, but an eclectic approach, used

Cayce as an adjunct to his practice for several years, styling him a Psychic Diagnostician, and he told an intrigued medical audience how Cayce functioned, according to Cayce's own description of his powers.

"Edgar Cayce's mind," Ketchum told a skeptical Boston medical group, "is amenable to suggestion, as are all other subconscious minds, but in addition it has the power to interpret what it acquires from the subconscious mind of other individuals. The subconscious mind forgets nothing. The conscious mind receives the impression from without and transfers all thoughts to the subconscious, where it remains even though the conscious be destroyed." Long before the humanist Jung advanced his concept of the collective unconscious, Cayce was apparently practicing what Jung only postulated. "Cayce's subconscious," Ketchum elaborated, "is in direct communication with all other subconscious minds, and is capable of interpreting through his objective mind and imparting impressions received to other objective minds, gathering in this way all knowledge possessed by endless millions of other subconscious minds."

Ketchum, who is still alive, and living in California, was particularly impressed because Cayce correctly told him he didn't have appendicitis, when seven doctors insisted he did, advising surgery. Cayce attributed the attacks to a wrenched spine, which had caused nerve impingements and peripheral pains, and recommended osteopathic adjustments. With Cayce's treatment, the condition cleared, and Ketchum was never troubled with "appendicitis" again. He had no quarrel with the doctors, for he had diagnosed his own case similarly—appendicitis.

As one examined his work, Cayce appeared to be not only healer but counselor and philosopher. Much before his time, he was aware that most bodily illness was born of the mind, of emotional frustrations, resentments, anger. He advised one woman to cleanse herself physically and mentally. "Keep the mental in the attitude of constructive forces. See in every individual that which is hopeful, helpful. Do not look for others' faults, but rather for their virtues, and the virtues in self will become magnified. For what we think upon, that we become." He told another woman bothered with chronic colds: "Instead of resentments, love; instead of snuffing, blow." It worked. She didn't have another cold for years, and her disposition today is sunny, her complexion the schoolgirl pink of a teen-ager, though she is in her sixties.

He applied the same philosophy to nations, stressing that as the body warred on itself, so did countries, feeding on jealousy, malice, hate. Once asked what could be done by the American people to bring about a lasting peace, he replied: "We haven't the American people [here at the reading]. The thing is to start with yourself. Unless you can bring about within yourself that which you would have in the nation or in any particular land, don't offer it to others."

As sound as he may have been medically, this was evidence of but one phase of his powers. There were those who thought that if Cayce was subconsciously infallible in this one respect, he was right in all respects, since the source was necessarily the same. "Why," said a grizzled old sea captain, whom Cayce had correctly diagnosed at a distance of a thousand miles, "why should he be so right about the cure for my aching back, and be wrong about anything else?" It was a question that I had to ask myself many times, as I looked into many of the other marvels he talked about in sleep: his truly earth-shaking prophecies and forecasts of world affairs, Atlantis, reincarnation, his detailed description of past geological changes that had caused entire continents to disappear. There was another intriguing point. Why, too, if he had unlimited powers of divination, had he not made himself wealthy, exploring for oil or gold, playing the races or the market, instead of being wretchedly poor most of his life?

Ironically, others did make fortunes out of his stock market readings; others did find oil, where he said it would be, and others, reportedly, won on the horses. But Cayce himself had never profited. Perhaps the answer lay in his own readings, which stressed repeatedly, that they were not to be used for material gain. In the end nobody gained, it seemed, when motivated only by gain. A stockbroker lost his fortune, achieved through Cayce, when he persisted in playing the market, contrary to Cayce's advice; a man who had won on the horses, misusing the Cayce gift, wound up in an asylum. Yet Cayce was uncannily accurate, predicting the 1929 stock market crash almost to the month, and saying there was oil in Dade County, Florida, when all anybody was thinking of was oranges and grapefruits, and pinpointing the end of the Depression. As he considered his own performance, Cayce felt that the stress on materiality was a negative force, defeating what he thought a God-given purpose. Whenever he read subconsciously for gain, his own or somebody else's, he suffered severe headaches, or in extreme cases, lapsed into aphonia, loss of voice. There was a notable instance of this. After the turn of the century, he had given a test demonstration, describing to doctors in Bowling Green, Kentucky, the precise movements of a real estate operator in New York, as he climbed up to his office, smoking a cigar and whistling "Annie Laurie." Since the report tallied precisely with his actual movements, the realtor immediately saw the possibilities. He took the next train for Bowling Green. His proposition was a simple one. "I'll take you back with me," he said, "and we'll make a fortune on Wall Street."

The newly married Cayce discussed it with his wife, Gertrude, a moving force in his life, and she felt it would be an abuse of his power, for which he would suffer. "Once you get away from helping people," she said significantly, "it always makes you ill."

When Cayce refused him, the New Yorker asked for a test reading. As the man had traveled a considerable distance, Cayce agreed. He fell into a trance, and when he awakened, the man had already left, with an armful of notes. That night, Cayce tossed and turned, unable to sleep. His head ached horribly. Later, that week, the explanation materialized. The real estate operator, taking advantage of Cayce's unconsciousness, had picked his subconscious mind. On information from the unsuspecting Cayce, he gleefully confided to friends, he had cleaned up twenty thousand dollars on the market in one quick coup.

After another demonstration, in which experimenting doctors thrust needles in him to test whether he was actually in trance, Cayce decided he would never give another reading, without somebody present whom he could implicitly trust. That person was his wife, Gertrude, who supervised thousands of readings thereafter.

With all his vaunted powers, Cayce was a humble man, religious, God-fearing, who read the Bible every day of his life. He would see anybody, at any time, if left to his own devices, though it was a strain to do more than two readings a day. He was twice arrested, once for practicing medicine without a license, another time for fortune-telling. Yet, he never gave a health reading, without an express request, nor did he turn anybody away because they couldn't pay. When he was most hard-pressed for money, during the Depression, with unpaid bills piling up, his sponsoring group, the Cayce Foundation, felt that clients who could afford it were chiseling in not contributing to the A. R. E. treasury, a usual requirement for a reading. This contribution was normally twenty dollars. So a beleaguered finance committee, wishing to cut off the chiselers, put a leading question to the sleeping Cayce: "To those who cannot pay, free help shall be given. To those who may well afford to pay and refuse to donate anything, either in services or money, shall further aid be denied? In this policy shall we be following the correct path?"

The answer must have been rather a disappointment to his chancellors of the vanishing exchequer, but it was typical of Cayce: "The rain falls on the just and unjust alike. Do not make such [denial to anyone, for any reason] an ironclad rule."

. Awake or sleeping, Cayce was no ordinary man. He had a way of putting people at their ease immediately, and strangers, otherwise shy and retiring, would walk up to this slim, stoop-shouldered man, with the kindly gaze, and shake his hand. Frequently, they would talk to him across his desk, discussing the most intimate problems, or they would write from every corner of the globe, and he would always write back, in a precise hand, which showed a clarity of thought, even when the spelling wasn't. He had a lively humor, enjoying a joke on himself. "Would you like to talk things over?" he once asked a woman visitor. "Yes," she answered, "but I want to hear what you say when asleep, Mr. Cayce, not when you're awake."

The shyest children approached him, and Cayce thought nothing of their friendliest overtures. It could very well be, he told himself with a smile, that he had known them before. One day, for instance, as he dropped into a Virginia Beach barber shop, a small boy casually climbed onto his lap. The father looked up from his haircut. "You mustn't bother that man," he said. "He isn't anybody you know."

The boy's arm tightened around Cayce's neck. "But I do know him," he said. "We were hungry together at the river."

This gave even Cayce a start. For in a reading, that only his family knew about, he had seen himself in a previous life on a raft on the Ohio River, fleeing from a band of marauding Indians. The Indians finally caught up to their quarry and massacred them, which was probably just as well, for they were slowly starving to death anyway.

In the year 1923, Cayce's direction took a startlingly new turn. Until then he had only given the physical or health readings. But in that year, prodded by the sharp questioning of Arthur Lammers, a Dayton, Ohio, printer interested in religious philosophy, Cayce began the life readings which traced man's experience in past lives. This was Cayce's introduction to reincarnation, the soul's return to earth in a different body—a concept, ironically, he was not yet ready to accept. Lammers, preoccupied with man's purpose in the universe, had thrown all sorts of questions at the psychic with an apparently endless fund of knowledge. Lammers asked what every sensitive man had been asking since the beginning of time:

"What is the human soul?

"Where does it come from, and where does it go?

"Is man but another of Nature's creatures, put on earth for a brief cycle, then turned to dust like the fallen trees?"

At these questions, the conscious Cayce could only shrug. "Try the Bible," he said, "the answer for everything lies there."

Lammers grimaced. "I've read the Bible, and I'm still asking you."

It had never occurred to Cayce to delve into the areas of life after death, and as a fundamentalist born, he balked at a philosophy not accepted by orthodox Christianity.

"Reincarnation," Lammers argued, "is simply a belief that the soul is eternal, at intervals appearing again in other physical bodies, so that it can continue as an instrument of its own development." He pointed out several Biblical references that apparently showed acceptance of reincarnation. "Those Jews who didn't recognize Jesus as the Christ," Lammers observed, "asked if he were Elias, here to herald the coming of the Messiah and He replied that Elias had already come and they knew him not." He quoted from the Bible: " 'Then the disciples understood that He spake unto them of John the Baptist.' "

Cayce was not convinced, but under the gentle prodding of Lammers and his friends, his subconscious began invoking past life experiences. These took the subjects back to not only such exotic known lands as ancient India, China, Persia, and Egypt, but to such legendary places as Lost Atlantis and sunken Lemuria in the Pacific. As these life readings progressed, they became at times more interpretative than narrative. Cayce outlined how past life experience had influenced the present, and what the individual must overcome to fulfill this life. Unlike many reincarnationists, indulging in flights of fancy about glamorous former incarnations, Cayce insisted that only one life could be lived at a time. "Life," he said many times, "is for the doing today."

As he got deeper into life readings, he frequently spoke alien languages in trance, chiefly the familiar Romance tongues. But once asked to speak Greek, by a Greek scholar, he broke into Homeric Greek, as though living in that period. Atlantis, of course, was born of his flights into reincarnation, since so many had "lived" there once before. In his discourses on Atlantis, describing its progress and collapse, he said the last surviving islands had disappeared in the area of the Caribbean about ten thousand years ago. He predicted that land would rise again one day soon in this area. However, the rise would be gradual, and freshly emerging land might not evidence itself for a while. The Atlantis story was esoteric but fascinating. With the age-old Atlantean breakup, Cayce had seen a dispersal of its superior culture to the Mediterranean, Central and South America, and even some parts of the United States. Archaeologists, digging behind Cayce, are now turning up records of "homegrown" civilizations in Peru, Mexico, New Mexico, where man had a culture going back some ten to twelve thousand years ago—dispersal time in crumbling Atlantis.

In time, examining his own readings, believing in The Information, Cayce came to believe in reincarnation—and Atlantis. The first appeared to put rhyme and reason in a fundamentally orderly universe, even in its seeming disorder, and the last was plausible, considering the catastrophes foreseen in the past and visualized for the future. Besides, there was the Bible. Had not Joshua, in the name of the Lord God, said to the people of Israel: "Your fathers dwelt on the other side of the flood in old time, even Terah, the father of Abraham, and the father of Nachor, and they served other Gods. And I took your father Abraham from the other side of the flood, and led him throughout all the land of Canaan."

As a doubter, it was rather intriguing at times to see how Cayce subconsciously applied the past experience of a subject to an understanding of very tangible problems in this experience. Consulted by a twenty-five-year-old woman, with a karma—or debit—of letting down others, Cayce advised, "That sown must one day be reaped. Ye disappointed others. Today from thine own disappointments ye may learn patience, the most beautiful of all virtues and the least understood."

Impatiently, the woman asked how she could marry the man she wanted. "What may I do to help the problem?"

"As the experience indicates," the sleeping Cayce said, "do not do too much. Rather be in that position to be the helper when needed. Do not push or advise, but listen."

"S—— and I quarrel and are unhappy with each other much of the time . . ."

(Cayce interrupting) "Would it not be expected, considering the positions?"

"Are we mated? Should we continue our relationship as lovers with the purpose of marrying, or would it be better to break off our relationship?"

Again, after counseling patience, Cayce delivered a piece of advice, apparently paraphrased from Frances Anne Kemble's *Faith*. "It is better to trust one heart, and that deceiving, than doubt one heart which if believing, would bless thy life with true understanding."

The young woman persisted. "Is it indicated that I should marry during this incarnation? If so, when and where will I meet the person?"

"Not until near the thirtieth birthday." She had five years to wait.

Undaunted, she adopted another tack: "What is my purpose and am I living a Godlike life so that I may reflect God and bring happiness to everyone?"

The answer hardly required a mystic. "Read what we have given. There has been much accomplished, and there is much to be accomplished. Be not hasty in thy choices, but know that it is not by might, but by the trusting wholly in Him."

It was plain, solid advice, and in keeping with the man. Nobody would have taken Cayce for a mystic at sight. As he grew older, his brown hair thinned out in the middle years. He had a sharp, quizzical face, a receding chin, and twinkling blue-gray eyes behind rimless glasses. He could have been a teacher, a country doctor, a store clerk, anything but an esoteric or occultist. When people came to see him for their readings, instead of sitting in their own parlors as he "found" their bodies, he greeted them humbly, and promised only that he would do his best. Sometimes The Information wouldn't come. "It isn't anything I can control," he would say apologetically.

He observed a regular ritual. Avoiding strictures of circulation, he would remove his jacket and tie, open his collar and loosen his cuffs, unlace his shoes. Then he would lie back on the couch in his study, placing his hands on his forehead. Often as not, he would smile pleasantly, before responding to the suggestion that he put himself to sleep. As a signal, Gertrude would lean over and touch his cheek. He would close his eyes, fold his hands over his chest, and begin to breathe deeply. Mrs. Cayce, and Cayce's secretary and trusted aide, Gladys Davis, would close their own eyes in prayer. As Cayce sighed, breathing evenly, as anyone would in a nap, Gertrude would speak softly, making the suggestion that induced the reading. "You have the body of M. L. before you, who is in Chicago [street and address were given]. You will go over this body carefully, examine it thoroughly, and tell me the conditions you find at the present time, giving the cause of the existing conditions, also the treatment for the cure and relief of this body. You will speak distinctly at a normal rate of speech, answering the questions as I ask them."

Cayce apparently not only visualized the health of the subject, wherever he was, but his surroundings as well. His subconscious would sometimes pick out streets as he groped about, naming them even when they weren't marked by street signs. Occasionally, he would hesitate, saying the subject had left the house. Once he broke off a reading completely, and the next day, it was learned the patient had died at that precise moment. Another time, tested by a medical committee headed by Dr. John Blackburn of Bowling Green, he described the distant room in which his subject lay. He pictured wallpaper, decorations, furnishings, even to a corner night table; described the bed and bedding, naming the manufacturer. The next day, it all checked out. On still another occasion, an ailing sea captain, forgetting his appointment, had left his ship at the time of the readings, but Cayce caught up to him anyway. "You see," the skipper explained, "Cayce had read for me before, and knew my habits."

Healthwise, Cayce had a virtually infallible record, when his recommendations were followed. Nevertheless, his advice was often disregarded, either because the treatment required so much time or effort, or the patient could find no therapist to implement the instructions. At times, impatience turned even Cayce's dearest admirers to therapy promising faster relief. Cayce's friend and biographer, Thomas Sugrue, trying Cayce's tedious cure of an apparent arthritic condition, began to bridle at his slow recovery. Cayce, stressing improvement would be slow, had recommended a cumbersome wet cell appliance with a gold chloride solution. Instead, Sugrue impetuously turned to the miracle drugs, which adversely affected his system, and a few months later he was dead, following an operation.

There was scarcely any activity, terrestrial or celestial, that Cayce's universal consciousness didn't explore. Longevity, or the absence of it, intrigued the sleeping Cayce. He synchronized long life with selflessness, pointing out that in time the age span would increase most in those nations practicing the greatest altruism. "Look to the nation where the span of life has been extended from sixty to eighty-four years, and you will judge who is serving God." In Russia, surprisingly, after his predicted fall of Communism, he saw a sharp age increase. As it is, Russia's life expectancy, reputedly second only to England's, stands at sixty-eight, provided only natural death is considered, not sudden demises brought about by political factors.

Cayce often intruded in the areas of science. Once he provocatively spoke of a death ray the Atlanteans had devised to eliminate deadly beasts. In the reading, given in 1933, he predicted a similar ray would be discovered here by 1958, as he described how it once worked, "And this [method of handling the environment] was administered in much the same way or manner as sending out from various central plants that which is at present termed the death ray—or the super cosmic ray—that which many are seeking, which will give their lives much, from the stratosphere—or cosmic rays—that will be found in the next twenty-five years."

What hogwash this must have seemed at the time, and what hogwash it would still appear, if not for passing press reports, such as this, out of Denver in December of 1961: "Scientists are developing a death ray weapon designed to turn anything it is focused on into a wisp of gaseous vapor. Dr. Carl L. Kober of the Martin Company plant disclosed the weapon would be partially nuclear-powered. It would accomplish its destructive work by throwing a fantastically hot beam on the subject . . . the disintegration ray, sounding like something from science fiction, would be designed for use in terrestrial warfare."

As science refines its methods of exploring the pre-historic past, new opportunities will constantly present themselves to test Cayce's unconscious. With the United States and Russia engaged in a little publicized race in "inner space," American ocean survey ships, a virtually unknown Little Navy, are coursing the globe, trying to explore the mysterious two-thirds of the world covered by the seas. Already, in a vast corridor between Hawaii and Alaska, they have discovered a thousand-mile-long mountain range, with peaks some six thousand feet from the ocean floor—and still two miles below the surface. Other oceanographers have turned up a river in the Pacific, flowing some thirty-five hundred miles along the Equator. Perhaps, as Cayce's unconscious insisted, great continents did crowd the North Atlantic and South Pacific at one time, eventually swallowed up by cataclysms, as other land masses may be one day if Cayce's a proper prophet. Nevertheless, despite all this foreshadowing of death and destruction, Cayce's message was fundamentally one of hope and faith: "Know and realize that the earth is the Lord's, with all its turmoils and strifes, with all its hates and jealousies, with all its political and economic disturbances. And His ways are not past finding out. By living them in the little things, day by day, may that surety in self, that sureness in Him be thine. For His promises have been and are sure. 'Let not your heart be troubled; ye believe in God.' Believe also in the Christ, who gave, 'If ye love me, ye will keep my commandments, and I and the Father will come and abide with thee day by day.' "

Chapter Two

CAYCE THE MAN

Although he many times warned of World War II, predicting its beginning and end, Edgar Cayce was as stunned as anybody else when the bombs dropped on Pearl Harbor. He brooded over the war, not only for the two sons called to the service, nor the young men fighting and dying on the seven seas, but for the passionate feeling he had that man had not learned to live with himself or his God. Ten days after America's entry into the war, he wrote a sister he loved dearly: "I do hope I won't bore you with all the burdens of my heart just now, but this war business about has the best of me. Have felt of course that it was coming about, but hoped against hope that it would not. But we are reminded continuously that 'God is not mocked, and whatsoever a man sows, that must he reap.' "

With customary candor, he acknowledged that he had no inkling, psychically, of the sneak attack. "Yes, we have much data that we are seeing coming about, but nothing was ever given as to what happened on the 7th." At the same time he expressed his concern for the Navy personnel, who had shipped out from the neighboring naval base at Norfolk. "Had, and hope have yet, some very good friends in Hawaii, haven't heard from them since, though had letters mailed just day or two before it happened. Some of them are in the Navy, but not on any of the ships reported lost, boys who seem to have gotten much from their contact with the Work; address me as Dad, even as my own boys—and have told me I was the sort of a father they would like to have had. So you may know about how anxious I am at this time."

Though surrounded by people who loved him, he was a lonely man. Like Lincoln and Lee, whom he admired, he carried his cause close to his heart, a cause even more universal than theirs, man's understanding of God's purpose for him on earth. Everything he said or did in his mature years was subsidiary to this. In his own work, he felt that he was fulfilling this purpose. It was the only thing that made endurable the years of doubt, of ignominy, of privation for the ones he loved most. "If I thought for one minute it wasn't helping, I'd give it up this instant."

At one of the low points of his life, after his arrest as a fortune-teller in New York City, he returned in black despair to his home in Virginia Beach, wondering why, if his work was worthwhile, he and his family should suffer one reversal after another. In his depression the lesson of the long-suffering Job appeared lost on this fervid student of the Bible. And so he gave himself a reading, his wife, Gertrude, asking why his power, if he had any, had not warned of the trap set by police. The answer was not what he was looking for. On his awakening, his wife, and his aide, Gladys Davis, told him what his message was: "A certain amount of scouring was essential for the better development of the soul." The much tried psychic shook his head and sighed heavily. "I seem to be able to help everybody but myself."

It had been that way with the search for oil, with investments, with simple real estate transactions, until Cayce got the feeling that he and materiality were never meant to join hands. At the same time, Cayce seldom fretted about money. His attitude toward it was almost child-like. Like an earlier mystic, Bronson Alcott, the Concord transcendentalist, he felt the Lord would provide. And he appeared to be right, though it was not unusual for his children to have patches in their clothes and Cayce to have holes in his shoes. One harsh winter, the family was without fuel. The children, huddled in their overcoats, looked up from a meager meal, to hear their father calmly asking the good Lord for firewood.

A couple of hours later, there was a knock at the door. It

was a road foreman for the power and light company. His crew was ready to cut down an old light pole in front of the house, and for the necessary permission they were willing to saw the pole into firewood and stack it on the lawn. On another occasion, a local grocery store had cut the Cayce family off the credit list—until a bill for $87.50 was paid. The harried Mrs. Cayce fretfully asked her husband to think of raising the money somehow. "Don't worry about it, Mother," he said calmly, "the money will turn up." And he calmly went fishing.

That morning, the postman arrived with a letter. Inside, was a check just large enough to cover the bill. Mrs. Cayce heaved a grateful sigh. "Now take it over to the grocery store, Edgar," she enjoined.

"All right, Mother," he said good-naturedly.

An hour later he was back with a new fishing pole and an armful of tackle. Mrs. Cayce looked at him with despair in her heart. "Edgar," she said, "you couldn't . . . ?"

"Don't worry about it, Mother," he said imperturbably. "The money will turn up somehow."

At one time, without money to buy family necessities or pay his secretary, he was asked to explain why he wasn't doing better. The question was put by his wife. "In consideration of the fact that Edgar Cayce is devoting his entire time to the Work, give the reason for his not being able to obtain sufficient financial support for his and his family's material sustenance, and how may he, Edgar Cayce, correct this condition?"

Mrs. Cayce looked up expectantly as Edgar's lips began to move: "Live closer to Him, who giveth all good and perfect gifts, and ask and ye shall receive; knock and it shall be opened unto you. Give and it shall be returned fourfold. There has never been the lack of necessities, neither will there be, so long as adhering to the Lord's way is kept first and foremost."

The seer's family would have been less than human had they not thrown up their arms. But, as the future was to show, Cayce was again prophetic. In every low spot, a door opened and the Lord provided.

Contrary to prevailing impression, Cayce was psychic, waking, as well as sleeping. He constantly saw fields of lights around people's heads—auras telling him about the state of their emotions and health. Once, a woman, fresh from a quarrel with a neighbor, came marching into his study. He looked up mildly from his Bible. "I see a red aura all around you. Come back next week when you're not angry any more."

Again he was concerned about a woman, who had no aura. Two days later, she was dead.

Since he was so acutely sensitive to everything about him, it was difficult to relax like the ordinary person. He had to make a continuous effort to close himself off. There were few ways he could detach himself. He liked to play cards, but once, without even glancing at the deck, he correctly read off fifty-two cards in succession to demonstrate that bridge would be a bore. Aside from the Bible, his only relaxers were fishing and gardening. He loved to sit for hours on the pier back of his house, casting into a fresh-water lake. Children would come and talk to him as he fished, and he would tell them stories, remembered from his own fanciful childhood. He fished when it rained, and when it blowed or snowed, for here he found refuge from himself.

On the gloomiest days he would work in his garden, talking soothingly to the plants. He could make flowers grow where they had never grown before, caressing them tenderly, as though they were people. He was keenly aware of every aspect of the outdoors, observing all life with an appreciative eye. On a particularly exhilarating spring morning he noted: "Lovely day—new bird songs today—appears to be an unusual number of birds, or am I just aware of their presence? The early morning song of the tomtit, the bluebird, lark, cat bird, robin, the mockingbird, and the new ones sound like canaries, but are red, with brown, and the female yellow and black, but lovely bird—used to call them weaver bird, but haven't seen any before in years and years. Oh, let's not forget the redwing, he is lovely."

There was an artless boyishness about Cayce that belied the mystic. As a young man, it kept bartenders from serving him, and poolroom operators from renting him their tables.

Looking for a job once, he walked into a shoe store, and began waiting on a customer. The manager, seeing him at work, absentmindedly sent the young stranger to the bank for change, and Cayce worked on for the rest of the day. That night, the puzzled manager asked how it all happened.

"Somebody asked me for something and I just gave it to them," Cayce replied simply. He stayed on for eighteen months.

He was constantly described as an illiterate by writers he never saw, but this was clearly a misnomer. For as the years went by, the sixth-grade dropout learned much from the outside world. Statesmen, financiers, professors, and scientists discussed their problems with him. He visited their homes, rubbing elbows with the great and near-great, and they visited him, drawn by curiosity and need. He read the newspapers, but rarely opened a book, except the Bible, which he read through each year, constantly finding it a new source of inspiration. As it did Lincoln, it influenced his conscious writing, making it precise and pointed, though his unconscious speech always remained florid and involved. He had been a failure in school, leaving at fifteen, because he could not harness his mind, already showing signs of subconscious development, to a relatively primitive learning process, patently absurd in the face of his own pipeline to the Universal Mind. Later in life, he scanned his own readings carefully, dispassionately regarding them as The Information, and he imbibed much from them, in such varied areas as health, homosexuality, astrology, and politics.

The universality of his faith crossed all religious lines. He was equally at home with Catholic, Protestant, Jew, Hindu, Buddhist. All reacted equally to the interest he felt in everybody. He had frequent soul-searching conversations with Father Brennan, the pastor of the Catholic Star of the Sea Church, across the way. The good Father never ventured upstairs in the Cayce home, but paid his ecumenical respects in other ways. One day when Cayce was out of town, a hurricane ripped through Virginia Beach, flooding streets and homes. Returning the next day, Cayce went down into his cellar to investigate. There, he saw the Catholic priest and a Presbyterian minister from down the street, ankle-deep in water, bailing out the basement as though their souls depended upon it.

For many with far more education and worldly distinction, he was an authority figure. Some respectfully called him Judge, others Captain, many called him "Doctor." His first biographer, Sugrue, knew him simply as Boss.

Like the mystic Lincoln, Cayce made friends easily, and had the same homespun way of spinning out a story. But again like Lincoln, because of the hypersensitive side of his nature, there were corners of his mind he could share with nobody. Everybody became an outsider when terrible visions flooded in on him, as they often did. One bright, sunny day in June of 1936, for instance, he was hoeing in his garden, when he heard a noise like a swarming of bees. He looked up, startled, and there in the sky saw a chariot, drawn by four white horses. He tried to persuade himself that it was pure imagination, when he heard a voice saying, "Look behind you." He turned and beheld a man, with a shield and helmet, knee-guards and a cape, but no weapon of any kind. His countenance was like the light, his armor of burnished silver. He raised his hand in salute, and said, "The chariot of the Lord and thy horsemen thereof." Then he disappeared.

Shaken by this daytime nightmare, Cayce dropped his hoe and rushed into the house. He brushed past his son, Hugh Lynn, and locked himself in his study. When he finally emerged hours later, he explained that he had seen the approach of World War II, with its millions of dead. It had been a jolt to his conscious mind.

In forming some friendships at sight, Cayce believed he had known the friend before. His belief in reincarnation, with its corollary of a karmic past, made him more tolerant of others, and devoid of vanity. Still, he had a rising regard for his own mission, and with reason. Once he was surprised in his study by a minister, who had come to question his powers. As the minister walked in unnoticed, Cayce was murmuring under his breath, "Thank you, thank you, oh Lord, for another life." Only a few moments before a grateful mother had phoned to thank him for saving her baby.

He tried to find time for everybody with a problem. Though his own readings said that he should read but twice a day, or risk disintegration, he stretched this to seven or eight readings a day during World War II because of demands not only from the ill, but from parents like himself concerned by sons away at war. However he pushed himself, the mail piled up. His own clairvoyance was some help. Once, as his aides helplessly eyed a huge sack of mail, not knowing where to start, he said, "Take the telegram, there is the greater need there." Down near the bottom of the bag, a telegramed request for a reading had been mistakenly placed.

Cayce had the ordinary instincts. He liked the companionship of pretty ladies, as he did that of intelligent men. He took a drink occasionally, making his own wine. He considered the grape a food. Ironically, he was a chain smoker. When admirers wondered about this, he would laugh genially and point to the heavens, "Where I am going there are no cigarettes."

He rarely fretted about his own health. At the dinner table one day an admirer noted with dismay that Cayce, tabooing pork in his readings, was consuming it with evident satisfaction. "But Mister Cayce," she said, "pork is bad for you."

The mystic smiled brightly. "If I couldn't raise the vibration of this poor little hunk of meat, I sure wouldn't amount to much." He was like the doctor who prescribed for everybody but himself.

His was a volatile temperament; he could be easily hurt or disturbed, but then his sense of balance would assert itself. Although he relied implicitly on the ubiquitous Gladys Davis, he would sometimes get annoyed, feeling she had assumed too much in interpreting a reading. He fired her a dozen times in waves of mercurial wrath. An hour or two later, he would look her up, smile and give her a friendly pat on the back. They were in business again—till the next time.

Gertrude was the partner who kept him on the track in moments of wavering, Gladys Davis the outlet for the petty frustrations that plagued his day. As a man has no secrets from his valet, Cayce had none from his secretary. She went to work for him at eighteen, lived in the house, and took down almost every reading from September 1923 until his death in January 1945. Despite close contact, under mundane circumstances, he always remained a hero to her. The Work, as they called it, dominated her life, and she never married until after his death, knowing that she couldn't serve two masters. Yet, she never considered it a sacrifice, sublimating her own maternal instinct to his family and that of her relatives. Cayce allowed her to keep her small nephew in the house, treating both as family. Typically, he kept an eye out for the nephew even when his own eyes were closed. One day, during a reading, Gladys looked out the study window, and saw the boy teetering precariously at the edge of the lake. Knowing he couldn't swim, she still couldn't bring herself to leave the reading uncovered. Cayce was on the couch, talking in trance, but he suddenly broke off, without batting an eye, to say peremptorily, "Go out and get the child." In a flash, Gladys dropped her stenographer's pad and raced out to the water, returning with the chastened boy. The reading continued, as though there was no interruption.

Cayce was not unlike the old family doctor with an anxious patient. "He had the ability," Gladys Davis recalled, "to make you feel that you were the most important person in the world. He gave his full attention to you, whatever else may have been on his mind before."

Early in their relationship, Gladys had a dramatic revelation of Cayce's remarkable gift. It changed her whole attitude toward her job. Before, it had been a pleasant chore working for an unusually kindly man. After that, it became a lifetime's devotion. She had been with Cayce for about two months, and was hampered by dull headaches off and on. While she wore glasses for close work, they didn't seem to relieve the strain. Desperate, she asked for a reading one day. The reading attributed the headaches to eyestrain resulting from deflected circulation due to bad posture. Simple neck exercises were recommended—stretching the neck up and down, sidewise three or four times, then rolling the head slowly in each direction a few times. This was a traditional Yoga exercise, though Cayce was not aware of this. He also advised a hand-machine violet ray three times weekly, and told her to discard her glasses. The effect was instantaneous. "Thirty years later I finally went back to glasses," she recalled, "when I couldn't find a number in the telephone book. But I never had another moment's eyestrain or headache."

Cayce was literally a dreamer, and he felt people could learn about themselves and the world about them by studying their own dreams. "Consciousness is sought by man for his own diversion. In sleep, the soul seeks the real diversion or the real activity of self." If he didn't understand a dream, he would lie down and interpret it in trance. In one dream, he saw himself climbing to a heavenly chapel to pray. A celestial custodian showed him a large room crammed with packages, beautifully wrapped and addressed to different people. They had not been delivered, and the custodian sorrowfully explained why. "These are gifts for which people have been praying, but they lost their faith just before the date of delivery." These gifts were latent talents and abilities, so seldom drawn upon by the owners. Was this a message for Cayce to get on with his work? He took it as such.

There was a period in Cayce's life when nothing appeared to work out. Through Morton Blumenthal, a New York stockbroker whom he had helped market-wise, he had been able to finally realize two lifelong dreams, the Cayce Hospital, and Atlantic University, both launched at Virginia Beach. The college, chartered by the Commonwealth of Virginia, was to stress research into parapsychology and the occult, while providing a general education and a Bachelor of Arts degree. The hospital, headed by an MD, Thomas B. House, a remote relative, was to treat patients from the readings. However, the collapsing stock market, which Cayce had ticked off for 1929, broke Blumenthal, who had inexplicably ignored Cayce's advice. Deprived of Blumenthal's backing, the hospital was subsequently closed. The college never really got started. On February 28, 1931, the last patients were moved out of the hospital, and Cayce sadly handed over the keys to the sheriff. Soon thereafter he lost his house, but the worst blow was in the offing. A few months later, in New York, looking for help to reinstate his hospital, Cayce gave a few readings for New Yorkers who had requested them, including a Mrs. Bertha Gorman.

When he came out of the Gorman reading his subject was watching him grimly. Mrs. Cayce and Gladys were sobbing softly. Cayce sat up abruptly. "Did I say anything to upset you, Mrs. Gorman?" he asked.

She flipped out a shield, with a number on it. "My name is Conwell, Bertha Conwell. I'm a policewoman and you're all under arrest."

The tabloids had a field day, with snide innuendos about the fifty-four-year-old Cayce and his twenty-six-year-old blonde secretary. One newspaper ran a photograph of Cayce and his "blonde secretary," artfully snipping Mrs. Cayce's likeness from the original photo. Some reports were as misleading as the picture. One reporter said Cayce had demanded seventy dollars for his reading, paid in marked bills. Cayce was exonerated, but Arthur Brisbane, the leading columnist of his day, lashed out at him anyway: "There is magic in words, much in a name, despite Shakespeare's saying about the rose. Edgar Cayce, his wife Gertrude, and their secretary, arrested for fortune-telling, were told, 'You must not pretend to tell fortunes, because you can't.' Things looked dark, but Edgar Cayce, who knows language, told the court, 'I'm no fortune-teller; I'm a psychic diagnostician.' Instantly, he, his wife Gertrude, and their secretary were set free to diagnose psychically to their hearts' content. When a lady asked, 'Is this the right time to make certain investments,' the psychic gave her the psychic answer. The law couldn't object to that."

It didn't happen that way at all. The Judge had heard of Cayce and his work through friends. In court, substantial citizens vouched for what Cayce had done for them. And Cayce had done no fortune-telling. The Judge listened intently to the simple recital of his work by a simple man, who candidly acknowledged that he wasn't himself sure how he functioned or how much good he did. And the Judge, like Brisbane, also recalled a line from Shakespeare, "There are more things in heaven and earth, Horatio, than are dreamed of in your philosophy." There was no case, the charge was dismissed. But the proceedings left their scars, Cayce wondering again whether he had been punished for readings motivated by material gain. Originally, he had rationalized that his stock market forecasts were purely motivated because they meant he would get his school and his hospital. Now both were gone. His name had been dragged through the mud, and he felt tired and discouraged. Perhaps he was on the wrong road? Maybe he should go back to work like everybody else?

Several times before, doubting the high purpose of his gift, he had given up the readings and turned to photographic work. But Gertrude, believing in him, had encouraged his return to the work she felt he was intended for. Again she comforted him, pointing out that the readings had saved both her and their son, Hugh Lynn. She had been suffering from lung hemorrhages, and the doctors had said that she could not survive another spasm. "If there's anything in this monkey business," one doctor suggested, "you'd better try it on your wife." It was the first reading for his own family. In trance, he prescribed a preparation to stop the hemorrhaging. A specialist, who sat in at the reading, was impressed but pessimistic. "Most wonderful discourse I've ever heard on tuberculosis, but I don't see how she can be helped." The druggists wondered whether the prescription would even compound. It did, and Gertrude showed immediate improvement. There was no more hemorrhaging. As she was convalescing, he had her inhale from an empty cask of apple brandy, which additionally soothed and relieved her. She was months mending, but her lungs never bothered her again. The story was almost the same with his son, Hugh Lynn. As a child, while he was playing with his father's flashlight kit, some of the powder flared up into his eyes. The doctors despaired of his sight, counseling surgery. The child, overhearing the consultation, propped himself on an elbow, and cried, "Don't take out my eyes, Doctor. My Daddy, when he's asleep, is the best doctor in the world. He'll tell you what to do."

The specialists shook their heads. "One eye is so damaged that it must be removed at once to save his life."

Cayce said grimly, "You will do nothing until I've taken a reading."

Gertrude supervised as Cayce spoke in his sleep. "Keep the boy in a completely darkened room for fifteen days, keep dressings soaked in strong tannic acid solutions on his eyes, frequently changing same. Thus will the sight be saved and restored."

Though the doctors considered the sight gone in one eye, and the other removable, they protested that the solution would irreparably damage the delicate tissues of the eye.

"Which eye," Cayce demanded, "the eye beyond hope, or the one you want to take out?"

There was an awkward silence, and then one of the doctors set about preparing the prescribed application. Twelve days later, the final dressings came off. The boy's eyes were clear and bright. "I can see," he announced gleefully.

As he looked now at his wife, and his son, Cayce knew that there had to be something to his gift. These two, dearer than any, were dramatic testimonials of his work. He felt that he must go on until the day of the long sleep.

There was little in Cayce's heritage to justify his strange gift. It was almost as though he had been plucked out of obscurity to manifest the unlimited possibilities of man and Creation. The Cayces were an old conservative Kentucky family. Edgar was born on March 18, 1877, on a farm near Hopkinsville, in Christian County. His father, Leslie, a justice of the peace, was known locally as the Squire. His grandfather, a farmer, may have been psychic. He reputedly could take two forks of a witch hazel tree, and dowse successfully for water. Despite his conventional background, Cayce was obviously different from other boys. He was interested in the Bible, enjoyed going to the Christian Church, an offshoot of the Presbyterian, and didn't care much for games. He was little more than seven or eight, when he reported a clairvoyant experience which was to eventually shape the direction of his life. Off by himself, in a secluded outdoor nook, he had been reading in the Bible of the vision of Manoah, for he loved dearly the story of Samson. Suddenly, there was a humming sound, and a bright light filled the glade where he usually hid to read the wonderful stories. As he looked up, he saw a figure in white, bright as the noonday light, and heard a voice:

"Your prayers have been heard. What would you ask of me, that I may give it to you?"

The boy was not startled. Even then it seemed natural to see visions. "Just that I may be helpful to others," he replied, "especially to children who are ill, and that I may love my fellow man."

It almost seemed as if somebody besides himself were speaking.

The figure silently disappeared.

Edgar was not a scholar. The next day, thinking of the vision, he bungled his classwork, and had to remain after school to write the word "cabin" five hundred times on the blackboard, as punishment for misspelling it.

That night, even more than usual, he seemed unable to concentrate on his lessons. There was an invisible barrier between him and his book. But his father had told him he would have to stay up until he had his lesson. At eleven o'clock, long past his bedtime, as his head nodded drowsily, he heard a voice within himself, as in a dream. It was the voice of the previous afternoon. It kept repeating, "Sleep, and we may help you."

He fell asleep for a few minutes. And when he awakened, as absurd as it may seem, he knew every word by rote in that particular spelling book. He had slept on it. This was Cayce's own story of how Universal Consciousness came to him. It was strange, hard to believe, but no stranger, no more incredible than the feats he was to perform in the years to come.

The incredible beginnings of an incredible career continue. Shortly thereafter, accidentally hurt by a thrown baseball, he told his parents to prepare a special poultice and put it at the base of his brain. Seeing him in a semi-stupor, they complied wonderingly, and in the morning he was well. It was his first health reading. As time went on, he gave others spontaneously for friends. They all seemed to work. But at this time he didn't know what he had or what to do with it. After leaving school, he worked on a farm, then in a shoe store, and later a bookstore. He fell in love with the neighboring Gertrude Evans. She had a knack of putting him at ease, encouraged his Bible work, and his teaching Sunday school. He wanted to be a minister, but had neither the money nor aptitude for higher education. When he confided his ambition to the touring Dwight Moody, the great evangelist observed, "You can serve God wherever you are, and with whatever you have." He always remembered Moody's advice.

Like Edgar's mother, who had a tender regard for the son who was different, Gertrude felt that he should use his burgeoning powers to help others. Even before their marriage, she discovered that when he concentrated on making money, instead of using his gift, something would always go wrong: either a blinding headache, an upset stomach, or loss of voice. Able to talk only in whispers, he had to give up a job as a salesman, taking one in the darkroom of a photographic studio where it didn't matter much whether he could talk or not. Because of his condition, he became an early cause célèbre. Professional hypnotists and doctors lined up to cure his baffling aphonia with hypnosis. But nobody could help until Al Layne came along. Layne was a frustrated healer. He had wanted to be a doctor, but instead circumstances had compelled a mail-order course in osteopathy and hypnosis. Layne varied the traditional hypnotic method. He put Cayce to sleep, as the others had, then allowed him to make the hypnotic suggestion to himself, instead of the hypnotist making it directly. "Your unconscious mind is looking into your body," he said. "It is looking at your throat. It will tell us what it sees wrong with your throat, and what can be done to cure the problem."

At the added suggestion that he tell himself to speak normally, Cayce's voice came in crystal clear. "Yes, we can see the body. The trouble we now see is a partial paralysis of the vocal chords, due to nerve strain. To remove the condition it is necessary only to suggest that the body increase circulation to the affected area for a short time."

Layne leaned forward, "Tell the circulation to increase to the affected area and to remove the condition."

As young Cayce's parents looked on incredulously, their son's throat began to turn a deep crimson. The blood was rushing to the trouble spot in response to Cayce's hypnotic suggestion. It was a truly amazing feat of self-hypnosis.

Now Cayce took over completely. In the same clear voice, he instructed Layne, "Now suggest that the circulation return to normal and the body awaken." This was done, and Cayce sat up in a few moments, rubbing his eyes. He started to ask what had happened, and then realized that he was talking normally. He was overjoyed. Layne, equally jubilant, was struck by the knowledgeable way in which Cayce had discussed his own ailment.

He turned to the smiling Cayce.

"When you were in trance," he said, "you talked like a physician looking down a patient's throat. Perhaps you could do the same with somebody else's body, just as you looked into those closed books your father told me about."

Cayce regarded him curiously. Was this what the vision in white had brought him? But he knew nothing about medicine, nothing about hypnosis, he was, in the last analysis, a sixth-grade dropout.

"What would be the purpose of it all, even if I could tell what was inside somebody's body?" Cayce asked.

"Perhaps," said Layne, "you could locate ailments, injuries, sources of infections that regular medical examinations might not turn up." He frowned a moment. "I have been sick for years," he said, "and yet the doctors don't know what's wrong with me. Maybe you could help people like me."

He took the young man's hand. "It might not work, Edgar, but if it did, what a wonderful opportunity to heal the sick."

Cayce came to a quick decision. "All right, I'm willing."

The next day the great experiment started. After putting Cayce to sleep, Layne planted the additional suggestion: "You have in this room the body of Al Layne. You will go over this body carefully, noting its condition and especially any parts that are ailing. You will give the cause of such ailments and suggest treatments to bring about a cure."

Cayce seemed to ponder in his sleep. And then suddenly he spoke out. "Yes, we have the body. We have gone over it carefully. Now, here are the conditions of that body as we find them . . ."

Layne's pencil flew across the pages of white paper.

Finally, Cayce opened his eyes. "Did I get anything?" he asked.

Layne laughed. "Did you get anything? You described my symptoms better than I could myself, and you told me what to eat and what medicines to take." He pointed to the pages which had fluttered to the floor. "It's all there."

Cayce blinked at the scrawled pages, and the unfamiliar terms. His jaw dropped a little. "How could that have come out of me?" He repeated some of the medical words, mispronouncing them. "I never saw these words before, not to mention knowing what they mean."

But the mail-order osteopathic student knew enough medicine to know that Cayce was on the track. "The drugs and herbs you recommended are well known. There's not a harmful ingredient in any of them."

Cayce sat silently, thinking, half-frightened at the prospect of getting into something over his head. He was twenty-four now, and all he really wanted of life was to marry Gertrude, and make enough money to bring up a family. He was a comparatively normal young man.

As usual, he talked things over with Gertrude. "Why should God pick out somebody like me, and give him this strange power?" he asked.

Gertrude smiled. "Jesus was a carpenter, and the apostles were ignorant, obscure fishermen and tillers of the soil."

Cayce wasn't convinced. Though Layne's general condition improved noticeably after a week, he avoided Layne, as though he actually had the plague. But his mother and Gertrude continued to encourage him. His mother reminded him of the childhood vision, and Gertrude allayed fears that he might inadvertently harm someone. "I don't think God would grant such a gift, and permit its misuse."

But the responsibility of delving into what he didn't understand, of controlling the lives and health of others, was too much for young Cayce. Despite his mother, Gertrude, and Layne, he decided against working with Layne at this time.

But as fate would have it, as he was telling the disappointed Layne of his decision, his voice faded into a thin reedy whisper.

He still wasn't convinced. "If God wanted me to be a healer, as you say," he whispered to Gertrude, "then why didn't he permit me to continue my education and become a doctor?"

Gertrude picked out one flaw in this reasoning. "If you were a physician, limited by the limitations of known medical practice, you would be in no better position to help than the brilliant doctors who have already failed with so many ailing people because of these limitations."

This was a rather plausible argument. And Cayce's last misgivings were dispelled when Layne stressed that he knew enough medicine to know whether the readings were consistent with established medical practice, and whether the remedies would at least be innocuous. Besides, didn't Edgar ever want to get his full voice back? This was the clincher.

Cayce preferred at first not to see the first few subjects who wanted his help, nor did he want to know who they were. This way, it was an impersonal problem, and he did not become emotionally involved. Originally he gave two readings a day, at 10 A.M., and again at 2 P.M. There was no charge for the readings. He awakened each time feeling refreshed, and hungry. Apparently, he was burning up lots of energy without depleting himself.

But while subjects were reporting improvements, generally, Cayce still doubted himself after weeks of readings. Then one day, a woman burst into Layne's office, a man staggering after her with a small girl in his arms. The girl was apparently choking to death. She was coughing spasmodically and couldn't catch her breath. Cayce got a quick rundown on her condition. The doctors thought there was an obstruction. But X-rays had shown no blockage in the windpipe. For the first and perhaps only time, Edgar Cayce raced to his couch. He quickly went into trance, at Layne's suggestion, and when he awakened, the couple and their child were already gone. But the father was back within the hour. Tears pouring down his cheeks, he gratefully wrung Cayce's hand.

The little girl had swallowed a celluloid collar button, and Cayce had specified exactly where it would be found in her windpipe. "It was just where you said it would be," the father said. He thrust his hand into his pocket, but at this stage, Cayce was adamant about not accepting fees of any kind. "If God has given me a special gift, it is so that I could help others, not profit by it myself," he insisted.

Cayce's first health reading occurred in 1901. Meanwhile, Cayce had gone back to work in Bowling Green, doing readings only occasionally, when he heard from Layne. In the summer of 1902, however, he received a phone call, which was to eventually change his life. Over the phone, C. H. Dietrich, the Hopkinsville school superintendent, pleaded with him to help his five-year-old daughter, Aime. She was apparently retarded from a siege of illness three years before. Cayce did not yet realize he could perform a physical reading at a distance. He returned to Hopkinsville on a weekend, and went directly to the Dietrich home. Layne was waiting. Cayce soon fell asleep. "The trouble is in the spine," he said. "A few days before her illness, the child slipped getting out of a carriage and struck the base of her spine on the carriage step. This injury weakened the area, and led to the mental condition."

Dietrich's eyes widened. He didn't know whether Cayce's diagnosis was correct, but he did know that Cayce had picked out an all but forgotten incident, the fall from the carriage, which had seemed of no consequence at the time.

Some spinal vertebrae were out of alignment, causing pressures on nerves. Layne adjusted the vertebrae specified by Cayce. There were three adjustments, and within five days, the child had improved noticeably. In three months, she was in school with other girls her age. The cure was complete. The grateful Dietrich could never do enough for Cayce, and it was through his testimonial that Dr. Wesley H. Ketchum was to later use Cayce as a psychic diagnostician, turning him to a career, professionally, that continued until death.

All through life, nonetheless, the modest mystic was to have self-doubts and misgivings and it was Gertrude's job to resolve these qualms. Knowing her husband's mind, she frequently suggested introspective readings, which they could study together. For Cayce had more respect for The Information, subconsciously given, than for his own fallible conscious. As she had, since he shied away from experimenters, Gertrude put the key question to her husband. "Is this information always correct?" she asked.

"Insofar," he replied, "as the suggestion is in the proper channel or in accord with the action of subconscious or soul matter."

The solicitous wife inserted a question of her own: "Will this work hurt the body?"

"This body," Cayce began, "is controlled in its work through the psychical, or the mystical or spiritual. It is governed by the life that is led by the person who is guiding the subconscious when in this state. As the ideas given the subconscious to obtain its information are good, the body becomes better." The reverse was true, if the motivation was base or mean. "The body should keep in close touch with the spiritual side of life if he is to be successful mentally, physically, psychically, and financially."

As he read back what he had said, Cayce could only sigh. That was always the problem, how to remain spiritual while trying to cope with a world of materiality.

Chapter Three

CAYCE'S TIME CLOCK

When Alaska became the forty-ninth state in 1959, it set the stage for the materialization of one of Cayce's early earth changes, slated to occur between 1958 and 1998. "The early portion," Cayce had said, "will see a change in the physical aspect of the west coast of America"—and that certainly happened in 1964, with the continent's worst quake ever. Repercussions of that quake are still being felt, for as *Current Science,* a weekly science report, pointed out, the quake shifted mountains an average of five feet, lifted the sea floor as much as fifty feet, and raised the entire continent of North America a half an inch. Its shock impact was even greater perhaps than Cayce had considered. "Tides surged eight feet higher than usual along coasts three thousand miles away. In Iran, the solid land rose and fell like a wave when earthquake waves passed through."

Actually, the Alaskan quake was only the most dramatic in a series of drastic earth changes presaging far more sweeping destruction visualized for later this century. Cayce also saw dramatic risings and sinkings in the Mediterranean, as a prelude to catastrophe elsewhere, and the eastern basin of Mare Nostrum has briefly subsided, while the sea floor off Morocco spectacularly shot up 3300 feet.

Already, new land has materialized in both the Atlantic and the Pacific, as Cayce foresaw more than twenty years ago, and the most specific forecast on his time clock—a dramatic land rise where Atlantis once supposedly stood—may be just around the corner, if the Cayce time clock is on schedule. Psychics traditionally have foggy notions about time, even in otherwise precise predictions, but Cayce definitely fixed 1968 or 1969, for new land to appear in the Caribbean.

Clockwise, great interest centers on the predicted destruction in Los Angeles, San Francisco, and New York with Cayce intimating this would begin in the latter portion of the '58–'98 period. While he put the California cataclysm before the devastation of Manhattan and coastal areas of Connecticut and New England, he made no distinction between Los Angeles and its sister city to the north, ruined by a quake sixty years ago.

In the Pacific, the tempo of subterranean rumblings appears to be stepping up along the Ring of Fire, in a wide arc from the Orient to the Western Hemisphere, just as Cayce said it would before the greater destruction. And in the Mediterranean area again, as a forerunner of havoc elsewhere, Etna has come dramatically alive.

In this dynamic forty years, Cayce also visualized parts of Japan sliding into the sea and cataclysmic changes in Northern Europe, both possible if present geological trends were to accelerate. As for Japan going into the sea, a crack geologist reported that, "one volcanic area in Honshu has experienced 87,000 recordable quakes in a six-month period in 1965–66, with eight thousand of these strong enough to be felt." And the Japanese geologist, Nobichiko Obara, reports that the Japanese archipelago has been steadily sinking into the sea.

Cayce predicted, too, that the Great Lakes would one day empty into the Gulf of Mexico, rather than the St. Lawrence, and the same expert geologist, studying Cayce, tied in disturbances to the Middle West with predicted inundations in the Carolinas and Georgia. There had been a sharp crustal break once before in the Midwest, in Missouri, in 1811, possibly repeating in the 1970s or so, together with an uplift north of the Great Lakes. "This area is tilting slowly, anyway," the Geologist noted, "and need only accelerate to shift the flow from the St. Lawrence to the Mississippi by way of the Chicago River."

Oddly, Cayce saw not 1958, nor even '78 or '98, as the most critical date on his calendar. He singled out 1936 as the key year in the world-wide power struggle, and as the year in which great changes would begin unnoticed within the earth's core with the shifting of the polar axis. Asked in February of 1932, to "forecast the principal events for the next fifty years affecting the welfare of the human race," he had replied: "This had best be cast after the great catastrophe that's coming to the world in '36 [1936] in the form of breaking up of many powers that now exist as factors in world affairs."

There was more about international affairs. "Will Italy adopt a more liberal form of government in the near future?" he was asked.

"Italy, too," he replied, "will be broken by what now is an insignificant or smaller power between those of the larger or those of the moment that are larger. These will not come, however, before the catastrophe of outside forces to the earth in 1936, from the shifting of the equilibrium of the earth itself in space, with those consequential effects on various portions of the world."

"What will be the type and extent of the upheaval in 1936?" Cayce was asked.

"The wars, the upheavals in the interior of the earth, and the shifting of the earth by the change in the axis as respecting the portions from the polaris center."

Looking back, 1936 was indeed a critical year—the League of Nations and collective security shattered, civil war in Spain, a dress rehearsal for a still bloodier engagement; Italy dyspeptic over Abyssinia; Hitler marching ominously into the Rhineland.

But the Cayce reference to a physical change within the earth itself far overshadowed any other forecast. Was this to be the agency of destruction foreseen for the predicted upheaval—the destruction of nearly all of New York, Los Angeles, San Francisco, the disappearance of hunks of Japan, and of northern Europe in the twinkling of an eye? As it might happen again, it may have all happened before in a planet undergoing cataclysmic changes for millions of years. The Frenchman, Georges Cuvier, father of modern paleontology, theorized that the dinosaurs of the distant past had disappeared because of spontaneous catastrophes, since almost perfectly preserved bodies of woolly mammoths have been found quick-frozen with their last meals still in their mouths.

Cayce and Cuvier were dramatically alike. "According to Cuvier," the Geologist said, "one major source of catastrophism was the tilting of the earth, its drastic upheavals creating oceans where there was once dry land, and dry land where there was sea." In this concept, as opposed to the theory of slow change, the first breakups would come where the earth crust was weakest, the so-called Ring of Fire which forms an arc of volcanoes ringing the Pacific in New Zealand, the Philippines, Japan, the Aleutians, Mexico, Chile. It had happened before, the scientists say. "In the deepest ocean trenches, water is forced down into the crust through earthquake faults, creating pressure changes resulting in violent eruptions. Man has obviously lived through such upheavals, with resulting climatic changes, but not since he was able to make a written record of the event." As time went on, the axis tilt would impart a slight wobble to the spinning earth, the Geologist noted, and the shifting momentum would cause the globe to alter its shape as it adjusted to a newly angled course.

And where would the earth give first? Obviously, if Cayce was correct, in the hot, plastic mantle of the earth, which was capable of movement hundreds of miles under the crust of the earth.

The Geologist's map showed different levels for crust, mantle, and the intensely hot inner core. "Even a small shift in the axis would have serious consequences to the crust," he said gravely. "Consider what would happen if the Atlantic seaboard were lowered only thirty feet—a relative trifle if a downward current affected the plastic mantle. Most eastern seaports would be flooded and large sections of the Carolinas, Georgia and Florida would come under water."

If the earth's axis shifted in 1936, why hadn't catastrophic changes reflected themselves thirty years later?

The Geologist smiled wryly. "Some may have begun within the core of the earth. Essentially, there is a natural lag in the effect of the earth's disequilibrium. Upheavals in the mantle would begin slowly, but gradually build up until they caused an actual shifting of the poles."

Exactly how earthshaking were Cayce's earth-shaking prophecies? They were certainly more credible than the H. G. Wells' stories a generation ago of death rays, atomic warfare, and men in space, certainly no stranger than stories passing for news in the press of the world.

Curiously, one of the most provocative headlines was from

a press report of May 1958, Cayce's year for the onset of worldwide catastrophe: *OCEANS MAY GULP NEW YORK, LONDON.* The story, by David Dietz, a science editor, reported: "New York, London, Paris and some other great cities may eventually disappear from the face of the earth, even though the nations succeed in avoiding World War III. It is possible that one day they will be submerged beneath the oceans of the world."

The writer attributed his rather startling report, not to some sleeping clairvoyant, but to hardheaded International Geophysical Year scientists working together to trace the world's physical past and future. An axis tilt, reversing the global seasons, could do it. "The level of the oceans would rise sufficiently to inundate many coastal cities and many large areas whose altitudes are not great, if the ice caps of Antarctica, Greenland and Iceland melted. Such melting would result in time from a rise in the world's climate. The question, therefore, is whether or not the world's climate is changing."

Although the earth's inner core may have been churning since 1936, not until 1958 were there to be signs of drastic change. One of the first Cayce prophecies, pointing up this period, came in January 1934 and embraced several continents:

"As to the changes physical again: The earth will be broken up in the western portion of America.

"The greater portion of Japan must go into the sea.

"The upper portion of Europe will be changed as in the twinkling of an eye.

"Land will appear off the east coast of America."

Cayce spoke of upheavals in the Arctic and Antarctic, and volcanic eruptions in the Torrid areas as a prelude to a polar shift with a striking reversal of global climates.

Already, the Geologist noted a sharp increase in volcanic activity in the Torrid area. "It has been gathering momentum in the Hawaiians since 1958. There was a violent eruption on Bali in 1963, a new volcano is being built over the shattered remains of Krakatoa [blown apart in 1883], and the Mount Irazu volcano near San Jose, Costa Rico, has been erupting continuously for more than a year."

With Cayce's prognosticated time clock of forty years came a prediction that some have loosely interpreted as foreshadowing a Second Coming. "And these [changes] will begin in those periods in '58 to '98, when these will be proclaimed as period when His Light will be seen again in the clouds."

Meanwhile, a literal reading of Cayce, always advisable, doesn't put the end of the predicted changes in this forty-year period—only the beginning! But, as noted, already there has been a beginning of the beginning. The earth has been broken up in western America, government geologists referring to the Alaska quake on Good Friday, 1964, as the greatest ever in North America, with a seismograph rating of 8.4, against the 8.2 that wrecked San Francisco sixty years ago. Fortunately, scores of tremors hit broad uninhabited expanses of land. Even so, many villages were wiped off the map, parts of Anchorage were destroyed, great hunks of land sunk and others rose. Even streams and lakes were affected. The Copper River got twisted around, and started running backwards, upstream. Uninhabited Montague Island in Prince William Sound, fifty miles long and fifteen wide, was thrust upwards thirty-three feet, along with other land masses from the Alaskan mainland near Cordova to Middleton Island and the continental shelf southeast of Kodiak Island. On Montague Island, a government geological team could walk where twenty-foot depths of seawater normally flowed even at low tides. Far from the center of the quake, thirty thousand square miles of land sank up to six feet, against some fifty thousand square miles involved in a more spectacular rise of thirty to fifty feet.

Since Cayce's death, there has been striking support for his picture of an earth turned upside down by the shifting poles. Every million years or so, some scientists report, the earth's magnetic field, triggered by its fluid, metallic core, reverses itself during a brief geologic interlude of ten thousand years. And we may be at this moment of history right now, the Geologist points out. In 1963, a U. S. Geological Survey team estimated that the last such reversal had been concluded some 980,000 years ago. "By studying lava formations, whose magnetized iron-bearing minerals duplicate the earth's magnetic field, they were able," the Geologist noted, "to determine where the north magnetic pole was at that time, testing rock formations from the prehistoric lava flows of Mount Etna and Hawaii."

The Geologist had done pretty much the same thing. Studying Cayce, it became apparent to the Geologist that there was a pattern to the foreseen changes. Cayce frequently mentioned quakes, volcanic eruptions, floods. Though he never referred to nuclear destruction, he did say that man could destroy himself as he had in Atlantis. Man could touch it off and Nature do the rest.

Cayce was often asked to specify when the various break-ups would occur, but he rarely gave more than hints, except to refer occasionally to 1958–98 as the key period when the axis tilt would make itself felt around the world. Instead of dates, he gave clues, when asked, as in 1932: "How soon will the changes in the earth's activity begin to be apparent?"

"When there is the first breaking up of some conditions in the South Sea [that's South Pacific, to be sure] and those as apparent in the sinking or rising of that that's almost opposite same, or in the Mediterranean, and the Etna area, then we may know it has begun."

"How long before this will begin?" the questioner pursued.

"The indications are that some of these have already begun, yet others would say these are only temporary. We would say they have begun."

And so devotees of Cayce looked with mixed feelings for signs of activity in the Mediterranean area, particularly Etna, after 1958. They found it. In July of 1960, the Associated Press reported a new resurgence within the volcano peak. "Villagers at the foot of the volcano said the force of the blast was unprecedented in their memory, and persons twenty-five miles away said it had the force of an atom bomb." And Etna keeps erupting with increasing violence. In February of 1964, the press again reported, "The most violent eruption of Mount Etna in years sent a river of lava streaming down its seaward slope."

Sinkings in the Mediterranean were first spotted in 1959, with drops of several feet around Greece. In 1960 there was a truly momentous "sinking and rising" in the Mediterranean, as a devastating quake razed most of Agadir, Morocco's southernmost port, killing twelve thousand people. A giant tidal wave poured in and the sea floor rose an amazing thirty-three-hundred feet in places. The geologist Tillosson noted the drastic changes in the water depths. "In one case," he reported, "the depth was found to be forty-five feet, where previously charted at forty-five hundred feet." There were other upsets in the Mediterranean basin. Lesser quakes rocked southern Italy, Yugoslavia, Turkey. The city of Skopje in Yugoslavia was laid in ruins. Meanwhile, on the other side of the globe, quakes shook Japan, Hawaii, the Philippines, and the Aleutian trench. Things seemed to be building up. As for the risings, there was a supplementary note in the *New York Times*: "Soviet Academy of Sciences reported research which indicates Italian scientists discovered that Mount Etna is twenty-five feet higher since its last eruption."

When Vesuvius stirred mildly recently, some felt the critical period of the Cayce earth changes had really arrived. "If there are greater activities in the Vesuvius or Pelée," Cayce said, "then the southern coast of California—and the areas between Salt Lake and the southern portions of Nevada—may expect within the three months following same an inundation by the earthquakes. But these are to be more in the southern than the northern hemisphere."

With an air of brooding expectation, Cayce cultists waited. But had they read Cayce closely, they would have realized their forebodings were in vain. For in the "greater activity," Cayce had indicated rather clearly, as researchers noted at the time, that there would have to be other, greater Vesuvius eruptions, before the stage was set for the rest of the prophecy to unfold.

"Cayce saw things in a pattern," the Geologist explained. "Vesuvius in the last analysis will have to blow off big in the present period—'58 on—to relate to the predicted activity. And Mount Pelée in Martinique hasn't been heard from since 1902."

In some respects, Cayce appears to be strangely conservative. For, as geologists have pointed out even more freely than Cayce, one of his most provocative forecasts can occur at any moment: namely, great destruction in California—San Francisco, Los Angeles and beyond. On television one day recently, a member of the U. S. Geodetic Survey, discussing earthquakes in California, described the prominent San Andreas earth fault, and the communities built up around its precarious length. California's next devastating quake, he said, could come in twenty, fifty or a hundred years, or even as he was making his telecast. It could be a giant-size holocaust. For his part, Cayce saw the California disaster in the "latter portion" of the '58-'98 span, presumably not before 1978 or '80. Only time would tell.

The Geologist, trained in California, was alert to California's cumulatively building up stresses internally. His familiarity with studies by geologists at the California Institute of

Technology bolstered his faith in geology—and Cayce. "Most geologists," reported expert Clarence R. Allen in 1961, "would not be surprised at a great earthquake along the fault's central or southern portion within the next twenty-five years. Certainly, the segment of the fault near Hollister and San Bernardino now appears far more dangerous than the segment of the fault near San Francisco which broke in 1906."

Earthquakes seemed indigenous to California, three major tremblors within a generation rocking Long Beach, Arvin, and El Centro. It was more difficult to credit the Cayce predictions of destruction elsewhere. For instance: "The greater change, as we will find in America, will be the North Atlantic seaboard. Watch New York, Connecticut and the like."

"When will this be?" Cayce was asked.

"In this period ['58 to '98]. As to just when . . ." Cayce's voice trailed off.

While quakes in this area seemed rather unlikely, the Geologist said they were quite possible, geologically. "It isn't generally known but there is an earth fault running down from Maine through the Boston area to New York and Philadelphia. Even so, quakes can occur where there are no known faults." He picked up a *Life* magazine report on the Alaskan earthquake, and read solemnly: "Earthquakes are not restricted to recognized earthquake zones. They can happen anywhere. Seismologist L. Don Leet of Harvard is particularly concerned about the seismic future of eastern North America. There has been increased seismic activity in eastern Canada, New England, and New York in recent years. Though this does not worry most seismologists, in Leet's view a big quake may very well hit at some unpredictable spot before the century is over."

By coincidence perhaps, the year 1958 seemed to touch off a chain of unusual events within the earth. An earthquake where there had never before been earthquakes was detected in 1959, the U. S. Coast and Geodetic Survey reported, in the northern Magellan Strait near the southernmost tip of South America. In 1960, the southern part of Chile was shaken by a series of massive quakes, others rocked the continent all the way north to Colombia and Peru. Two hundred earth tremors a month have been recorded in the Peruvian Andes recently. The Chile quake was particularly ominous, the Geologist pointed out. There were four severe shocks on the first day, then a shock of great magnitude—8.5—surpassing even the Alaska tremblor of 8.4. According to a report by the Earthquake Engineering Research Institute, "the sequence of shocks in Chile was more than equivalent to all the destructive earthquakes in California during the past sixty years." The tidal effects were noted throughout the Pacific Ocean, and life lost as far away as Japan from resulting inundations.

Some changes have been taking place in the Greenland area, amid reports that the climate is actually getting balmy for that part of the world. "Recent measurements of crustal upwarping in the Canadian Arctic, Spitzenberg, and Greenland," the Geologist observed, "show relatively rapid rates of uplift due to unloading by recently vanished ice masses. In the last six thousand years, because of these meltings, the oceans have risen roughly twenty feet, according to Francis Shepard of the Scripps Institution of Oceanography. It wouldn't take much acceleration of this thawing process to flood low points in southeastern coastal areas of the United States; it has already brought about land rises in the Atlantic, as parts of Scandinavia, Labrador, and Newfoundland, once held down by glaciers, are bobbing up like a life-preserver released by a strong hand."

Except for the hint Cayce himself gave, there seems little clue to the timing of the prophesied destruction in California and New York. If Cayce is right about Los Angeles and California, New Yorkers can then govern themselves accordingly, particularly if they dwell on Manhattan.

Cayce indicated the changes were to build up gradually, though there is obviously nothing gradual about upper Europe being changed "as in the twinkling of an eye." As he noted more than once, "Many portions of the East Coast will be disturbed, as well as many portions of the West Coast, and the central portions of the United States." But it would not happen all at once. "In the next few years," he said in 1941, "lands will appear in the Atlantic as well as in the Pacific. And what is the coast line now of many a land will be the bed of the ocean. Even many of the battlefields of the present will be ocean, will be the seas, the bays, the lands over which the new order will carry on their trade as one with another. Portions of the now east coast of New York, or New York City itself, will in the main disappear. This will be another generation, though, while the southern portions of Carolina, Georgia, these will disappear. This will be much sooner."

One Cayce forecast wasn't long in fulfillment. In the Galapagos Islands in the Pacific, due west of Ecuador, in 1944, a four-mile stretch of seabed suddenly heaved up forming a new land rise. In 1957, a volcanic island thrust itself up near the Azores before sinking again as Atlantis presumably did, and an Atlantic island rising off Iceland in 1963 is a reminder that a minor Cayce prophecy has materialized. In 1960, new land rose again in the Pacific. "An island more than a mile long, one hundred yards wide and 125 feet high at some points has emerged from the Pacific off Ecuador," the *New York Times* reported. "Two witnesses to the island's birth said it was heralded by trembling of the earth and underground noises."

Cayce picked out some points of safety, including the place where he chose, psychically, to live with his family. "Then the area where the entity [the subject] is now located in Virginia Beach will be among the safety lands as will be portions of what is now Ohio, Indiana, and Illinois and much of the southern portion of Canada, and the eastern portion of Canada; while the western land, much of that is to be disturbed as of course, much in other lands."

Obviously, great earth changes were nothing new. As the Geologist pointed out, mountains rose and fell with the great glaciers, and even in recorded history there have been drastic changes in the earth's crust. Cayce several times referred to destruction on both coasts, almost as though he was issuing a warning. In September 1942 a New York businessman, worried about enemy bombings, had asked in what must certainly be the epitome of self-engrossment, "Is the present location of business safe until expiration of the lease [in January 1943]?"

Cayce saw no immediate upheaval. "After that period, change to other environs, these on the mainland, not on Manhattan Island." His suggestion might have been interpreted as merely advice to free one of big-city tension, except for the cryptic reference to the mainland.

"Should the danger of bombing or other upheaval be given any consideration in making this decision?" the careful merchant asked.

"Not for the present," Cayce replied.

The mechanism for destruction was again not even hinted at. The New York metropolitan area's only noticeable quake had occurred on Long Island back in 1884, causing some damage, but nothing on the scale visualized by the sleeping prophet.

His prediction of Atlantis rising will of course be his first major test, but he promised further Atlantean revelations. "Yet, as time draws nigh when changes are to come about, there may be the opening of those three places where the records are one, to those that are initiates in the knowledge of the one God. The temple [on Atlantis] will rise again; also there will be the opening of the temple of records in Egypt, and those records that were put in the heart of the Atlantean land may also be found there. The records are one."

For the Geologist there was nothing inconsistent about Cayce's prospective land rises. "Presumably such uplift in the Atlantic," he observed, "would be compensated for by sinking of adjacent land areas [like the portions of Carolina and Georgia]." The Geodetic Survey has shown a land subsidence of four inches in the Savannah, Georgia, area, chiefly since 1933, insignificant in itself, without acceleration.

In the Pacific's so-called Ring of Fire, where the earth crust is most sensitive, sub-surface activity seems to be reaching an ominous crescendo. In the Kermadec Island group, six hundred miles northeast of New Zealand, Sunday Island had a bizarre geological experience after being hit by a series of tremors in November 1964. When a crater erupted, steam, rocks, and mud were flung 2500 feet into the sky. The water level in a fresh lake rose fifty feet, and its temperature soared from a normal forty degrees to over two hundred. The water level in surrounding Denham Bay rose a hundred feet, as gas bubbles frothed to the surface.

Cayce's earth-shaking predictions often came during readings for people concerned only with their own immediate problems. Usually, he gauged his predictions to the individual's lifetime, but even so it was difficult to pinpoint the chronology he had in mind. Reading for a twenty-seven-year-old woman early in 1944, he said, "Changes are due in the earth through the period of the entity's sojourn." Again, for a woman, fifty-one, in 1943, he put the approaching breakups in the next generation, comparing them in destructive intensity to the havoc in Atlantis. "Before that, the entity was in Atlantis when there were the periods of the first upheavals and the destructions that came to the land, as must in the next generation come to other lands." In still another reading, in August, 1936, Cayce indicated that by the year 2000 a new cycle would be in full swing.

Apparently concerned that the '58 to '98 cycle would destroy civilization, as we know it, a millennium-minded individual had asked, "What great change or the beginning of what change, if any, is to take place in the earth in the year 2000 to 2001 A.D.?"

With Cayce's axis change in effect for some sixty years by then, the seer saw at this time a resulting shifting of the poles, "When there is a shifting of the poles, or a new cycle begins." That was for the year 2000 A.D.

Postulating that the Cayce predictions were accurate, the Geologist weaved together a prophetic pattern of his own. Twice at least Cayce had warned about lean days ahead. "Anyone," he said once, "who can buy a farm is fortunate, and buy it if you don't want to grow hungry in days to come." Again, in 1943: "The hardships for this country have not yet begun, so far as the supply and demand for foods is concerned."

As these forecasts, still unfulfilled, had no time tag, the Geologist projected these predictions to others that might affect them. "If the southern portions of the Carolinas and Georgia sink beneath the sea," the Geologist theorized, "this would cut off rail and truck traffic to Florida; meanwhile, breakups in California, which accounts for 30 percent of the fresh-vegetable production, would interrupt food transport to the rest of the United States. The two states, together, control the citrus market, and Florida, additionally, is second in beef."

As an inveterate Bible reader, Cayce drew on the Book as a source of prophetic inspiration, but his Scripture-like forecasts were as cryptic as those in Daniel and Revelation: "These changes on earth will come to pass, for the time and times and a half times are at an end, and there begin those periods for the readjustments. For how hath He given? 'The righteous [the meek] shall inherit the earth.' Hast thou, my brethren, a heritage in the earth?"

Frequently, he was asked, "How should we regard those changes that do come about?" His answer again smacked of Scripture. "What is needed most in the earth today? That the sons of man be warned that the day of the Lord is near at hand, and that those who are unfaithful must meet themselves in those things which come to pass in their experience."

And what boded "the day of the Lord is near at hand?"

"That as has been promised through the prophets and the sages of old, the time and half-time, has been and is being fulfilled in this day and generation, and that soon there will again appear in the earth that One through whom many will be called to meet those preparing the way for His day in the earth." And when would this implied Second Coming materialize?

"When those that are His have made the way clear for Him. Don't think there will not be trouble, but those who put their trust wholly in the Lord will not come up missing, but will find conditions, someway and somehow, much to be thankful for."

To be in harmony with Cayce—and his time clock—one must obviously be as optimistic as he. It certainly would be incongruous to move about, as some may, to avoid the long arm of destiny. And if Cayce is right, and the Bible—as we profess to believe—life is of the spirit, anyway. There is little doubt about Cayce's optimism. In 1943, he heralded the dawn of a new age—Atomic, Space, or Spiritual—beginning with the Axis defeat. "When those that have gradually forgotten God entirely have been eliminated, and there has come, and will come at the close of this next year, the period when there will be no part of the globe where man has not had the opportunity to hear, 'The Lord, He is God,' and when this period has been accomplished [when God's word is supreme], the new era, the new age, is to begin."

To paraphrase Winston Churchill, the world is either at the end of the beginning or the beginning of the end. According to Cayce, the choice is its own.

Chapter Four

CHECKING HIM OUT

"It's absurd," the Geologist said, "the way some geologists insist that nothing happened in the past, unless it was part of a process that we can directly observe." He made a face. "In other words, since we do not at the moment observe a continent sinking rapidly into the sea, then we cannot assume that any did in the past." He looked at me rather grimly. "What rubbish."

He had been brought up, geologically speaking, in the world of uniformitarianism, which apparently overlooked the fact that there may have been a pattern of catastrophe in the pre-historical past. As the head of geology in a major university, he had himself believed and taught uniformitarianism, until he began to check into the earth changes of the mystic Cayce, and they showed every sign of checking out. The deeper he delved into Cayce, the more he rebelled at a concept that didn't look beyond its geological nose. And so he quietly withdrew from his university post, no longer able to teach what didn't seem to tally with the new evidence that he was accumulating. Other geologists, knowing nothing about Cayce, were beginning to share similar views of the world's catastrophic past, and a possibly catastrophic future, but since he was now oriented in Cayce, he clung to his anonymity, thinking his professional status—and influence—would be jeopardized by open conversion to Cayce-ism.

What intrigued him about Cayce was his universality, his concept of the universe as a place of infinite possibilities, rather than a meaningless system of flying masses of matter. Even in predicting catastrophe, Cayce was not a catastrophist. "In his visualized destruction of Atlantis, he said very clearly that man's misuse of natural forces was the cause of the first catastrophe and that man's going against Divine Law had an effect on natural processes. Actually, this was a message of hope, since it countered a purely materialistic interpretation of the Universe."

It had helped the Geologist in his own approach to life. "Cayce tied everything in together, the spiritual and material, and this was especially meaningful because seven years of college and graduate school had almost brainwashed me to the point of believing in the mechanistic interpretation of life—that is, we come from matter, live a while, and then die, disintegrating completely in death."

Originally, he had been attracted to the Cayce readings, learning that Cayce had attributed history's Great Flood to the sinking of the last great remnants of Atlantis, and not alone to the melting icecaps of the frozen north. He had already considered this possibility from more tangible evidence of ancient ocean sediments. Therefore, Cayce's Atlantis readings found him only slightly incredulous.

But even as he looked into Atlantis, the scientist in him realized he would have to check out Cayce on something tangibly at hand. He happened on two readings capable of verification from old records. Imminent earthquakes had been foreseen in each reading, while one additionally described unusual storms a few months hence. Though it was now many years later, the Geologist shot down to Washington, to the Seismology Division of the U. S. Coast and Geodetic Survey, to prove or disprove what Cayce had forecast. The first reading had been for a man concerned about the prospects of earthquakes in his home town. "Will San Francisco suffer from such a catastrophe this year? If so, give date, time, and information for the guidance of this body, who has personal property, records, and a wife, for all of which it wishes safety." Here was motivation indeed.

This question had been asked on January 21, 1936, three years after a quake had been felt generally through the San

Francisco Bay area. The Geologist duly noted Cayce's answer: "We do not find that this particular district [San Francisco] in the present year will suffer the great material damages that have been experienced heretofore. While portions of the country will be affected, we find that these will be farther east than San Francisco, or those south, where there has not been heretofore the greater activity."

The young man in the Seismology office was helpful. He produced a booklet entitled, *Stronger Earthquakes of California and Western Nevada*. Eagerly, the Geologist thumbed its pages, finding only one quake for 1936, and that on May 10, at Bishop, California. The quake was felt in east-central California and Nevada. "Bishop," the Geologist recognized with a tiny thrill, "was east of San Francisco, and somewhat south of it."

Encouraged by this check-out, the Geologist moved on to the U. S. Weather Bureau to see if a more complicated reading would hold up. Could Cayce foresee windstorms as well as earthquakes? In August of 1926, a man interested in grain futures had asked about weather conditions in the ensuing months. Cayce's reply was highly suggestive as to planetary influences on storms and quakes. "Jupiter and Uranus influence in the affairs of the world appear the strongest on or about October 15 or 20," Cayce said, "when there may be expected violent wind storms—two earthquakes, one in California, another in Japan—tidal waves following, one to the southern portion on the isles near Japan."

Now shooting over to the Weather Bureau library in Suitland, Maryland, the Geologist checked the *Monthly Weather Review* for October 1926. He quickly came to what he was looking for: "October was an exceptionally stormy month. In the vicinity of the Kuril Islands [near Japan], the westerly winds increased to hurricane force on October 14 and 15." He turned back to his seismological records. "On October 22, California was shaken by three tremblors, quakes hit Japan on October 19 and 20." Cayce couldn't have been more right.

The Geologist was hooked. Reading on in Cayce, he was tantalized by a reference to the early habitation of the earth by souls in human-like bodies. Cayce put this over ten million years ago, a figure ten times too high, in view of prevailing scientific opinion. However, the Geologist stumbled across Professor de Terra's erudite study of fossil fragments in Tuscany, Italy, which concluded that human-like creatures [hominids] had lived there as early as 'the lower Pliocene or Miocene' period, ten to eleven million years ago. Cayce was again in good company.

The study of polar shift, as a factor in drastic earth changes in the past, was gaining support in geological circles, twenty years after Cayce's forecast of a gradual change in the axis. The Cayce statement that "the polar regions were once turned to where they occupied more of the tropical and semi-tropical regions" touched off the Geologist's own studies of the 'magnetic grain' in ancient rocks, revealing to his satisfaction that uniformitarianism "could be what you want to make of it, catastrophic or gradual change."

Atlantis was of special interest to the Geologist, since it apparently straddled past, present and future. Land on the continental shelf of the Eastern United States had been rising for years, and an additional twenty to thirty foot thrust, the Geologist pointed out, would produce hundreds of square miles of new land in the Caribbean alone. "With the exception of parts of the Bahamas," he noted, "the readings placed the submerged empire seaward of the continental slopes, those precipitous features of the earth's morphology that represent the boundary between continents and ocean basins." How could science dismiss Atlantis because the ocean floor revealed little of a lost culture, when it was patently impossible for significant artifacts to have survived the slime and corrosion of centuries? "Certainly, if Atlantis foundered 17,000 and again 10,000 years ago, as the Cayce readings suggested, the resulting upheaval would have covered the ancient land surface with reworked sediment and debris. The relatively short coring tools used by marine geologists could hardly penetrate to recognizable remains of the Lost Continent. As for Atlantean mountain peaks in the region of the Bahamas—Cayce's 'highest portion left above the waves of a once great continent'—these would have been completely covered with coral sediments laid down during ten thousand years of rising sea levels, brought about by the continually melting glaciers."

In his own way, the Geologist tried to check out the size of Atlantis, given in the readings as equal to "that of Europe, including Asia in Europe—not Asia, but Asia in Europe." He mapped out an area similar to that described by Cayce, and jigsawed it into the North Atlantic basin. The eastern part fit snugly over the Azores, and the northwest boundary was at the edge of the Grand Banks, and the southwesterly roughly parallel to the Atlantic slope. Bermuda fell within the projected mass. This was a puzzler because there was evidence, geologically, that Bermuda was a rather ancient formation. But the first breakup 17,000 years ago was of such cataclysmic proportions that it would be reasonable, he surmised, to expect a volcanic mountain or two to be thrust up at the time. This could have been Bermuda. There was one "leading scientific interpretation suggesting that the ancient soils of Bermuda could have been formed within the Atlantean breakup period." Atlantis posed a number of problems. To accept Atlantis, he would have to accept the whole fabric of the Cayce story, of a race technically superior that gradually brought on its own destruction through greed, and immorality.

I found the Geologist's interest in a mythical continent rather surprising. "Just because Cayce was right in his health readings, doesn't mean he was right about Atlantis," I pointed out. "In order to motivate him successfully, somebody with a need had to request a reading, or he seemed to have trouble functioning."

"That was only in the beginning," the Geologist rejoined, "before Cayce realized his own potentiality. However, I certainly wouldn't have accepted Cayce if Atlantis was all there was to go on." He found some reassurance in the findings of the International Geophysical Year, as the seismologists, meteorologists, geologists, and other scholars of the IGY got around to presenting their picture of an earth in constant change. With acute professional interest he examined an article in *Life* magazine, in November 1960, entitled "The New Portrait of Our Planet." For a Cayce fan, it was an old story. But still, as a scientist, the Geologist was always seeking confirmation of what he already felt was true. With some interest, he noted the heading in *Life:* "Science charts the structure of not-so-solid earth." Then: "Well-known places, apparently rooted with comfortable firmness, now seem to face uncertain futures. California, for example, may be gradually splitting away from the rest of the continental U.S. as part of a great shifting of the Pacific floor. The Hawaiian Islands, surrounded by a deep moat, seem to be slowly sinking into the ocean. Scientists observed Hawaii in the throes of massive palpitations, moving up and down four inches a day under the moon's gravitational pull. New land appears to be rising in the Red Sea, in the Caribbean, and in the Gulf of California."

As he scanned the report, the Geologist realized he had read something like it before, and he knew exactly where. He turned to a reading given by Cayce back in 1934. It discussed certain changes that the late mystic foresaw for the period from 1958 to 1998. A scientific report couldn't have been more explicit: "The earth will be broken up in many places. The early portion [of the forty-year period] will see a change in the physical aspect of the west coast of America. There will appear open waters in the northern portions of Greenland. There will be seen new lands off the Caribbean Sea, and dry land will appear . . . South America will be shaken from the uppermost portion to the end; and in the Antarctic off Tierra del Fuego will be land, and a strait with rushing waters."

Already, there were signs, the Geologist pointed out, of earth tremors of the type that turn up new land rises, stirring up underwater volcanic upsurges of sufficient strength to form islands. From his file, the Geologist took out a seismological report from Science Service, dealing with developments in the southern tip of South America. "An earthquake, where there have never before been earthquakes, has been detected," I read. "A large quake took place recently [1959] in the northern Magellan Strait." The U. S. Coast and Geodetic survey reported that twelve stations recorded the quake. It was a deep one and quite strong, running well over 7 on the seismograph scale, a significant quake considering that an 8.2 tremor virtually destroyed San Francisco in 1906.

The *Life* report was studded with parallels to the Cayce readings of many years before. For instance, in the captions for the *Life* map of the North Pacific ocean basin, the Geologist noted with satisfaction: "A feature akin to the mid-Atlantic [submarine] ridge is the newly charted East Pacific rise which extends along the west coast of the Americas and may underlie California." The Geologist saw here striking confirmation of the Cayce readings which pertain to the Lost Continent of Lemuria, a sort of Pacific version of Atlantis, which Cayce readings put in the southern and eastern-central Pacific. The Cayce reading, in 1934, was quite specific. "And when there came hearsay, in which it was told those portions of the land were discovered from what was left of Lemuria, in what is now lower California and portions of the valleys of death [Death Valley], the entity journeyed there to see and to know."

The Geologist saw more evidence of Lemuria, and Atlantis, too, in a descriptive report of the floor of the South Pacific ocean, though the scientists themselves were not as imaginative: "In the South Pacific, the 3000-mile-wide East Pacific Rise loops from South America around Australia toward the Indian Ocean to join the mid-Atlantic Ridge, making up a 40,000-mile-long, world-circling submarine range. Summits of the rise lie 10,000 feet below sea level except where they rear up into the Galapagos and Easter Island. IGY found the amount of heat radiating from the crust of the rise near Easter Island is seven times greater than heat flow elsewhere on the earth's surface, leading to a surmise that the rise is welling up with molten rock from the planet's depths and may some day be dry land."

It was more than surmise to a Geologist oriented to Cayce, and it almost seemed that the expert on Cayce earth changes welcomed validating signs of a coming crackup, though certainly not unmindful of the lives, including his own, that might be lost. For his face became solemn as he turned again to *Life*'s report on IGY prospects: "These shiftings, crackings, upwellings, and volcanic explosions are nearly always accompanied by gigantic heavings of the crust that create mountains. During most of its history, the earth has been fairly quiescent. But on about a dozen relatively brief occasions, violent mountain building has taken place. The whole of man's time on earth has been spent within such a period, which is still going on. According to some recent opinions, this restless activity is now stepping up."

As part of the restless step up that he saw, Cayce, in 1934, had foretold crustal upheavals near the two polar points, as a warning of greater upheavals in the critical 1958–98 period: "There will be upheavals in the Arctic and in the Antarctic that will make for the eruption of volcanoes in the Torrid area; and there will be then the shifting of the poles, so that where there has been a frigid or semi-tropical climate there will be a more tropical one, and moss and fern will grow."

The Geologist thumbed through his files, pulling out, finally, an article from the good, gray *New York Times*. It was dated January 3, 1961, and headed: *Antarctic Hears of a Second Volcano*. The dispatch was from the other side of the globe, Christchurch, New Zealand, and could very well be, the Geologist considered, a precursor of much bigger things. He read from the clipping with gusto. "It appears that Antarctica has two active volcanoes, not just one, according to a shortwave radio report received here. Plumes of steam were said to be seen issuing from a crater atop 10,148-foot Mt. Terror, thirty air miles from the U.S. main Antarctic base at McMurdo Sound. Previously the only active volcano known on the Antarctic Continent was Mt. Erebus, also on Ross Island, about eighteen miles from Mt. Terror." And in the Arctic, in 1963, a volcanic island abruptly appeared off Iceland, in the Westerman group.

As part of the geological speedup, the sleeping Cayce foresaw certain symptomatic activity in not only the South Pacific but the Mediterranean area—risings, sinkings, volcanic eruptions, quakes. Now, even more than the South Pacific, the Mediterranean has come strangely alive, almost as though trying to attract notice as a harbinger of Cayce forecasts for other fronts. In June of 1959, the Geologist was intrigued by the reports of unexplained sinkings in the Mediterranean. There was a glint in his eyes as he read from a clipping of the St. Louis *Globe-Democrat*. "The water level in Greek harbors has been dropping recently," the Geologist began, "but scientists have been unable to explain why." It was quite a drop off, exposing several shelves of the great inland sea, and noticeably affecting coastal shipping. "The drop, which in many places exceeded three feet, first was noted after strong northerly winds and a drop in temperature. At Nafplion Harbor, in Southern Greece, small boats 'sat' on the sea bottom after the level of the waters fell by three feet. This low level was constant for a week. At Tolos, near Nafplion, fishing boats have had difficulty in approaching the wharves. The bottom of the old Venetian harbor, at Heraklion, Crete, has appeared in many places. Similar phenomena were reported from Rhodes Island in the Southeast [Mediterranean] and Lefkas Island, off the western coast of Greece." The sinking was of such an unusual nature that hydrographic services ordered sea level reports from all Mediterranean harbormasters. It was a curious phenomenon, the Geologist agreed. "Some scientists naturally attributed the drop to strong winds or an undersea quake. But the water remained low even when there were no rough winds, and seismographs failed to record even the slightest tremor along the Greek coast." The Geologist dismissed the sinkings as "only temporary," the precise term used by Cayce in describing them years before.

It was curious how Etna had become suddenly active. It had been strangely quiescent for years. But a year later, idly speculating about Cayce's references to stepped up subterranean activity in the Mediterranean area, the Geologist picked up a current copy of the *Bulletin* of the Seismological Society of America. On July 18 and 21, of 1960, he read, three earthquakes rocked the Terni area, fifty miles north of Rome and 350 miles from Etna. Then: "The day before, Mount Etna erupted with a violence unmatched in modern times."

Was this the Etna activity that Cayce had foreseen? Certainly, too, there seemed indications that the weather was changing. In New York City, for instance, in parts of Canada, the winters were becoming strangely mild. Was climatic history repeating itself?

Apparently confirming the dim past, IGY research bore out Cayce's subconscious recollections of climatic changes from polar slippage. "Paralleling Cayce," the Geologist pointed out, "the IGY revealed a relatively weak layer of the earth's crust at a four-hundred-and-thirty-mile depth. And at this level, the 'more solid skin of the earth may slide over its inner part, as though the skin of a grapefruit were to slide over its pulp.' "

And how did global slippage induce climatic changes?

The Geologist turned back to the article. " 'Some geophysicists believe that the whole upper part of the earth has done this slide over from time to time in the past. They find evidence that the lands and seas which are now at the north and south poles once were in quite different locations. During IGY, coal, which is the remains of temperate-climate plants, was found in the Antarctic. One cause of this might have been global slippage of the upper rock layers.' "

The Geologist looked up triumphantly. "Now listen to what Cayce had to say about these changes: 'The extreme northern portions were then the southern portions, or the polar regions were then turned to where they occupied more of the tropical and semi-tropical regions. The Nile entered into the Atlantic Ocean. What is now the Sahara was an inhabited land and very fertile. What is now the central portion of this country or the Mississippi Basin was then all in the ocean. Only the plateau existed, or the regions that are now portions of Nevada, Utah, and Arizona formed the greater part of what we know as the United States. That portion along the Atlantic seaboard formed the outer portions, then the lowlands of Atlantis. The Andean or the Pacific Coast of South America then occupied the extreme western portions of Lemuria. The Urals and the northern regions of it were turned into a tropical land. The desert in the Mongolian land was then the fertile portion. The oceans were then turned about. They no longer bear their old names.' "

The Cayce concept of a shifting pole was in keeping with latest scientific research, the Geologist stressed. "Studies of the direction toward which bits of magnetic minerals in rocks point give clues as to the position of the magnetic north and south pole at the time the rocks were formed. Each magnetic grain is a little compass needle that faithfully points toward magnetic north at the time it is hardened into rock. Scientists are thus able to map the movement of the wandering north pole by measuring the 'magnetic fabric' of samples of rocks of different ages. If the magnetic north pole has always lain close to the geographic north pole, as standard geologists believe, then significant movements of the north magnetic pole should be interpreted as great shifts of the geographic pole."

Since nobody knew why the poles shifted, how could they categorically say when or how it might behave? "At the beginning of the Ice Age, possibly one million years ago," the Geologist said, "the north magnetic pole was in Antarctica. Some scientists have held that, for some unknown reason, the earth's entire magnetic field simply 'changed polarity' [did a complete flip-flop] during that time."

Cayce, he pointed out, had seen the geographic pole shifting most recently between fifty and eighteen thousand years ago. "This shift may have been rather slow but it seems to have been responsible for the final destruction of Lemuria in the Pacific and of most of the huge animals that roamed the earth then. These animals, Cayce said, were a cause for great concern in the communities of the time."

The Geologist had taken nothing of Cayce—or geology—for granted. He had himself measured magnetic traces in Pleistocene sediments to check the Cayce polar shift. It checked out, his measurements placing the north magnetic pole in southern Canada during one of the last great glaciations of the Pleistocene Age (approximately 600,000 B.C. to 10,000 B.C.). But the Geologist found that most colleagues didn't believe him any more than they did Cayce. "They just refused to break with tradition, and accept, logically, that the geographic north pole, moving with the magnetic pole, had also traveled southward at this time."

There was other evidence for Cayce's allusion to the "Arctic or north Arctic regions being in that region of the tropics." In this presumed shifting of the poles, Alaska would have been in the region of the tropics from at least 230,000 B.C. to perhaps 50,000 B.C. Researcher J. W. Gidley found remains of a camel, elephant, and other animals in Alaska and believed these fossils added "proof in support of the supposition that milder climatic conditions prevailed in Alaska" during most of the Pleistocene period.

Cayce had discussed an international conference on Atlantis to find ways and means of getting rid of the "enormous animals which overran the earth" during a Pleistocene period in which areas of Canada, Europe, northern United States, and northern Asia were sometimes covered by great ice sheets. Now, C. O. Dunbar, a historical geologist, points out: "Throughout the Pleistocene epoch, North America and Europe were both inhabited by great game animals, fully as varied and impressive as those of modern East Africa." These included giant elephants, tall, rangy imperial mammoths of the southern Great Plains, fourteen feet high at the shoulder. There were seven species of buffalo and one, the bison, was a "colossal beast with a horn-spread of fully six feet."

At times, the Geologist appeared to be stretching Cayce a bit. In the curious formation of weathered stones at Stonehenge in England, he saw evidences of an age-old transplanting of a Middle East culture, as described by Cayce. In January 1944, Cayce had noted: "In the Holy Land when there were those breakings-up in the period when the land was being sacked by the Chaldeans and the Persians . . . among those groups who escaped in ships and settled in portions of the English land near what is now Salisbury; and there builded those altars that were to represent the dedication of individuals to the service of a living God."

In the Encyclopædia Britannica, the Geologist found support for the Cayce picture of an exodus from the Mideast about four thousand years ago. He picked out the ancient Phœnicians, a seagoing tribe of Semites who founded Carthage and may also have ventured to England. "In the course of the Twentieth Century BC," the Encyclopædia reported,

"the towns still left in Transjordan after generations of no-
madic incursions seem to have been destroyed. This phase of
devastation coincides closely with the first successful wave of
north-west Semitic [includes Chaldean] conquest. The incursions of desert nomads into Western Palestine also led to destruction west of the Jordan. By 1900 BC, the population of
Palestine had probably reached one of the lowest levels in its
history."

Stonehenge itself is very much a reality, though still a mystery, as the Encyclopædia points out: "Stonehenge, a circular
setting of large standing stones surrounded by an earthwork,
situated about eight miles north of Salisbury, Wiltshire, England . . . belonging to the late Neolithic period. This date is
confirmed by a radioactive carbon determination [1848 B.C.
plus or minus 275 years]. The structures are unknown elsewhere in prehistoric Northern Europe and imply influence
from the contemporary Mycenaean and Minoan architecture
of the Mediterranean. The probability of such influence was
startlingly confirmed in 1953 by the discovery of carvings of
Bronze Age weapons on three of the sarsen stones."—a form
of sandstone. One of these was a "carving of a hilted dagger,
which with some confidence can be identified as a type used
at Mycenae between 1600 and 1500 B.C., but not found elsewhere in northwestern Europe."

The people who built Stonehenge were apparently highly
resourceful. Scientists have pointed out that the monumental
array of stones at Salisbury, some weighing up to a hundred
tons, were correlated, astronomically, with the key positions
of the sun and moon, providing an instrument of rare precision for checking the changing seasons—helping with the
planting, harvesting, etc. By observing the lines drawn
through the major stones, correlating them with a computer,
Professor Gerald Hawkins of the Harvard-Smithsonian Ob-
servatory, found that the ancient network of holes and lines
served as a natural computer, anticipating positions of the
sun and moon, and their effects, three hundred years ahead
of time. From the pattern that emerged, he observed, too,
that eclipses of the sun and moon inevitably occurred when
the midwinter moon rose over the heelstone, an upright stone
just outside the Stonehenge circle. Even the handling of the
huge stones reflected an advanced technology. The heaviest
stones were brought from quarries at Marlborough Downs
twenty miles away, and some ferried from Wales, one hun-

dred and fifty miles to the west. It seems impossible that two hundred thousand-pound stones could be moved without modern machinery, but the same problem must have confronted the ancient Egyptians as they built their pyramids. The Geologist had his own ideas about this. "Isn't it logical to assume a connection between the two stone-moving cultures, with perhaps a common cultural source, the Atlantean, pervading the Middle East and Egypt, as Plato indicated, after their island home went down?"

Cayce had thrown some light on the moving of the giant stones that formed the pyramids. According to Cayce, it was no problem. The Egyptians just happened to be ahead of us, mechanically. In July of 1932, the mystic was asked how the Great Pyramid of Gizeh was built. He replied, "By the use of those forces in nature as make for iron to swim. Stone floats in the air in the same manner. This will be discovered in '58."

The explanation was right down the Geologist's scientific alley, and he noted pedantically: "Weber reports on work done in 1958 on the detection and generation of gravitational waves, stating, 'Methods are proposed [for the generation of gravitational waves] which employ electrically induced stresses in crystals.' Also, Furth reports on recent experiments with magnetic pressure, which can move mountains of metal or plasma for the engineer, and atoms for the physicist."

It was impossible to be interested in Cayce, and not be interested in everything from vitamins or water on the knee to the Einstein theory of relativity. "Long before Cayce came along," the Geologist pointed out, "there had been theories in medicine and bio-chemistry that the remedy or cure for every human ailment existed somewhere in a benign nature. The nostrum only had to be found and isolated." This, too, was the concept behind the Cayce readings, that in an orderly Nature was the counterbalance for every disorder.

"Syphilis and gonorrhea, for instance, were the scourge of mankind, until the accidental stumbling onto a moldy fungus revealed the wonders of penicillin. Penicillin was as startling as some of Cayce's cures, but it had the backing of the medical establishment, while only a few hardy pioneers in medicine and osteopathy followed Cayce during his lifetime. However, regularly, since his death, there have been reports confirming treatments he advocated years before for specific complaints." Back fifty years ago Cayce prescribed gold chloride for a multitude of ills. Asked once what gold chloride would cure, if anything, he characteristically replied: "Chloride of gold—any condition wherein there is any form of the condition bordering on rheumatics, or of rejuvenating any organ of the system delinquent in action."

A report on the rejuvenating powers of gold, confirming all and more that Cayce held out for it, appeared in the Washington *Star*, September 5, 1965. "Doctors here," it began, "are fashioning the fanciest bandages ever—out of gold leaf. 'Nobody knows why,' one said, 'but damn it, it works. It seems to relieve pain and stop the oozing from severe burns and skin ulcers and sores. Best of all, it apparently speeds the wounds' healing.' Patients, who might ordinarily heal only after weeks in a hospital, the doctors reported, make such rapid progress that they were sometimes able to continue with their jobs while the gold did its repair work." The experiments were the work of Drs. John P. Gallagher and Charles F. Geschickter, working together—and their report was originally carried in the *Journal of the American Medical Association*.

Gold was also used effectively in treating patients at the Hebrew Home for the Aged in Washington. As the press reported: "Thin sheets of gold have given spectacular results when applied to big, open wounds and sores. Dr. Naomi M. Kanof, a dermatologist, applied the gold to long-standing, deep and open skin ulcers resulting from injuries, diabetic and varicose conditions, and from the deterioration known by the mild name of bedsores."

"In private practice here," the report continued, "the gold leaf has been used even on gangrenous ulcers and, in at least one case, on an open wound from X-rays used in treating another condition."

Cayce had recommended "three almonds a day" as a guard against cancer. No reason was advanced, as nobody asked the sleeping seer why almonds were beneficial. But it was well-known that a substance, laetrile, was contained in almonds, and also in apricots and lima beans. Recently, a book was put out by a Glenn D. Kittler, titled *Laetrile, Control for Cancer*. A Mrs. Alice Howell of Ojai, California, sent a copy to the Cayce Foundation, together with the report that a friend, dying of cancer, used laetrile, and her cancer was brought under control.

Cayce's observations on health, generally, intrigued the Geologist. The mystic pointed out, surprisingly, that "overalkalinity is much more harmful than a little tendency for acidity." In December 1962, the National Health Federation Bulletin carried a report on research into this area by Dr. George A. Wilson. "Dr. Wilson has found, over a series of tests on hundreds of patients over a fourteen-year period, that most sick persons are too alkaline, not too acid, as has been more generally thought. More so is this true, he says, of the chronically sick persons, who are all, with very few exceptions, highly alkaline."

Long before endocrinologists were astonishing their colleagues with experiments demonstrating the importance of the ductless glands, primarily the pituitary, Cayce had noted in his readings, "We find that which connects the pineal, the pituitary, may be truly called the silver cord, which is the creative essence in physical, mental, and spiritual life; for the destruction wholly of either will make for the disintegration of the soul from its house of clay."

Years later, the *Medical Center Memo,* of the Stanford University Medical Center News Bureau, reported the honoring of experimental anatomist, Dr. Philip E. Smith, for his pioneer research into the unique function of the pituitary. His findings were considered so important that he was elected to the National Academy of Sciences, made a Chevalier of the French Legion of Honor, and became the first American to win the Sir Henry Dale Medal for supreme medical achievement. And yet he only discovered what had been proclaimed years before by the untutored Cayce. The medical organ reported: "Dr. Smith demonstrated conclusively that the gonads, the thyroid and adrenal glands cannot develop or function without the pituitary gland, which is located at the base of the brain. Once the pituitary was removed [from test animals] the three glands wasted away. By injecting the pituitary into these animals, he found that these glands could be restored to their normal functions."

Nobody upgraded the pituitary more than Cayce. "The pituitary is the door," he said, "through which physically all of the reflex actions penetrate through the various forces of the nervous system. It is that to and through which the mental activities come that produce the influences in the imaginative system as well as the racial predominating influences, or the

blood force itself. It gives judgment and understanding, toler-
ance, and relationships to the determining factors of one's
life."

At one time, erroneously, some thought that because of the
peculiar way he behaved as a child that Edgar Cayce might
well be epileptic. This would have explained his once climbing trees and wallowing in mud as a boy. But this phase
passed quickly, without the characteristic convulsive seizures
of epilepsy. Yet Cayce had a strong abiding interest in the
disorder, and read helpfully for people suffering from it. He
pointed out epilepsy was universal in nature, could affect almost anybody, regardless of race or social background. He
stressed that its cure lay in balanced treatment, expanding the
activities of the individual, not restricting them. He recommended exercise in the open—walking, swimming, calisthenics, games, and sports.

One doctor, poring over the Cayce files on epilepsy, was
profoundly impressed by the Cayce appraisal of the epileptic
problem. After his own research at the Cayce Foundation, he
found a report on the malady by an eminent physician which
corresponded with Cayce's own observations. "Most persons
suffering from convulsive disorder, with proper care, can live
essentially normal lives," the authority had observed. "The attitude toward those suffering from convulsions has changed
greatly. We now recommend little or no curtailment of activities because of a diagnosis of epilepsy."

When vitamins first became a fad, Cayce warned they
could not take the place of vitamins in food, nor would they
be helpful except for specific deficiencies. Continued use,
even where they were at first efficacious, would minimize
their effect: "Do not take the concentrated form of vitamins,
but obtain these from foods. The circulation carries within
the corpuscles such elements or vitamins as may be needed
for assimilation in each organ." He stressed: "All such properties as vitamins that add to the system are more efficacious
if they are given for periods, left off for periods, and then
begun again. For if the system comes to rely upon such influences wholly, it ceases to produce the vitamins, even
though the food values are kept normally balanced. It is
much better for these vitamins to be produced in the body
from the normal development than supplied mechanically,
for nature is much better still than science."

Again, Cayce was way ahead of his time. *Newsweek*, in

1960, the Geologist found, carried a warning by the American Medical Association to vitamin-pill addicts: Don't munch too many. There is a widespread belief, said the *Journal* of the AMA, that to keep healthy people must consume multivitamin pills. "On the contrary, only in a deficiency state or in an anticipated deficiency state are vitamin supplements necessary." An overdose of vitamins, added the *Journal,* can cause loss of appetite, irritability, skin eruptions, liver enlargement.

In his own experience, the Geologist could recall a pesky itching consequent to a large dosage of high potency B-complex. His doctor only wagged his head wisely. "It could never happen," he said, "not in a million years."

Cayce was a great believer in laboratory research, and foretold many of its strides. Discussing the blood as a barometer of the whole body, he asserted, "The day may yet arrive when one may take a drop of blood and diagnose the condition of any physical body."

He was not far off. In February 1960 newspapers carried reports of a *new,* revealing laboratory analysis of a single drop of blood, or tiny patch of tissue. "Drs. R. L. Hunter and C. L. Markest," the Washington *Daily News* reported, "with financial support from the American Cancer Society, hope by observing and analyzing the enzymes to trace the changes which take place in the process of growth from the embryonic stage to old age." In this way, observers reported, it was hoped to study the chemical changes that accompany various diseases and "make possible the diagnosis of some diseases, perhaps cancer among them, before clinical symptoms have appeared."

Cayce was still at bat.

Chapter Five

CALIFORNIA—EARTHQUAKES

Cayce wasn't the only one making predictions about California. The scientists were making them, too, and they were as foreboding as anything Cayce had gotten off. At California Institute of Technology, famous for its Nobel prizewinners in science, Professor Hugo Benioff pointed out that Los Angeles, and its wonderful new high-rise buildings—a comparatively recent innovation—could be devastated at any time by a severe quake. His fellow Cal Tech professor, D. E. Hudson, an expert in the mechanics of quakes, went him a little better, observing that everyone of the seventeen million people in California was living on or near a potential earthquake. "More people are going to be killed in the future than have been killed in the past," Hudson predicted, "and more buildings are going to be damaged and destroyed, simply because the earth is filling up with people and their buildings. A few years previously, the Good Friday earthquake in Alaska would have done comparatively little damage and killed few people. There was nothing there to damage and nobody there to be killed."

The chief villain, of course, is the San Andreas fault, which runs down most of California, coming into the continental shelf above San Francisco. It has help, too, from the Hayward fault, recently discovered to have a tributary under

San Francisco College. The San Andreas is lined with communities for hundreds of miles. It won't take an Alaskan quake to wreak havoc in thickly populated centers. "Small quakes," the Geologist pointed out, "could do considerably more damage in areas with numbers of thinly constructed buildings." As an example of low-magnitude quakes which did a disproportionate amount of damage, Hudson cited the Santa Barbara jolter of 1924, the Long Beach quake of 1933, and the Tehachapi and Bakersfield quakes of 1952, in Kern County. Actually, California has had only three high-magnitude quakes since the land was taken over from the Spaniards, one occurring in 1857, when the San Andreas fault was ruptured for hundreds of miles, as far out as San Bernardino. Another, in 1872, in Owens Valley, and the San Francisco quake in 1906, rupturing the fault for miles. The quiescence is ominous rather than heartening, as it indicates tension mounting in the earth below since the last real ruptures, sixty years ago in central California, and more than a hundred in Southern California. "This certainly suggests," Professor Hudson observed, "that something exciting is being prepared at the lower end of the fault."

The Geological Survey of the U. S. Department of the Interior describes the San Andreas as the "master" fault in an intricate network cutting through the rocks of California's coastal region. Besides the Hayward fault in west central California, several in the southern area branch out from the main fault. These are the Garlock fault, the White Wolf, Elsinore, San Gabriel, San Jacinto, Death Valley. "The San Andreas fault," the Survey reported, "forms a continuous break from northern California southward to Cajon Pass. From Cajon Pass southeastward, the identity of the fault becomes confused, because several branching faults such as the San Jacinto, Mission Creek, and Banning faults have similar characteristics. Nevertheless, the San Andreas type of faulting continues unabated southward to and under the Gulf of Lower California."

The Survey presents a vivid surface picture of the San Andreas: "Over much of its length a linear trough reveals the presence of the fault, and from an airplane the linear arrangement of the lakes, bays, and valleys appears striking. Undoubtedly, however, many people driving near Crystal Springs Reservoir, along Tomales Bay, through Cajon or Tejon Passes, do not realize they are on the San Andreas fault zone. On the ground, the fault zone can be recognized by long straight escarpments, narrow ridges, and small un-drained ponds, formed by the settling of small blocks within the fault zone."

The fault moves predictably. "Essentially, blocks on oppo-site sides of the San Andreas fault move horizontally, and if one were to stand on one side of the fault and look across it, the block on the opposite side would appear to be moved to the right. Geologists refer to this as a right-lateral strike-slip, or wrench fault. During the 1906 San Francisco earthquake, roads, fences, and rows of trees and bushes that crossed the fault were offset several feet, and the road across the head of Tomales Bay was offset twenty-one feet, the maximum re-corded. In each case the ground west of the fault moved rela-tively northward."

The Survey had no idea when the next quake would strike. "But there is every reason to believe that the fault will con-tinue to be active as it has been for millions of years. An-other earthquake as strong as that of 1906 could happen at any time."

The Geologist had many times trudged along the fault, fas-cinated by the ragged terrain—and its implications. "The fault is traceable, from its topographical expression alone, for 530 miles southeastward from Point Arena north of San Francisco," he observed. "Throughout this distance, it is marked by nearly straight valleys, generally at the foot of equally straight mountain fronts. At many places the valley that coincides with the fault has resulted from erosion along a belt much broken up and weakened by multiple faulting. North of San Francisco, this depression helps form Tomales Bay and Bolinas Lagoon, which partly cuts off the Point Reyes peninsula from the mainland.

"A number of faults that trend parallel to the San Andreas cut through San Francisco proper, but the San Andreas itself cuts the earth some five miles south of the city limits. A prominent stream valley, varying one-quarter to three-quarter miles in width, marks the fault where it parallels the west side of Route 35 [Skyline Drive]. About three miles south-west of San Bruno, [just south of San Francisco], a stream in the great rift valley has been dammed to form San Andreas lake. Up and down the rift valley, from each end of the nar-row, two-mile-long lake, one sees the exploitation of once forest-clad slopes by land developers. Here the trees are

cleared and the steep slopes bulldozed into perches for individual homes as well as small clusters of houses. This activity
continues, notwithstanding the fact that numerous landslides
took place during the 1906 quake, and its aftershocks a week
later, on hill slopes more stable than those being formed by today's bulldozers."

There already seems to be signs of increased activity. "One
of the busiest seismic regions in California right now," the
Geologist pointed out, "is Hollister, just at the end of the segment of the fault torn by the 1906 quake. Who knows when
the sleeping monster will wake with a jolt?" Cayce obviously
knew of the San Andreas fault, because he was already
"reading" when the destruction of San Francisco flared across
the front pages, but he never explored, subconsciously, the
mechanics of the destruction that formed his prediction some
thirty-five years later, as he seldom asked for trouble without
being asked about it first by others.

Actually, one didn't have to be a Cayce to see destructive
quakes where they had been before. It was more how, why,
and when. Constantly, inexorably—visibly almost in
places—trouble is building up along the San Andreas, deep in
the core and mantle of the earth, where scientists can only
speculate about what is happening.

The fault itself is the best known earthquake source in the
world. A solid fracture in the earth's surface, it is some two
thousand miles long and fifteen deep. On one side of the fault
line, the crust is moving north two inches a year, on the other
south. Below, great land blocks are jammed tightly together.
There is no movement, no relief of pressure, until suddenly,
easing the strain, two enormous land masses may slip off
from each other with a rumble felt halfway around the
world.

Clearly seen in places from the highways, the fault is a
morbid curiosity for the people most closely affected. "It is a
case," the Geologist observed, "of the small fish hypnotized
by the shark about to gobble him up." Because of its very
cohesiveness, the fault poses an added problem. "Little tremors along its length, or even major rumbles short of rupture
strength," the Geologist advised, "do not sufficiently ease the
strain along the entire fault. Eventually, accumulating tension
must be released by a tremendous jolt that will again break
the fault wide open."

Carefully, the Geologist considered the plausibility of

Cayce's California forecast. He had lived there for years himself, studying geology at a San Francisco Bay school, overlooking the San Andreas area, and he was very much aware that certain farsighted geologists had built themselves steel-reinforced homes against the day of reckoning. Like so many other scientists, he felt that an enormous earthquake could shake the land at any time. After college, he had moved out of California, not wanting to cope with the uncertainty of living on a perennial "land mine," even before he knew of Cayce. Since then, he had studied the revealing map issued in 1958 by Cal Tech seismologist Charles F. Richter, giving a general picture of the earthquake intensities that might be expected around the State on the basis of past shocks. Black shaded areas showed quakes of maximum intensity. The fault line cut from above San Francisco down the Western part of the State, branching out near Los Angeles past San Bernardino, but continuing to El Centro at the Mexican border. A whole plethora of cities, besides Los Angeles and San Francisco, were perched on or near the active fault lines in the Richter map: Berkeley and Oakland, San Mateo, Palo Alto, San Jose, Santa Clara, Salinas, Santa Cruz, Pasadena, Palm Springs, Indio, Riverside. There were plenty of people and buildings within the high magnitude quake zone now, where there had been little or nothing a century before.

The Geologist, for all of his scientific detachment, could not look upon the prospect serenely. "At any time, activity along these faults, in response to movements beneath the earth's crust, could prove disastrous to many people." Cayce had mentioned inundation by earthquakes, and tsunamis, sea waves generated by submarine quakes, had in the past wrecked whole cities. Some had occurred recently, in Chile, America's southern hemisphere, where Cayce had foretold eventual breakups greater than anything to the north. "The tsunamis that developed in response to the Chilean earthquakes of May 1960 had great destructive power," the Geologist observed. "At the height of this tidal wave, a 11,000-ton cargo vessel actually floated over the town of Corral before being carried back to sea again."

Just as there were warnings about the shaky ground in Alaska, before the great quake, there have been similar warnings about dangerous land foundations elsewhere—around Boston, in the Puget Sound area of Washington State, but California remains the critical area. "Wherever possible," the

Geologist recalled, "my professors built houses on solid rock." However, big developments, braving the future, were rising on all sides of the faults in the Bay area, with the knowledge of almost everybody concerned, including the householders. First glimmerings of the Californians' ostrich-headed attitude toward their earthquake potential came to him as he prepared a college term paper on the effects of the great San Francisco quake. "I clearly remember that the bulky reports written a few years after the quake had documented the problem of shaky soils and faults in the San Francisco area. And yet as I branched out, I found that a smart residential district just below San Francisco's Telegraph Hill had been built on filled land liable to slide away with the next major quake. Other housing developments were mushrooming on shoreline landfills, bulldozed hillsides, and other unstable areas, posing great dangers for the future."

This was in the mid-1950s, in a State with the strictest building codes. But under the pressures of a statewide population explosion and resulting real estate boom, apparently overlooked were the original reasons for the stringent code. But the Geologist had another and greater shock waiting. A decade or so later, now a fullfledged geology professor, he returned to California for a series of scientific meetings. He was flabbergasted by what now confronted him. "In the face of a bigger and better building boom, ordinary prudence seemed to have been tossed away. There was a wholesale disregard of the most elementary safety measures." On the San Andreas fault zone, a few miles southwest of San Francisco, a real estate developer had brought in heavy equipment and filled in part of the valley that marks the course of the fault. "There he had built a large subdivision centered essentially over the great rift. This subdivision could very well be demolished the next time the San Andreas breaks."

As he viewed the thousands of houses built around the giant fault, the Geologist recalled how Cayce had attributed Atlantis' downfall to a flouting or perversion of the orderly processes of Nature, with a consequent decline in morality. "Having been exposed to Cayce's readings," he said, "I thought of the greed and ignorance at work in California, and how this seemed to mirror reputed conditions in the last days of Atlantis." Wherever he turned, he encountered the same frivolous contempt and disregard of nature. Just across San Francisco Bay and to the east, construction was fanning out from the clearly outlined Hayward fault—an ominous zone of rocks slowly shearing past one another near the hills bordering the east side of San Francisco Bay.

There was ample cause for alarm. "The fault zone, varying in width from five hundred to ten thousand feet, can actually be traced by the creeping damage it is doing to houses, railroads, and pipes," the Geologist pointed out. "In 1966, a U.S. Geological Survey reported the cracking of a culvert pipe under the University of California stadium, cracks in the Claremont water tunnel in Berkeley, and in Fremont, the shifting of railroad tracks, and the splitting of concrete warehouse walls."

The Geologist considered the Bay area more than ready. "If Cayce was right in saying that gradual changes will be accelerated after 1958, then such an area will be a prime subject of acceleration. The San Francisco Bay area, with San Andreas on the west and Hayward on the east is now at 'ground zero.'"

The southern California problem was equally serious, complicated as it was by constant withdrawal of great underground reservoirs of oil, directly resulting in noticeable subsidence of the ground surface and some earth faulting. It seemed incredible that oil operations would be allowed to continue in areas where they might induce destructive quakes. The Geologist smiled rather grimly. "In the 1930s, quakes were generated in the Long Beach area after billions of barrels of oil had been pumped out, and they're still pumping." He shrugged. "Indicating the delicate balance in fault areas, a series of quakes were recently triggered in Colorado, when wastes were forced down a deep well at the Rocky Mountain Arsenal, near Denver." Penetrating into a deep-lying fracture zone, the waste waters lubricated the faults enough to release tension and touch off the quakes.

Recent quakes in the Long Beach district have been minor and shallow, occurring as the ground mass subsided after oil withdrawals from the Terminal Island area had created empty earth pockets. "These tremors are continuing," the Geologist stressed, "and have sheared off oil wells from time to time, though very little is said about it."

He laughed rather mirthlessly. "In December of 1963, the dam holding back millions of gallons of water in the Baldwin Hills reservoir cracked, sending a disastrous torrent over houses and roads located down valley. This was caused by a

movement along a fault that passed under the reservoir and
dam. The movement along the fault, in turn, was caused by a
dramatic sinking of the land surface in the nearby Baldwin
Hills oil field."

To the north, around Bakersfield, subsidence due to oil
withdrawals has caused gradual slippage along a fault in the
Buena Vista hills, east of Taft. "Late in 1949," the Geologist
said, "a crack in the ground surface two miles long developed
about fourteen miles north of Bakersfield. Apparently, however, there has been no directly resulting earthquake—yet."

In California, as in other earthquake zones, inhabitants
have as much to fear from the shallow aftershocks of a major
earthquake, as from the original shock itself. "For example, a
local aftershock of the 1952 Kern County earthquake, distributed over a far wider range, caused far more damage in
the city of Bakersfield, twenty-four miles away, than did the
main shock one month before."

Since faults don't go away, earthquakes have a habit of
coming back. The Owens Valley quake, eighty-five miles east
of Fresno, is generally considered the biggest quake in California history. More recent big shakes were the disastrous
Long Beach quake of 1933, the Imperial Valley quake in
1940, the 1952 Kern County shaker, also known as the Ar-
vin-Tehachapi.

In light of this history, it would be interesting to know
what had been done to minimize future quakes.

The Geologist smiled thinly. "There have been some efforts
to zone building areas off from faults and decree certain
types of reinforced housing, but not enough. There are also
plans to study the way quakes strike, and try to anticipate
them. But it's a lot like trying to catch the wind." There had
been an Earthquake Hazards Conference in San Francisco, in
1964, and he considered it a step in the right direction, but
wasn't sure how much good had come out of it. At the conference, addressing some three hundred geologists, geophysicists, and engineers, Hugo Fisher, of the Resources Agency
of California, stressed that while nobody knew when the next
quake would come, they felt it would be capable of great
damage to life and property. Cal Tech's Clarence Allen commented wryly on the building boom, "Far too many people
are buying and living in houses on soil conditions where most
geologists would never raise their own families." Very few
recommendations about regulating construction came out of

the conference. "With nearly everyone in the Golden State working and making good money," a California colleague of the Geologist's observed sardonically, "who would be so bold as to put limitations on the boom?"

The Geologist saw some bright spots. "Los Angeles had sufficient vision to pass a city ordinance in 1964 requiring all major new buildings to install strong-motion seismographs to study the movement of buildings under tremors and to gather data for improving future design. However, much remains to be done about the building of earthquakeproof structures, beyond providing the lateral bracing and reinforced walls prescribed in most quake areas. Buildings should not be built too close together, if architects want to minimize the risk of horizontal damage, as was apparent in the Alaska quake."

He brooded for a moment. "Not all damage can be avoided, whatever you do. It can be minimized by not crowding into obvious danger zones, protecting against the kind of building collapse that would cause death or injuries." A faraway look came into his eyes. "You know, if Cayce was right, Los Angeles should have plenty of data for its strong-motion seismographs. It should be an interesting study."

Cayce seemed to understand earthquakes. Asked about their causes, back in 1936, he replied somewhat like a Greek oracle: "The causes of these, of course, are movement within the earth, and the cosmic activity of other planetary forces and stars. Their relationships produce or bring about the activities of the elementals of the earth—the Earth, the Air, the Fire, the Water—and those combinations make for the replacements in the various activities."

The Geologist was rather impressed by this summation, as he had recently come to suspect that just as the moon affected the tides and man, other planets did influence changes in the earth. "What Cayce had said was precisely right: the interplay of rocks, gases, heat, and fluid, influenced by gravitational and magnetic forces in the solar system result in subterranean movements that in turn produce earthquakes."

Quakes, the Geologist stressed, keep recurring where the earth's crust is weakest. "In this geological age, the crust is weakest around the margins of the Pacific Ocean, the great half-circle from New Zealand in the southwest to Cape Horn in the southeast, extending north to Japan and Alaska. In the great area enclosed by this Ring of Fire, in the deepest ocean trenches, the water is forced deep into the crust through earthquake faults, into regions of intense subsurface heat, leading to eruptions." This was the earthquake belt and it included California. "The earthquakes occurring in this zone account for eighty percent of the earthquake energy released throughout the world, and the area is full of deep fractures indicating giant upheavals in the past. There were three known major fractures of the ocean floor between Hawaii and the Aleutians—the Molokai, Murray, and Mendocino—and now they have turned up an eight hundred mile crack to the north, fifteen miles wide in places, so new that it hasn't been named yet."

These giant troughs may have been formed in massive undersea upheavals that displaced great land masses. "According to Cayce," the Geologist observed, "there was once a large continent in the South Pacific called Lemuria. This supposedly sank beneath the sea as the earth's north pole turned to its present position [from one in South Africa]. As Cayce described it, one side of Lemuria had included part of the Andes and the west coast of South America. The crust broke along the length of what is now the Chile-Peru trench and the scar along this coast of South America is still active. Earthquakes in this trench periodically set off giant tidal waves and volcanic eruptions, and quakes from Ecuador to the southern tip of South America regularly wreak havoc on the inhabitants."

And what of Lemuria?

The Geologist shrugged. "It could very easily be identified with the South Pacific rise."

Quakes were one of the hard facts of life. There were a million a year, one hundred thousand strong enough to be felt by humans, and perhaps a hundred powerful enough to damage buildings. "Actually," the Geologist noted, "there are only about a dozen quakes of any magnitude each year. But of course we notice them more now, since our communities are spreading out over once barren land. If the Alaskan or Chilean quakes—both stronger than the San Francisco jolts—had occurred in the San Francisco or Los Angeles areas instead, Cayce's prediction of a California holocaust might already have come true."

The Alaskan quake had shaken a land area of five hundred thousand square miles. A report by the U. S. Coast and Geodetic Survey presented an eye-opening picture of raw nature at work. "In places as distant as Illinois, New Jersey, and Florida," a review of the report noted, "water-well levels precipitously dropped two to ten feet. In the main shock area, centered about seventy-five miles east of Anchorage, a four-hundred mile long subterranean rock formation extending down the coastline and out to the southern tip of Kodiak Island was rent asunder. On one side of this enormous fracture, the land—including part of a mountain range—dropped as much as eight to ten feet; on the other side, the coast—and one off-shore island—rose as much as thirty to fifty feet. Later measurements showed that the fracture had permanently displaced the earth's crust as far west as Hawaii."

These were the most dramatic far-reaching effects, revealing not only the magnitude of the quake but the cohesion of the earth.

The Geologist was intrigued with the report. "Now just look, briefly, at what the quake did locally in a veritable wilderness, and translate this in terms of a similar tremblor hitting the heart of Los Angeles or San Francisco. In the main shock area, huge avalanches, landslides, crevasses, and mud spouts knocked out all utilities, roads, transportation, and communication. A giant, thirty-foot seismic sea wave or tsunami, generated by the main shock, and many shorter-range but taller waves, dashed upon the coast, wiping out Alaska's fishing and canning industry, and spreading havoc as far south as California. Small coastal towns, such as Chenega and Valdez, all but disappeared. Seward lost its entire waterfront, and Anchorage sustained the greatest amount of total damage to schools, offices and homes. There, two small boys playing in their yard, suddenly disappeared down a yawning crevasse. In one night of primordial terror some 115 lives were lost and over $350,000,000 in damage was sustained."

All it had taken was two or three minutes.

Obviously, the impact on any great metropolitan center could be calamitous. "Yes," the Geologist agreed, "it certainly would be bad for business, particularly the real estate business."

He was familiar with history's deadliest quakes, and didn't feel any were greater, seismically, than the Chilean or Alaskan quake—or the one now potentially building up somewhere. Casualties in the past had been formidable. "Over 140,000 people perished in the Tokyo and Yokohama quakes in 1923. In Lisbon, in 1755, 60,000; in Martinique, Cayce's Pelée, some 40,000 died in 1902." The greater the population center, the greater the risk of life. "The worst quake ever shook China way back in 1556, killing some 830,000 people."

It was difficult to see how they could have counted the bodies in such a disaster.

The Geologist observed with scientific detachment, "Well, they knew what they had in their towns, and when the towns were wiped out, I suppose they just added the losses up from the census figures."

There were areas in the United States that on their record appeared safe from tremors—Louisiana, Michigan, and Minnesota. But one of the country's great quakes had once rocked relatively secure Missouri, near New Madrid, with repercussions as far north as Canada and to the Gulf Coast to the south. Four hundred miles away in Cincinnati, chimneys were toppled from rooftops. However, the Geologist's major concern was California, not only because of Cayce and the giant fault, but the extension of a restless crest of the East Pacific rise under the West Coast. "The Gulf of California, cut from Lower California," he said, "is a notable example of previous breaking up of the western continent. The northward extension of the axis of the Gulf is marked by a line of geologically youthful, but presently extinct volcanic craters, indicating subterranean activity all along this route at one time."

In a recent work of the distinguished European geologist, R. W. Van Bemmelen, the Geologist saw striking confirmation of Cayce's portrait of the earth in change. "Van Bemmelen saw one section of an enormous current in the lower mantle of the earth rising beneath the North Atlantic basin, from the equator to Iceland. A slight upward push in the vicinity of the Bahamas and the Azores, in accordance with the Van Bemmelen concept, would produce thousands of miles of new land. Because of these currents, Van Bemmelen says that the North America mass is drifting westward, causing huge faults and trenches, and an inevitable crumpling of the earth's crust in western North America, against the South Pacific rise which extends below the west coast."

Van Bemmelen and Cayce appeared to share a basic view, the Geologist felt. "Now, if as Cayce says, these upheavals in the earth's interior are accelerated, beginning in 1936, then we can expect renewed uplift in the North Atlantic basin [Atlantis rising], breakups in western North America, and more downdropping of the blocks of the earth's crust along the U.S. East Coast, from New England down to the Carolinas and Georgia. So actually Van Bemmelen and Cayce are very close, only Cayce speeds everything up and gives us the source of all of the energy for the 'commotion in the ocean'—the axis tilt."

Once asked the extent of the 1936 change, Cayce had replied, "The war, the upheavals in the interior of the earth, and the shifting of same by the differentiation in the axis as respecting the positions from the Polaris center." As he indicated many times, the changes would be world-wide, and might awaken people to the universality of the deity. "Ye say that these are of the sea. Yes, for there will be a breaking up, until the time when there are people in every land who will say this or that shows the hand of divine interference—or that nature is taking a hand—or that this or that is the natural consequence of good judgments. In all of these times, let each declare whom ye will serve: a nation, a man, state, or thy God."

As he saw illness and infirmity from inside the human body, so did the X-ray eye of Cayce apparently perceive the changing earth clear through its 1800-mile mantle to the deep inner core. What he saw might not show on the surface for many years, just as disease builds up inside an organism for a period before it manifests itself externally. In this connection, there was an interesting Cayce colloquy in 1932, dealing with predicted changes in Alabama's topography.

"Are there to be physical changes in the earth's surface in Alabama?" an interested southerner inquired of Cayce.

"Not for some period yet," the mystic replied.

"When will the changes begin?"

"Thirty-six to thirty-eight."

"What part of the state will be affected?"

"The northwestern part and the extreme southwestern part."

"Are the changes to be gradual or sudden?"

"Gradual."

"What form will they take?"

Cayce, after dealing with his favorite theme of man's behavior reflecting itself in his environment, foresaw that parts of Alabama would sink under water. "As understood, or should be, by the entity," he said, "there are those conditions that in the activity of individuals, in line of thought and endeavor, often keep many a city and many a land intact, through their application of the spiritual laws in their association with individuals." But apparently Alabama wasn't thinking right. "This will take more of the form here in the change, as we find, through the sinking of portions, with the following-up of the inundations by this overflow."

Two years later, in 1934, he made his sweeping forecast of earth changes, including the breakups in western U.S., and the sliding of most of Japan into the sea. Already, as the Geologist saw it, there has been a blow forming for Japan. As a prelude to a perhaps bigger show, the town of Matsushiro, some 125 miles north of Tokyo, has been shaken, beginning in 1965, by more than five hundred tremors a day. Most of the jolts have been minor, hardly felt, but one day, in the spring of 1966, as the quakes accelerated, local earthquake headquarters received one hundred reports of damage. One shock tore a 130-foot gap in a street, pushed over a bulldozer, cut power lines and water mains; others altered the habits of an apprehensive populace. Instead of living in buildings that might crash down on them, many in the community of 22,000 people took to spending their nights in tents, and wearing protective helmets. More recently, the affected area appears to have spread to the neighboring city of Nagano, population 170,000. But fortunately, none of the tremors—so far—have been of any magnitude. Japanese authorities at first attributed the quake town's "rock around the clock" to underground volcanic activity, but later ascribed the tremors to a distortion inside the earth, apparently coinciding with Cayce's shifting axis.

At best, the Geologist saw Japan sitting on a rather flimsy foundation, especially vulnerable to the deep quakes which have been recurring more regularly of late. The highly concentrated population was no help. "The four main islands—Hokkaido, Honshu, Shikoku, and Kyushu—together with numerous smaller islands are so aligned as to form a slightly bent arc off the eastern fringe of the Asiatic continent," the Geologist pointed out. "Relatively high mountains are located in the center of the islands, with narrow coastal plains supporting the swarming millions. The Japanese economy has leaned heavily on agriculture and fisheries, which require great reclamations of land around the bays and estuaries, all shaky. If Japan were severely shaken by a series of great tremors, many of the reclaimed areas would conceivably slide into the sea. As it is, Japan is disaster-ridden, plagued by the typhoons of the western Pacific, and by seismic sea waves generated off Chile, Alaska or Japan itself. The land seems to be constantly shifting. After a tremor destroyed much of Yokohama and Tokyo, soundings in Sagani Bay before and after the quake showed depth changes of a thousand feet due to submarine landslides. Vast blocks of the earth's crust moved downward twenty feet and laterally thirteen feet. Along a ninety-mile stretch of the northeast coast of Honshu, the crust is sinking; if it speeds up devastating earthquakes will then occur, with cataclysmic tsunamis, as Japan reacts to the wobbling of the earth from the continuing shift of its axis."

And so there would be great earthquakes, as before, in the South Pacific, South America, California, and Japan. Yet it seemed hardly likely that the same agency of destruction—could affect "New York, Connecticut and the like."

To New Yorkers, Cayce's quakes seemed rather remote. "Too bad," my editor commented calmly, "that Cayce didn't say how all these places would be destroyed. Of course, I can visualize California, a series of earthquakes and then the tidal waves." He looked up with a puzzled frown. "But what could happen to New York City—Manhattan, as I understand?" He shook his head doubtfully.

I agreed. "An H-bomb would certainly knock out more than Manhattan—Staten Island, New Jersey, Bronx, and Brooklyn, too."

With the problem undisposed, I hurried off to an appointment with a retired executive of New York's giant utility, Consolidated Edison, to learn about the recent power blackout.

Engineer David Williams, Con Ed's authority on underground power cables, while explaining the great Northeast power blackout of November 9, 1965, had a lively interest in the earth-shaking prophecies of Edgar Cayce.

"Maybe Cayce had something," Williams said, looking over at me quizzically. "You know, of course, about the Fourteenth Street fault?"

"If you're talking about Manhattan," I said, "I thought it was planted solidly on bedrock, making all those great skyscrapers possible."

He rejoined matter-of-factly, "In the event of a major earthquake in this area, all of Manhattan from Fourteenth Street south could very easily drop into the bay."

In many years as a reporter, I had never heard a whisper of such a fault, though I had known vaguely of an earth fracture passing under the East River, parallel to the island of Manhattan.

But it was no wonder, for the Fourteenth Street fault was a closely kept secret. It was re-discovered, quite inadvertently, in 1962 when Con Ed planned to build the world's largest generating plant next to its existing facilities in Manhattan, at Fourteenth Street and the East River. To test the foundation strength, heavy drills explored the ground below for some two hundred feet until they hit apparent bedrock. Bids were then taken for the steel pilings that would have to be driven into the ground before construction could begin. Some engineers, remembering the fault under the river, suggested drilling as a further safeguard with still heavier equipment. The result was startling. "At two hundred feet or so," Williams recalled, "the heavy drills plunged through into a vast underground chasm. It ran diagonally from Fourteenth Street northwest, branching out from the river, until Fifteenth or Sixteenth Streets, where Con Ed's property lines ended." The fault, of course, kept going.

Very quietly, plans to build the huge generator at Fourteenth Street were abandoned. Instead, it was put up across the river on Long Island and the company made a playground out of the original site, as a goodwill gesture toward its customers, the people of the city of New York. "The articulate adversaries of air pollution, who had opposed the project from the beginning," Williams noted drily, "felt they had scored a memorable victory."

In a way, perhaps they had.

As usual, where it concerned quakes, the Geologist had the last word. He brought out a map, in a volume titled *Geomorphology* by Professor A. K. Lobeck of Columbia, which established that the Fourteenth Street fault was really old-hat, and merely cut into Manhattan at Fourteenth, crossing over from the Brooklyn Navy Yard under the East River, and slanting northwesterly under the island to the Hudson River at about Eighty-sixth Street. There were other faults in the northern end of the island. "The northernmost," Professor Lobeck reported, "is followed by the western end of the Harlem

River. The second one determines the Dyckman Street valley. A third one is at One Hundred and Twenty-fifth Street, where it causes the Manhattanville depression over which the subway and Riverside Drive are carried on viaducts."

New York City had something to think about, too.

Chapter Six

WORLD PROPHECIES

In addition to all the destruction he saw, Cayce also saw the passage of world events. He saw wars and peace, depressions, racial strife, labor wars, even the Great Society, which he saw doomed to failure. He saw things for individuals, as well as for nations, predicting that they would marry, divorce, have children, become lawyers, doctors, architects, sailors, and marines. Most of his prophetic impressions came during his sleep-readings, but he was spontaneously psychic in his waking state, and fled from a room full of young people once because he saw instantly that all would go to war, and three would not come back.

His batting average on predictions was incredibly high, close to one hundred percent. He may have missed once or twice, on Hitler's motivations, which he thought essentially good in the beginning, or on the eventual democratization of China, but so much of what he said has come so miraculously true, that even here there are some who give him the benefit of the doubt—and time.

He not only foresaw the two World Wars, but picked out the years they would start and end. He saw not only the great worldwide Depression of 1929, outlining the stockmarket crash with uncanny detail, but forecast when that Depression would begin to lift, in 1933.

One of his most celebrated predictions, yet to be realized,

concerns Soviet Russia. It was almost one of his last major predictions, made a few months before his death. He not only saw the end of Communism in Russia, but saw that country emerging as the hope of the world: "Through Russia comes the hope of the world. Not in respect to what is sometimes termed Communism or Bolshevism. No. But freedom, freedom! That each man will live for his fellow man. The principle has been born there. It will take years for it to be crystallized. Yet out of Russia comes again the hope of the world."

As many have begun to suggest plausibly, in view of the growing peril to the West from China, he saw Russia eventually merging in friendship with the United States. "By what will it [Russia] be guided? By friendship with that nation which hath even placed on its monetary unit In God We Trust."

Cayce was perhaps the first to visualize the approaching racial strife in the land, sounding his original warning back in the 1920s. He also predicted, in 1939, the deaths of two Presidents in office, tying these deaths in, time-wise, with an additional prediction of racial and labor strife and mob rioting.

It certainly had all come to pass between the time Franklin D. Roosevelt died in April 1945 and John F. Kennedy was assassinated in November 1963. Riots in Little Rock, Birmingham, Chicago, New York, had shown only too well how right Cayce was. And his prophecies, which live in the files of the A. R. E., where they can be checked and rechecked, carry a foreboding picture of the days ahead: "Then shall thy own land see the blood flow, as in those periods when brother fought against brother."

Cayce was not a prophet in the conventional sense. He didn't enjoy making predictions, or drawing attention to himself. Often he restrained himself from telling people what he saw, as he did not want to influence their free choice. In the choices that the individual made for himself, Cayce recognized his opportunity for growth, even though the result might be destined.

Perhaps because gain was not a clear motivation, Cayce was never good at making money for himself. But he did make fortunes for others out of fiscal predictions, and even after his death, people have been making thousands anticipating the real-estate boom he foresaw for the Norfolk-Newport News area.

Those honoring the prophet in his home town, were able to make money with him twice again, beginning forty years ago when he predicted that property values in Virginia Beach would move north, and in 1966, when he said this trend would end, and the south beach build up, as was happening before my eyes.

Some who made money with Cayce lost it when they stopped following him. Some six months before the 1929 crash, Cayce warned Wall Street friends to sell every share of stock they owned. But they had been doing so well for so long on a rising market, they attributed some of the success to their own judgment. They wouldn't listen, and went broke.

Other predictions only appeared clear in retrospect. In 1925, in a life reading, Cayce said of a young man, "In the present sphere [life], he will have a great amount of moneys to care for. In the adverse forces that will come then in 1929, care should be taken lest this money, without the more discretion in small things, be taken from the entity."

Just as he forecast the Depression, so in 1931 did Cayce see the precise upturn. "In the spring of '33 will be the real definite improvements." As most battle-scarred veterans of the Depression can recall, Franklin Roosevelt, inaugurated on March 4, 1933, sent confidence—and business—surging through the nation with the cry that "all we have to fear is fear itself."

Speculators did well with Cayce. Asked what portions of the country would first respond economically, he mentioned Pennsylvania, Ohio, and the Midwest, attributing the incline to "adjustments in the relative valuations in stocks and bonds from the automotive and steel interest"—not to mention the railroads.

As a prophet Cayce was unique. Nearly all psychics are loathe to time their predictions, explaining there is no such thing as time. Cayce was a slumbering calendar, dates reeled out of him, full of portent, crying for verification. Long before World War II, he picked out the year, 1936, as the critical turn away from peace, and he could hardly have picked a greater year of decision had he written the history book himself. For not only did Hitler declare his intentions that year, marching into the Rhineland, but Italy mopped up in Ethiopia, the major powers chose sides in the Spanish Civil War, and the League of Nations collapsed, bringing an end to the post-World War I dream of collective security.

Nobody was more prophetic about the major events of his time. Before the Foreign Offices of the world even began to suspect, he foresaw, in 1935, the juncture of Austria and Germany, with later on "the Japanese joining this influence." At this time, the Japanese were professing their love for the United States.

Frequently, in reading for individuals, he caught the overtones of great events affecting millions. For instance, in August 1941, four months before Pearl Harbor, a young man, debating whether he should enter the Army or Navy, wanted to know how long he would have to serve. "How many years are these conditions [wartime] likely to last?"

"Until at least forty-five ['45]," Cayce advised.

Cayce also caught the turning point of the war, before we were even in it, for in November 1939 he noted, again implying our entry, "A sad experience will be for this land through forty-two and forty-three ['42 and '43]."

Through the affairs of still another subject, Cayce again correctly foresaw the end of the war, before its beginning. In August of 1941, a business executive asked about business, and Cayce saw his civilian affairs blocked for the duration, but picking up thereafter. "For through the efforts of the entity much may be accomplished when in '45 to '46 peace again rules the earth." Peace came halfway through 1945.

America's entry into the war was revealed through a reading in July 1939 for a retired naval commander, who had asked, "Am I likely to be recalled to active service within two or three years?"

Cayce saw the conflict, but hopefully looked for a way out. "The only likelihood will be in '41. This, too, if the people pray, and live as they pray, will pass."

Did he mean the likelihood, or the war, would pass?

Probably Cayce's most dramatic vision of World War II was the "horse dream." In vivid color, it foreshadowed the death of millions in the bloodiest of all wars. And coming at the time of the apparently irresistible Nazi surge into Russia that summer of 1941, surprisingly presaged the successful counterattack of the Red hordes of Communism against the "white knights" of Germany. The dream, as sometimes happened, came to Cayce during a reading, which he remembered on waking. In its rich symbolism, the dream was reminiscent of the Book of Revelation: "I saw that the man was Mr. R. [the subject of the reading]. Then I saw another horse coming, a very red horse. As it came closer I saw that the rider was Mr. R., but he had on a white and a blue armor, and there were hordes of people following him. Then as the two horses came together, it seemed that Mr. R. disappeared and the two groups clashed. The followers of the first horse were well-armed, while the others were not. Yet, there were such hordes following the red horse that they seemed to march right through the ranks of the well-armed group, though millions were slain while doing so."

Cayce seemed almost obsessed with the fate of Russia, as though he suspected that world peace would eventually pivot about this unpredictable Brown Bear. "On Russia's religious development," he said at the height of the Stalin tyranny, "will come the greater hope of the world. Then that one, or group, that is the closer in its relationship [to Russia], may fare better in gradual changes and final settlement of conditions as to the rule of the world."

A few years later, shortly before World War II, he still saw Russia emerging, but not until it knew freedom at home. "A new understanding has and will come to a troubled people. Here because of the yoke of oppression [under the Tsars] has risen another extreme. Until there is freedom of speech, the right to worship according to the dictates of conscience, turmoils will still be within."

Cayce frequently stressed how the spiritual life of individuals reflected itself in the values of the community or nation. "Each nation, each people," he said about the time of the appeasement at Munich, "have built by their very spirit a purposeful position in the affairs not only of the earth but of the universe. The peoples of France, then, have built a dependence and independence that makes for the enjoying of the beautiful, a reverence for the sacredness of body." This was a way of saying perhaps that the French put their national emphasis on sensuous pleasure, a costly preoccupation with the Nazis on their frontiers. Elsewhere, the whole was also the sum of its parts. "Just so is there the result in England, just so the conglomerate force in America. Just so are there the domination forces in Japan, China. Just so in Russia is there the new birth, out of which will come a new understanding. Italy—selling itself for a mess of pottage. Germany—a smear upon its forces for its dominance over its brother, a leech upon the universe for its own sustenance."

Cayce hadn't always seen Hitler's Germany in this unenviable light. Shortly after Hitler came to power in 1933, Cayce was asked about the Führer by a group of German-Americans sympathetic to the Third Reich: "Will Hitler be able to take the control of German banking out of Jewish hands?"

"It is in all practical purposes in that position now."

"Will you give us any other information regarding Hitler and his policies that will be of interest and help to us?"

"Study that which had been the impelling influence in the man, in the mind as it has acceded to power. For few does power not destroy."

Had he stopped there, Cayce would have been clearly ahead. But he continued, "Yet this man unless there is material change will survive even that." Those believing Cayce infallible insist that Hitler must have changed.

However, Cayce was not long taking after Hitler and the dictators, prophetically. In June of 1938, while warning the French of softness, Cayce also foresaw the end of the Nazi, Fascist, and Communist regimes. These governments he saw oppressing their peoples, as likewise Spain, China, and Japan. The Russian social experiment could not survive. The attempt to rule "not only the economic, but the mental and spiritual life" of the ordinary Russian was not only iniquitous, but fortunately ordained for failure. "This brings and works hardships where they should not be. And such is true in other lands, whether under the Communist, Fascist, or Nazi regimes. When mass distinctions arise between groups, then there is only a class distinction and not 'Love thy neighbor as thyself.' The Lord is not a respecter of persons [the dictators] and these situations cannot long exist."

Before the war, Cayce's subconscious clearly saw the Nazis as the villainous breakers of the peace, and observed mounting resistance to Hitler. "Thus an unseen force, gradually growing, must result in almost direct opposition to the Nazi or Aryan theme. This will gradually produce a growth of animosities. And unless there is interference by supernatural forces or influence, active in the affairs of men, the whole world will be set on fire by militaristic groups and people who are for power and expansion."

For his own America, the man with twin portraits of Abraham Lincoln and Robert E. Lee over his door, counseled the broad moderate middle-of-the-road. He predicted that regimentation would never work in this country, no matter the announced objective. "Such attunements are to be kept by which the country itself may define what freedom is, whereby each soul by its own activity is given an opportunity for expression, for labor, for producing. All individuals are not to be told where or what, but are to seek through their own ability, their own activity to give of themselves."

Even before World War II, in June of 1938, Cayce was giving the blueprint for the welfare state of the future, including our own Great Society. "A new order of conditions is to arise. There must be greater consideration of the individual, so that each soul becomes his brother's keeper. Then certain circumstances will come about in political, economic, and whole [human] relationship, in which a leveling will occur, or a greater comprehension of the need for it. The time or period draws near for such changes. It behooves all who have an ideal—individuals, groups, societies—to practice faithfully the application of this ideal." But he warned: "Unless they are up and doing, there must come a new order for their own relationships and activities."

Cayce was sympathetic with the working man, but in 1939 foresaw almost ceaseless strife between labor and capital, with first labor then capital making demands that would feed the fires. He made an almost direct commentary on union featherbedding: "There must be more and more a return to toil upon the land, and not so much make-work for labor in specific fields. Unless this comes, there will come disruption, turmoil, and strife."

But capital was not blameless. "Unless there is more give and take, consideration for those who produce, with better division of the excess profits from the labor, there must be greater turmoil in the land."

As a Southerner, from a border state, Cayce had a lively consciousness of the approaching integration problem. Believing in the brotherhood of man, he was aware that the coming confrontation could only be solved by good will, but his subconscious told him the situation was to be badly handled. He visualized the sectional strife that has risen in many areas of the land over the racial issue, in one of his most dramatic forecasts: "Ye are to have turmoils, ye are to have strife between capital and labor. Ye are to have division in thy own land, before ye have the second of the Presidents who will not live through his office. A mob rule."

Even then, he anticipated the opportunism of politicians

catering to bullet or bloc votes, rather than to ending the ine-quities which have brought about so much discord. True equality, Cayce pointed out, was not the indiscriminate lump-ing together of groups, not false, artificially contrived integra-tion, but of judging individuals by merit, regardless of skin.

"What should be our attitude toward the Negro?" he was frequently asked.

He replied, "Those who caused or brought servitude to him, without thought or purpose, have created that which must be met within their own principles and selves. These [Negroes] should be held in an attitude of their own individual fitness, as in every other form of association."

Cayce constantly called the Negro "brother." And in his most provocative forecast of racial strife, harking back to the Civil War for an analogy, he made a prediction which ob-viously has not yet been fulfilled. The prophecy has an al-most Biblical cadence in its solemn urgency: "When many of the isles of the sea and many of the lands have come under the subjugation of those who fear neither man nor the devil; who rather join themselves with that force by which they may proclaim might and power as right, as of a superman who is to be an ideal for a generation to be established, then shall thy own land see the blood flow, as in those periods when brother fought against brother."

There was a distinct pattern to the Cayce predictions. Every word or phrase had some special meaning. Brother against brother, meant just that, citizen against citizen, civil war. At the time the forecast was made, during an A. R. E. conference in Norfolk in 1940, the conferees had no doubt of the meaning. The only misgivings were as to timing, iden-tifying to the evil power with which the prophecy was linked. It could be Russia, China, or X, the unknown, waiting to "proclaim might as right."

But the Negro must have his chance. Cayce himself thought the interpretation clear. He was clairvoyant enough, waking, to visualize years of racial ferment. "Being my broth-er's keeper does not mean that I am to tell him what to do, or that he must do this or that, regardless. Rather, that all are free before the law and before God."

There was no easy path to integration or racial harmony. "More turmoils will be from within." Repeatedly, he attacked the sincerity of some trying to resolve the racial problem.

"There is lack of Godliness in the hearts of some who direct the affairs of groups."

In the midst of the world's greatest war, he was asked about peace, and he warned that the losers—Germany and Japan—might soon rise again if their land was not occupied and democratized.

"How," he was asked, "might we cooperate in setting up an international police force in such fashion that our recent enemies will not be antagonized?"

"They have expected it. And unless something like it is created, they will always feel that they have won the war—no matter how much they declare their willingness to quit!"

"Can the re-education of the Geman people in the principles of democracy be conducted in such a fashion that their own cooperation will be enlisted?"

"Who can set a standard for democratic education of a Germany who considers itself already wiser than all the democracies? Rather teach Germany God, how to search for and find Him, how to apply his laws in dealing with their fellow man."

In the spring of 1966, from normal hindsight, this was a rather striking commentary on an unrepentant Germany. Idly perusing a newspaper one day, I came across an article describing the increasing desecration of Jewish cemeteries in free Germany. Not having a living residue of Jews, the resurgent Nazis were venting their frustrations and hate on the unforgotten dead. Germany, as Cayce visualized, had much to learn of God.

But Cayce was not always macabre or gloomy, not even when he was being asked to foresee disasters. In January of 1942, for instance, a fretful, war-worried New Yorker inquired, "Should I feel safe in New York City from bombings and enemy attacks?"

Cayce replied drily, impersonally, "Why should he not, if he lives right?"

Often meanings were read into Cayce prophecies that he hadn't intended. As he said himself of the Bible once, in commenting on controversial reincarnation, with Lincolnesque humor, "I read it in, and you read it out." So perhaps for this reason, the sleeping prophet's prophecies didn't always seem to stack up. In 1943, reading for a publisher bound for China on an educational mission, he predicted that "in the next twenty-five years" China would lean toward the Christian faith. This would hardly seem likely, witnessing the supremacy of Communism in Red China today. However, Cayce threw in two modifying phrases. First, "it may appear to some at present that this is lacking"; secondly, "it will be more in the last five years than in the first ten."

China still had to 1968 to turn democratic. Cayce stressed that China would witness a consolidation of its various castes and sects, with "these united toward the democratic way. More and more," he added, "will those of the Christian faith come to be in political positions, and this in China will mean the greater rule in certain groups, according to how well these manifest. And these will progress. For civilization moves west." This was an old thesis of Cayce's, the westward trend of the dominant culture, with the mantle eventually falling on the U.S., if it was spiritually up to it.

On his return from China, the publisher advised Cayce that he had correctly anticipated his reception abroad. However, on a global level, Cayce had apparently missed. Certainly Mao and Chou En-lai were hardly the Christian leaders of a democratic people. But some Cayce students didn't see it this way. They somehow picked out a democratic trend. The great Chinese mainland was now unified, the Japanese had been thrown out, and China had a "democratic" free peoples government, with a so-called parliament. "It may not be the kind of democratic state we can live with," a devotee said evenly, "but it is certainly more democratic than anything they had before. And there are reports of a simmering pro-Christian underground in both China and Russia. Who knows what a few years may bring?"

In Formosa, across the straits from China, the *Reader's Digest* reported twelve million people enjoying a rebirth of freedom under Chiang Kai-shek. But the great Chinese mass traditionally could not be hurried. "The sin of China?" Cayce pondered. "Yea, there lives the quietude which will not be turned aside, which saves itself by slow growth, like a stream through the land, throughout the ages, asking to be left alone, just to be satisfied with what is within itself." But had not the sacred queue come off with Christianity? "It awoke one day and cut its hair off! Yea, there in China one day will be the cradle of Christianity, as applied in the lives of men. It is far off, as man counts time, but only a day in the heart of God. For tomorrow China will awake."

Cayce could be irritatingly wordy or as concise as the Bible he loved. At the height of World War II, when Hitler was everywhere triumphant, he was asked, "What is Hitler's destiny?"

In one breath, he replied, "Death."

At times, Cayce declared absolute prophecy improbable, since it obviated free will and the power of prayer, both of which he believed in consciously. Nothing, he stressed at these times, was predestined, except as a possibility. Yet elsewhere, in the absoluteness of the predictions he made subconsciously, he recognized that the individual had little personal option, as during a war or holocaust, except as he reacted, cheerfully or drearily, to the blows of destiny.

He seldom made waking predictions, as he felt the implanted suggestion might over-influence the individual. However, there were exceptions, as the time he warned a passing woman not to ride in a car on that particular day; the car was wrecked a few hours later. "His prophecies," an intimate observed, "were given as hopeful possibilities or helpful warnings, not to alarm or impress anyone, or prove him a prophet." Still he thought enough of his own gift to be staggered when he saw a war that would kill three young friends. Not for a second did he take comfort in the recourse of free will, nor doubt his moment of illumination.

From a practical standpoint, prophecies were meaningless unless they could be counted on, and being misleading, could even hurt those putting their trust in the prophet. Back in the 1920s, as pointed out, when Virginia Beach realty values were at a premium on the south beach, Cayce counseled buying to the north, without knowing the first thing about real estate. His own headquarters was acquired accordingly, and those believing in him, picked up what land they could in this direction. Some became wealthy. Even small lot owners prospered. "A north lot I paid $500 for twenty years ago," a Virginia Beach housewife told me, "is now worth nearly $20,000."

Had Cayce been wrong, those nearest to him could have been painfully affected. Meanwhile, without any noticeable display of free will, other Cayce faithful have profited from his long-range predictions of a Tidewater boom. In 1958, about the time of the stipulated boom, a Virginia Beach businessman bought eighty acres of unwanted Cape Henry farm land for $125 an acre. In 1965, he was offered $1250 an acre, for a cool profit of $80,000 on a $10,000 investment. "All I did," he said modestly, "was follow Cayce."

In 1932, Cayce had been asked what, if any, changes would take place in the Norfolk-Virginia Beach area. Around 1958, he said, there would be changes making the section "eventually more beneficial as a port." He forecast that Norfolk with it environs—Newport News, Hampton—would become within thirty years "the chief port on the East Coast, not excepting Philadelphia or New York." U.S. census figures show that by 1964 the Norfolk complex had far surpassed any rival, its vast shipments of coal and grain and other cargo, exceeding sixty million tons, as against forty-eight million for New York and twenty-one million for Philadelphia.

It was curious to trace the developments that years later made a killing for one Cayce believer. In 1957, about the time fixed by Cayce, the Hampton Roads Bridge Tunnel was opened, facilitating auto and truck traffic; construction of the two hundred million dollar Chesapeake Bay Bridge Tunnel, the longest fixed-crossing in the world, was authorized. This artery, eliminating tedious ferry travel, consolidated the area and started a building boom. The realty rise was consequently enormous. Another local entrepreneur, heeding Cayce, acquired sixteen acres near the Virginia Beach end of the Bridge-Tunnel in 1960, even while the span was under construction. The cost: five thousand dollars. In 1965, with the tunnel completed and the area expanding, he turned down $100,000 for his land.

The fortunate investors may not be long grateful to the dead seer, but they would have certainly been disillusioned if the land values had gone down instead of up. And no talk of free will would have consoled them. However, some may now consider free will the big factor in their gain. "It was a combination of events," one lucky speculator told me, "that made me buy the land. Cayce's pinpointing the year 1958, together with his forecast of rising values thirty years before, made me perk up when I saw plans for the new tunnels and bridges connecting the area. But I still had to consolidate the Cayce information with what was actually going on, and then follow my hunch. That's free will."

But how much free will entered into what was going on?

That was a poser for a Cayce.

After many years, looking for a reason for his unique ability, Cayce came to have a healthy respect for what he called "the Information." He didn't tamper with it himself, and didn't want others bending it to their own inclinations. He wrote clearly, consciously, with Lincoln-like precision, adapted from his own Bible readings, but would not edit or streamline his own roundabout phrases delivered in the apparent infallibility of his subconscious. Consequently, many were perplexed by the seer's involved sentence structure. But the answer was there if the interpreter was ready. Groping with Cayce's dangling participles, a subject once asked how the readings could be presented to provide the fullest meaning.

"Better the understanding," Cayce replied drily.

Studying the readings, particularly the prophecies, I found myself gradually seeing a pattern not immediately discernible. Even so, some forecasts ostensibly didn't lend themselves to verification.

Browsing through the A. R. E. library, I had stumbled across a Cayce reading on World Affairs, June 20, 1943, at the height of World War II. Unusual even for Cayce, it pinpointed an event of a decisive nature within a few days. Cayce, speaking of peace, generally, suddenly particularized: "On Friday next, strange things will happen which will determine how long, how many and what will be necessary."

Could it be a portent of the war? What else? But the war, as I recalled clearly, had lasted another two years.

Cayce was then asked: "Is there any indication of the time at which hostilities will cease between this country and Italy, Germany, Japan?"

Again, he mentioned a period in late June, as a possible turning point.

"These are in thoughts and principles of men. They will be able to determine a great deal in respect to more than one of these countries by the 25th of June."

Cayce evidently was pointing to an action stemming out of thoughts already established; and an interpretation obviously required some insight into these minds. I thumbed inquiringly through almanacs and encyclopedias, but found nothing of significance for late June of 1943.

I worked late at the A. R. E. library, poring over the Cayce files, and retired to my hotel after midnight. Despite the hour, I decided to relax over a copy of *Barbarossa*, an authoritative account on the Russian-German conflict by the Englishman Alan Clark. Barbarossa was the German code name for the Russian invasion, begun so optimistically by Hitler on June 22, 1941.

I soon came to a chapter, "The Greatest Tank Battle in History," describing a titanic struggle, with masses of men and machines arrayed against each other on a broad front around Kursk. The pick of the German military, directed by Hitler himself, was there: Keitel, von Kluge, Manstein, Model, Hoth, Guderian. By itself, "Hoth's 4th Panzer army was the strongest force ever put under a single commander in the German Army." The Russians, too, had the cream of their military available: Marshal Zhukov, the Soviet hero, who had never lost a battle; Vasilievski, Sokolovski, Koniev, Popov. The German operation was so vast that it had its own code name: Zitadelle. It seemed good reading to drowse off with, and then my eye suddenly stopped. "Certainly, by any standard other than that of the Soviet formations opposing them," Clark wrote, "the German order of battle, as it finally took shape in the *last days of June, 1943*, looked very formidable."

A tiny chill went up my spine, as I read on: "In the last days before the attack a *strange* feeling, not so much of confidence as of fatalism, pervaded the German tank forces—if this strength, this enormous agglomeration that surrounded them on every side, could not break the Russians, then nothing would."

The author and Cayce, it struck me, had even used the same word to describe the mood of the gathering action. The word was "strange."

The action was critical enough to warrant a special message from the Führer: "Soldiers of the Reich! This day you are to take part in an offensive of such importance that the whole future of the war may depend on its outcome. More than anything else, your victory will show the whole world that resistance to the power of the German Army is hopeless."

The reverse was also true, and the Russians were more than ready. Everywhere, the Germans were pushed back. Meanwhile, in another theater, "other thoughts and principles" were to affect the fighting in Russia. The Allies had mounted their invasion of Italy. The German action, already in trouble, now faced diversion of its main striking force. "Hitler," Clark related, "sent for Manstein and Kluge and told them that the operation should be cancelled forthwith.

The Allies had landed in Sicily and there was a danger of Italy's being knocked out. Kluge agreed that it was impossible to continue."

Cayce had been asked about Italy, Germany and Japan, and he had said that more would be known "in respect to more than one of these countries, by the twenty-fifth of June." The attack on Italy had been thought out, mounted, and a date fixed at that time, though the actual thrust was not made from North Africa until early July.

How decisive was Zitadelle in the final outcome of the war—all decisive, according to the most astute of the Nazis, Gestapo chief Heinrich Himmler. "One member of the Nazi hierarchy, at all events, was not deluded," Clark observed. "Heinrich Himmler saw that the failure of the Zitadelle offensive meant that the war was lost. The question which now exercised him was how to moderate defeat and save his own skin."

Cayce had observed, "There is nothing new, nothing strange." It was apparently all part of a universal order in which there was no such thing as chance, even to picking a paperback named *Barbarossa* off the rack of a Virginia Beach drugstore.

Cayce was clearly prophetic in his health readings, for he not only made diagnoses, but prognoses, predicting whether a subject would get well, how, and when. He once told biographer Tom Sugrue that he would recover from his crippling arthritis only if he was patient, and warned against the high-fever cabinet therapy that eventually left the writer helpless. Subsequently, before Sugrue undertook the Cayce biography, the clairvoyant forecast that his mind would develop brilliantly in a crippled body— "a *mind* only working through a body that is not active at all." When Sugrue, having disregarded the Cayce advice in his impatience to get well, did come to Virginia Beach in June 1939, a year after the reading, he was completely helpless, a stretcher case. He could not use his legs, sit up, or control his arms. When he left Virginia Beach two years thereafter, having belatedly followed the readings, he had written two books, including *There Is a River,* could use his arms and hands to typewrite, and was practicing walking on crutches. The readings said he could have full use of his limbs if he continued to follow treatments, but the Naugatuck Irishman was an impatient, impulsive free spirit, who lived and died in accordance with his own restless whims. Before Sugrue's death, Cayce, loving him like a son, made many predictions for him, including the memorable one, where he suggested the title, *Starling of the White House,* for a book collaboration with the veteran head of the Secret Service, Colonel Starling, and then named the publisher, Simon and Schuster, and prophesied a national best-seller, which it was.

One of Cayce's most singular predictions developed in a health reading which came too late to help the person for whom it was requested. The reading dates back to 1919, but living proof of the Cayce power is very much in evidence today. In this instance, Cayce had given a reading for a pregnant mother, who lay dying, and, contradicting the doctors, he said her baby would be born alive, though he agreed that the mother would die. "When Cayce was consulted," a sister of the dying woman recalled recently, "all hope had been abandoned for both mother and baby. Edgar Cayce was in Selma, Alabama, my sister was in Kentucky. He was told nothing of the nature of the case."

Nevertheless, Cayce had gotten the situation immediately in trance. "There are two living to be considered. It is too late to save the mother but she will live to give birth to the baby. The baby will live, and let there be no fear for her. The condition under which the mother is living during pregnancy will not affect this baby, and she can live a normal happy life."

The prognosis was contrary to the unanimous verdict of a trio of eminent doctors. "The most famous surgeon in the South was called into consultation," the sister said, "and assisted by our local surgeon, performed two operations, too late to benefit the patient. It was predicted by the three doctors—Dr. Haggard of Nashville, Tennessee, Dr. Gant Gaither [later president of the Kentucky Medical Society], Dr. Ed Stone—all in attendance, that this baby could not live."

It was mid-July, and the child was not expected until August. The mother clearly could not last that long. Nevertheless, the desperate family did as Cayce suggested in the way of treatment, hoping to save the child somehow. "He had prescribed an unheard of concoction comprised of simple ingredients with a base made of a brew from the bark of a slippery elm," the sister said. "We went to the forest, obtained the bark of the slippery elm, prepared the formula, gave it to my sister as directed." The dying woman became more comfortable right away. A few days later, on July 18, at the stroke of midnight, the baby prematurely arrived. "My sister died easily after naming her child. The baby was pathetically weak, so tiny the doctors advised us not to give her the name suggested by the mother. They said we would be wasting a family name."

The rest of the story is a happy one. The child somehow perked up and help was forthcoming. "A good Christian mother heard of our distress and offered to nurse the baby with her own child. After about six weeks, the baby was put on a formula and gained weight rapidly." She grew to womanhood, married, and gave birth to two daughters of her own. In 1961, at the age of forty-one, she became a member of the A. R. E. Cayce had been right again.

Occasionally, particularly in time of stress, Cayce could foresee things for himself, even if he had to dream them. During the latter years, though penniless, he seldom worried about money, convinced from one of his own readings, that the Lord would always provide in extremity. However, others in his family were not always as sublimely confident in the face of adversity. During the Depression, as Cayce's principal backers went broke, and the hospital and the university closed, the Cayces had no place to live. Hugh Lynn suggested a reading.

Subconsciously even, Cayce was unperturbed. "Why don't you do something about this?" he inquired.

Hugh Lynn drily asked for suggestions.

"Why not buy a house?"

"And what will we use for money?"

"Buy the house across the lake; the money will be provided."

On waking, checking over the reading, Cayce looked up the house that he had said was for sale, and purchased it. He agreed to make the initial down payment in thirty days, and the family moved in. On settlement day, there wasn't any way of beginning to make the payment. And then came an unexpected reprieve. The seller telephoned on a Friday to say that he could not come out until the following Monday to pick up the five hundred. He would be there at noon.

At ten that Monday morning, Cayce looked into the mailbox and took out an envelope. Inside was five hundred dollars—a check from somebody he had once read for.

A few years later, another crisis developed with mortgage

payments, and it looked like Cayce would lose his house. Again Cayce had nowhere to turn—except God. As happened often during personal crisis, he had a dream, this more singular than most because it visualized Jesus Christ, with whom Cayce felt a lifelong communion. In this dream, recorded in May 1937, when the world was avidly following the romance of the Duke of Windsor and the American Wally Simpson, Cayce had attended a concert. After the performance, he noticed the Duke and Wally walking out in front of him. At that moment, a wraith-like figure approached Cayce with a smile. The lineaments were those of Jesus. All four then adjourned to a sidewalk restaurant—in Paris. The bill came to $13.75, but Cayce, searching his pockets, found only three cents. "I can't pay this bill," he said desperately. The Duke and Wally had disappeared.

"Never mind," the visioned Jesus said, "here is the $13.75. Don't worry. On the wedding day of the two who have just left us, your troubles will be over."

On June 3, a woman came into Cayce's office and gave him a sealed envelope. It had been entrusted to her in Paris, by a woman who had told her about being helped by a Cayce reading. Cayce tore open the envelope. In it he found $1375, the precise amount he owed on the house.

That same day, the former King of England and Wally Simpson were married.

Chapter Seven

THE DOCTORS AND CAYCE

The shingle said WESLEY H. KETCHUM, M.D. But it might as well have said "Dr. Ketchum—and Cayce." Wesley Ketchum, still hale and hearty, was the first of the accredited physicians with a medical degree to use Edgar Cayce as an adjunct to his professional career. He employed him quietly, not letting most patients know who was actually diagnosing and treating their cases, and then one day, before a group of doctors, he discussed his most unusual case—Cayce. Instead of a degree of acceptance, he found only criticism. "Why spend years studying medicine," an outraged doctor said, "if some illiterate lying on a couch with his eyes closed can diagnose and prescribe better than any physician?"

Even when they viewed Cayce's wonders, and saw what appeared to be miracles, conventionally oriented doctors of medicine blinked unbelievingly and turned their heads. There were exceptions, of course, and Ketchum was one, using Cayce in more than a hundred cases, to the consternation of his colleagues. Perhaps because of this general non-acceptance by the medical profession, in these early days, the slumbering Cayce turned subconsciously to osteopaths, physiotherapists, and chiropractors who had more open minds about his treatments. Cayce was an empiricist, dealing with anything that worked, and in his waking state, soliloquizing about his own cures, he often mentioned that in a providential nature lay the cure for every disorder, including cancer, if treatment could be invoked in time.

With the youthful of any age, Cayce had a better chance of a favorable reception, since the young, congenitally, weren't rooted in tradition. Shortly after the turn of the century, when he settled in Hopkinsville, Ketchum was in his mid-twenties, and eager to make his way. As a damyankee from the wrong side of the Ohio River, in a community still fighting the Civil War, he had little to lose with Cayce, since he was an "out," anyway, in a place where one could only be born "in."

He heard of Cayce through another Ohioan, the local school superintendent, C. H. Dietrich, whose daughter Cayce had miraculously helped. Ketchum was impressed that a man of Dietrich's substance so implicitly accepted the unacceptable. Even so, he did not look up Cayce for another year. And then it was an extreme case, a chance to crack the Hopkinsville "carriage trade," hitherto monopolized by the "ins." The patient was a college student, from a wealthy, aristocratic family. During a football scrimmage, he had suddenly keeled over, unconscious. When he came to, he seemed completely out of his mind. He could only mumble a few inarticulate words. His eyes wandered. He had violent seizures, and sat in a chair for hours, staring speechlessly in front of him. The family consulted specialists all over the country. It was put down as a hopeless case of dementia praecox. They had tried every doctor in Hopkinsville, and Ketchum was all that was left.

Ketchum spent two hours examining the young man. He was normal physically, but was as responsive as a slab of cheese. "He wasn't capable of answering the simplest questions," Ketchum recalled. "If you looked at him, he would say yes or no, indiscriminately, and then clam up." He was in constant custody of two attendants. But he usually sat around like a vegetable, showing no interest in anything. Ketchum didn't have the slightest idea what was wrong, but agreed to take the case if the family gave him a free hand for a year. Having no alternative, they complied. Money was no object. At this point, Ketchum was still sticking to orthodox treatment. He took his patient to New York and let the brain specialists take a look at him. They put him in a hospital, locking him up in a padded room for fourteen days, while they gave him tests and kept him under observation. In the end, they shook their heads sagely, and concurred with the prevailing diagnoses: "A hopeless case of dementia praecox." Next, a trip to Cleveland and a consultation with a top neurologist, one of Ketchum's former teachers. Again, dementia praecox, but this time an added bit of advice, "Seat him in front of you on the train; he's a powerful young man." On that train back to Hopkinsville, the thought suddenly came to Ketchum: "How about Dietrich's friend, the freak, Edgar Cayce?"

Instead of phoning Cayce directly, Ketchum put in a call to another physician, Dr. T. B. House, whom he knew to be vaguely related to the Cayce family. House not only was not encouraging, but warned against calling in Cayce. "The less you have to do with him, the better for you. You've almost lived down being a damnyankee, but if you get mixed up with Cayce you'll be in trouble."

But Ketchum, remembering Dietrich, and thinking of the vegetable that was his patient, wasn't easily dissuaded. In the end, House agreed to introduce him to Cayce, and took him to Bowling Green, Kentucky, where Cayce had a photographic studio. He introduced Ketchum as a friend of Dietrich's, and said Ketchum had a case for him. Cayce promptly took off his stiff starched white collar, and lay down on a couch. Rather dubiously, Ketchum wrote down his patient's name and address on a slip of paper, and handed it to House.

The impression of that first reading has remained with Ketchum for sixty years, even with retirement, in southern California, where he is now verging on ninety years of age. As Cayce lay in shallow trance, breathing gently, House said in a casual voice, "You have before you the body of M . . . of Hopkinsville, Kentucky. Go over this body and tell us what you find."

Cayce lay there a while, and then said, as though just stumbling onto something, "Oh, yes, yes, we have him here." He hesitated a moment, and then, though not given any indication of the patient's condition, raced on, "His brain is on fire. The convolutions in his brain are all red, as red as fire. His mind is distorted. In a very short time, unless something is done for him, he's going to be a raving maniac. It all dates 'way back."

Ketchum was impressed not only by the diagnosis, a mental disturbance, but the prognosis, rapid deterioration, which was what the specialists in Rochester, Minnesota; New York, and Cleveland had foretold.

House indicated that Ketchum could question the slumbering figure.

"What treatment do you suggest?" Ketchum asked.

The answer came back clear and bold. "Specific treatment, put to the limit." He mentioned a little-known drug.

"Anything else?"

"That's enough."

And it was, for Ketchum knew exactly what the procedure was.

Still, he watched fascinated, as House, with the reading over, put a waking suggestion to the reclining man, not only to get him out of trance but to disassociate him from the youth he had just read for. "You will no longer see the subject," House suggested. "You'll wake up feeling perfectly all right."

In a couple of minutes, Cayce was sitting up, rubbing his eyes. Ketchum was bursting with questions. "You used some very interesting language," he said, "now what do you know about convolutions?"

Cayce smiled ruefully, "Nothing at all."

Ketchum looked sharply at the slim figure with a slight stoop. "You're either the most interesting man in Kentucky or the biggest liar," he said.

Cayce smiled good-naturedly. He had heard it all before. "I make no claims," he said mildly.

The two men shook hands. "You'll hear from me one way or the other," Ketchum said.

Ketchum had not mentioned his visit to Cayce to anybody, the youth's family included. And he didn't have to worry about House telling anybody. Cayce was a medical man's pariah.

Directly from the train, Ketchum went to a Hopkinsville drugstore and got the recommended remedy. He started his patient on it immediately. Ten drops in the morning, eleven at noon, twelve at night, with the dosage gradually increased until it ranged up to twenty drops. He went through the first bottle without any noticeable patient improvement.

With the second bottle, he stepped up dosage to forty

drops. Normally, heavy doses brought on cold symptoms, swelling the delicate membrane of eyes and nose. In this instance, the patient showed no reaction. Ketchum started buying bigger bottles, tripling the amounts, beyond the ordinarily safe level. He then dropped back to the original starting point, and began all over again. Still no reaction, not even the slightest inflammation of the eyes. Three or four weeks had now elapsed, with the patient treated at home or in Ketchum's office. And then one morning the telephone rang. It was the boy's mother, a new urgency in her voice. Ketchum held his breath.

"Dr. Ketchum?"

"Yes."

And then her voice floated over the wire. "Good morning, miracle man," she said.

Just a few minutes before, her son had come down the stairs and spoken intelligibly for the first time in a year. It was as though a veil had been lifted from his mind. "Good morning, Mom, what are we having for breakfast?" That was all he said, but that was all he had to say. He was back where he had been before his collapse on the football field.

Ketchum took all the credit, since he didn't dare mention Cayce at the time, and of course, he did deserve credit for daring to consult Cayce and persisting with his treatment. Thereafter, when Ketchum couldn't diagnose a case promptly, or it seemed out of the ordinary, he would contact Cayce in Bowling Green and ask if he would "sleep" on it.

One day a laborer named Homer Jenkins, shoveling in a local brick works, tumbled over in a faint. He was piled on some straw in a road wagon and carted off to his home. Ketchum had no idea what was wrong. Cayce said it was a severe case of malnutrition. "Too much hominy and grits." He suggested a well-balanced diet with plenty of green vegetables.

It was the first case of pellagra Ketchum had ever seen, and it helped him diagnose and treat other cases which local doctors had been wrestling with for a year without being able to diagnose. "Prior to this," Ketchum recalled, "the only pellagra I had ever heard of was in Italy. But now they began picking up cases of pellagra from all over, where the people had been eating nothing but hog and hominy."

Again Cayce didn't get credit. One of the Hopkinsville

doctors, whose patients had been helped, read a paper on his diagnosis of pellagra to the Kentucky Medical Society, but he didn't mention Cayce, or Ketchum, for that matter.

Nevertheless, Cayce was quietly but surely enhancing Ketchum's reputation. Five Southern doctors, all seasoned veterans, and the neophyte Ketchum were called in for consultation when wealthy contractor, George Dalton, shattered a leg in a fall. As the doctors wisely communed, Mrs. Dalton came out of the sick room and announced, "Mr. Dalton is willing to trust his case to the Yankee boy."

It was a heavy responsibility for Ketchum—and Cayce. There was no hospital, and patients were treated at home or in the doctor's office. And Ketchum had never treated a compound fracture before. There was a hurried consultation with Cayce. And Cayce suggested rather radical treatment for that time: boring a hole in the kneecap, nailing the bones together, then putting the leg in traction.

Ketchum had some misgivings. He had never heard of anything like this. "They used splints then," he recalled, "but metal screws were still in the future. However, I went down to the nearest blacksmith, and he made up an iron nail like a large roofing nail, with a big head on it." Then with another doctor and two nurses helping, Ketchum bored a hole in the patient's knee and nailed it, and then put the leg in traction, with a pulley at the foot of the bed.

As the story got around that the Yankee doctor was hammering nails into Dalton's leg, Ketchum became uncomfortably aware of spiteful side glances, and of wagging tongues saying, "That damyankee. He'll kill old Dalton before he's through." He went to Cayce for reassurance, and got it. Meanwhile, he carried a double-barreled shotgun in his buggy with him. He realized that his survival, as a local doctor, anyway, hinged on Dalton's recovery. It took months, but he was vindicated. The leg was as solid as ever, and the iron nail stayed in, Dalton taking it to the grave with him thirty years later.

Still nobody knew that he was using Cayce. And Ketchum himself couldn't get used to the idea that this slumbering illiterate, who had not gone beyond the sixth grade, knew more about medicine, anatomy, and chemistry than an honor medical graduate like himself, and any of his distinguished colleagues or professors. Even seeing it happen, it seemed incredible. He kept testing. Once he asked the sleeping Cayce what the shortest muscle in the body was. Without hesitating, the unlettered youth replied. "Levator labii superioris alaeque nasi—in the upper lip." He asked Cayce to name the longest muscle, and with equal accuracy the sleeping phenomenon replied, "Sartorius"—the muscle flexing the hip and knee joints. Sometimes the words spilled out of Cayce, with all their intricate technical terminology, other times he seemed to be groping, like a bloodhound off the scent, and then would quickly recover as though he had picked up a fresh trail. At such times, Ketchum recalled, he appeared to be peering inside the subject, and it all seemed very clear to him.

Cayce seldom recommended operations, indicating that his subconscious considered surgery overworked. Any and every method that appeared favorable to the particular situation came out of him clairvoyantly. "He was an advocate of the new treatment of osteopathy that had just come in at that time," Ketchum noted. "He recommended it for cases that chiefly had to do with spinal adjustment or manipulation. Often we would ask if an operation was necessary, and he'd say, 'No operation needed.' Instead, he'd refer the patient to the nearest osteopathic doctor." There weren't many osteopaths around in those days, and Cayce would sometimes supply the therapist's name and address, and then describe the treatment in detail.

Yet, he was as partial to drugs when they suited the purpose. Ketchum was an often startled witness to Cayce's singular facility for picking out drugs that were not generally known, not yet on the market, or out of use. "One day," Ketchum recalled, "there were a couple of doctors and druggists in Cayce's studio on a complicated case, for which Cayce prescribed balsam of sulphur. They began scratching their heads. Nobody had ever heard of it. One of the druggists, an elderly man named Gaither, was convinced there was no such thing. They pored over a copy of the dispensatory, listing all available therapeutic drugs. There was no balsam of sulphur. Then, in an attic, they stumbled across an old defunct catalog, put out fifty years before. They dusted it off, opened it, and there found balsam of sulphur."

Almost every aspect of the Cayce phenomenon was observed by Ketchum in their years together. But each new wonder left him as surprised as the last. After a while he was convinced that Cayce's mind traveled in space, settling in the immediate vicinity of the person he was reading for. The clincher came one night when Cayce was reading in Hopkinsville for a patient in Cleveland. Suddenly, in the middle of the reading, Cayce broke off. "He's gone," was all he could say. He seemed to be groping about aimlessly.

Ketchum awakened him.

Later, Ketchum received a letter from a doctor friend in Cleveland. His patient had died at 8:20 P.M., the very moment that Cayce missed him.

Ketchum was a self-assured young man with a strong sense of balance. It stood him in good stead. Gradually, though he didn't talk about it himself, at this time, word had gotten around that he was associated with a clairvoyant possessing remarkable healing powers. Even so, people resorting to Cayce had usually exhausted all other remedial sources. There were all kinds of phone calls, from the rich, poor, trusting, cynical. Ketchum felt a little like Sherlock Holmes of Baker Street, able to pick and choose the most interesting cases that came his way. One day the phone rang, and a man announced that he'd like the services of Wonder Boy Cayce. He was a millionaire, living in a Midwestern city, and he was ready to pay handsomely, throwing in a princely bonus if Cayce was effective. It seemed the usual, last-ditch case, as Ketchum mulled it over, but it was to reflect Cayce's apparent omniscience in such a way that even Ketchum was left shaking his head weakly. As with Holmes' best cases, the beginning was rather ordinary. The patient, the wife, was apparently suffering from paralysis agitans, shaking palsy. The devoted husband had taken her to clinics, hospitals, baths all over the world, and had finally brought her home, hoping that care and rest would at least make her comfortable. When he heard somehow of Cayce, he thought it worth a chance. "All I ask," he said over the phone "is that you bring Cayce to our city to give her a diagnosis."

Ketchum didn't give him an answer right off. "Give me your wife's name and address," he said, "and I'll let you know." As often as Cayce had been successful, Ketchum still had to reassure himself each time that the performance was genuine—and repeatable. So with the man's request, and the wife's whereabouts, he asked Cayce for a preliminary reading, presented to the mystic like any other request. As a stenographer sat by, taking notes, Cayce raced on with a complete history of the woman's problem, induced largely by nerves. Ketchum studied the report, then called the man to tell him he was on his way. He had decided against taking Cayce, as he was still playing down the association publicly.

On his arrival, he checked into a hotel and phoned the husband.

"Did you bring the boy with you?" the man asked.

"No," Ketchum said.

The man's voice fell. "Well, what are *you* going to do?"

"I have with me a typewritten description of your case." He explained that it was from Cayce.

There was an awkward pause on the other end of the line. "Very well," the man said finally. "As long as you're here, you may as well come over."

Hundreds of miles away, in trance, Cayce had described the unknown patient as being in a wheelchair and said of her condition, "She is as rigid as a piece of marble. She can look neither to the right nor the left. She had two trained nurses with white caps." As used as he was to Cayce, Ketchum's jaw dropped when he drew up to the patient's home. "There was the wife sitting on the front porch, at the top of the steps, in a wheelchair. On either side stood a trained nurse in a white cap."

Because of the nature of the report in his pocket, Ketchum needed the reassurance he had just received to proceed confidently. The party moved into the living room, the nurses withdrew, and the husband eyed Ketchum darkly. "How can you proceed without the Wonder Boy?" he asked.

Ketchum permitted himself a smile. "I have the Wonder Boy right here with me," he said, taking out the typewritten report. He was not about to go into a description of how Cayce functioned when he didn't understand it himself.

The woman sat stoically, hands trembling, eyes staring ahead. Her husband was at her side, never lifting his gaze from the visitor. Ketchum sat close to the woman, as he read from Cayce. The patient had a nervous disorder, but not what was diagnosed. As Ketchum read on, he appeared to grow embarrassed, rare for him. "As a young woman," he said, "the patient had a secret sin." She moved her head a bit, showing her first sign of interest. Ketchum forged ahead. "This secret sin was masturbation."

The patient flushed from forehead to throat. Her husband looked bored. He had never heard of anything so ridiculous. But Ketchum had caught the woman's startled look. He went on bravely. Because of this sin, riddling her with guilt, the woman had delayed marriage until she was thirty-nine. She had then married happily, it seemed, had two children, and then fallen ill. The husband's interest perked up a little at this, since Cayce had hit the broad outline of their life together.

As Ketchum finished the Cayce report, the woman turned to her husband. "Would you please go into the other room? I want to talk to the doctor alone."

As the door closed, she fixed her gaze on the youthful physician. "Dr. Ketchum," she said, "what kind of man is this Cayce? I did have a secret sin, from the age of eighteen until I was thirty-nine. But only I and my God have even known of it. How in the name of God could this man have told you this?"

They chatted for a while, Ketchum explaining that Cayce was a clairvoyant, who somehow tuned into the subconscious. Apparently he had hit upon the suppressed guilt which had built up inside the woman all these years, gradually reflecting itself in her physical condition. As Cayce had so often indicated, mind and body were unified, and the one could not suffer without the other following suit.

Cayce had recommended certain drugs to help with the condition; talking it out seemed to do the rest. Recovering gradually, the woman lived normally for several years. The husband, nevertheless, was not overly impressed. He couldn't get out of his mind all that hogwash about a secret sin.

Ketchum never ceased marveling at Cayce's apparent universal knowledge. It was an arsenal, which he frequently drew on for his own curiosity, as well as to help others. With Cayce in his corner, it was difficult for patients to keep secrets from the doctor. At the same time, with his omniscient backdrop, it gave the young physician a sense of authority, broadening his jurisdiction over patients, even when he knew them only scantily. Whatever it was, he felt that Cayce knew best. And so he counseled. One time, around the Christmas holidays, a mother had made an appointment for her daughter, who had arrived home on college vacation in a state of depression. The appointment was for nine the next morning.

That evening, Ketchum consulted Cayce, giving him the girl's name and address. Cayce was very quiet for a few minutes, as though trying in trance to appraise what he was receiving, and then said with almost a sigh, "The trouble with this body is right here, right here. There is a new life developing here in this pelvis. As a result we have nausea, vomiting, otherwise known as morning sickness."

Ketchum's face fell. "What a case," he thought wryly.

But since he was testing Cayce, he felt he might as well do a thorough job.

"What treatment do you suggest?" That question could very well be a poser, since the girl was certainly not married.

"No treatment at all," Cayce replied. "It's perfectly physiological. Nature takes care of those things."

Before waking Cayce, Ketchum washed the girl out of the sleeping mystic's conscious mind. "Very well," he said, "you will not see her any more."

Mother and daughter arrived promptly at nine. The girl was pale and wan but beautiful, with fine features, and a refined way about her. If she had given herself to anyone, Ketchum sensed, it would only have been out of love. He turned to the mother, "May I talk to your daughter alone?"

In the privacy of his office, he said gently, "Now tell me all about yourself."

She flushed and swallowed a few times, then said in a tight little voice, "Nobody knows about it, but I've missed two months." It was by no means an unusual story, even for that day and age. She had been dating a young man at a college nearby for a year and a half, and they had fallen in love. Now she was pregnant.

Ketchum was only a few years older than the girl, but he had Cayce to borrow from. And Cayce had proposed that Nature take care of the problem.

Ketchum thought he would help Nature. "The first thing we must do is tell your mother," he said.

The girl was horrified. "Please, not that."

"Of course, your mother will know exactly what is best."

The mother was surprisingly calm. She turned to her daughter, asking how she felt about the young man. The girl sobbed that she loved him, but was too ashamed to let him know what had happened. "I don't want him to have to marry me."

The mother looked questioningly at the young doctor who seemed to have such easy command of a difficult situation.

Ketchum was still pushing Nature. "Take my advice, contact this young man right away, and have him come here for a talk." He threw one sop to her female pride. "I wouldn't ask any man to marry a girl unless she is the one for him. If you feel the same, then slip off to another state, get married, and spread it across every paper in town. If you keep it under cover, you'll only make people curious." In forty-eight hours, it was all settled. The pair eloped, and then went back to their classes, graduating in June, the baby arriving almost with the Commencement Exercises.

As Ketchum kept using Cayce, other doctors in Christian County began to take an increasingly dim view of him and "The Freak." On his part, the bumptious Ketchum was feeling a growing annoyance with a medical fraternity that looked on him suspiciously. He was also quietly aware that some who had been quick to denounce him to the local medical societies had clandestinely used Cayce themselves.

Cayce's own attitude toward M.D.s was sharply edged with reserve. His distant kin, Thomas House, later to head up the Cayce Hospital, had used him, without understanding how the power worked. But at least he conceded what did work, without the customary medical observation, that it would have cured itself anyway. Long before Ketchum arrived, the M.D.s had stopped the unlicensed Al Layne from practicing medicine. Cayce had keenly felt their ending Layne's work with him, when they seemed to be helping people. He had agreed, nevertheless, to work with a committee of youthful physicians headed by Dr. John Blackburn, who had been impressed by his work with the Dietrich child, among others. Blackburn, superseding Layne, had even helped Cayce once, when his aphonia, or voice lapse, had suddenly recurred, having Cayce suggest to himself that his blood circulate properly. His voice promptly came back.

But even so, the committee of doctors, constantly testing, put a strain on the brooding mystic, since at this indecisive stage, he was looking for assurance, not misgivings or doubts, to justify going on with the work. Some doctors had stuck him with pins when he was sleeping to make sure he wasn't faking, others had exerted themselves to show his treatments utterly false. Once, the committee thought they had him. It seemed an open-and-shut case. Specialists had urged an immediate operation for a woman with abdominal pains, bleeding internally. She went to Cayce. Cayce told her that all she had was an abrasion of the stomach wall. He advised long walks every day and a raw lemon sprinkled with salt. It was so patently absurd that the doctors decided to use this case to show up Cayce as a fraud. They held off the operation, though they considered surgery imperative. Three weeks later, the woman was hiking ten miles a day and the abdominal pains had disappeared. She was completely cured.

Shortly before he met Ketchum, Cayce decided that his

gift, if it was that, would have to stand on its own. There would be no more experiments, with him as the guinea pig. While he and Ketchum were worlds apart temperamentally, he recognized in Ketchum a pragmatic acceptance of what worked, and it gave him a chance to help people under competent supervision. Ketchum of course had profited. In three or four years of backstopping by Cayce he had achieved an enviable reputation as the doctor who could help when nobody else could. But he had no objection to Cayce as a partner, if Cayce was willing, for he realized that the only objections would come from doctors, not patients interested only in being helped. So he tossed a trial balloon in the air, choosing with his flair for the dramatic a most suitable stage—a convention of doctors. The occasion was a meeting of the National Society of Homeopathic Physicians, at Pasadena, California. As he listened to his fellow physicians discuss their most unusual cases, Ketchum rose leisurely one day and told them of his most unusual case. This was in July 1910.

Most of his listeners were incredulous, of course. But one, a Dr. Krauss, from Boston, approached Ketchum and asked if he would prepare a paper on Cayce for the American Association for Clinical Research meeting in Boston that September. Without much more ado, Ketchum sat down and dashed off his description of Cayce with a lead pencil, and handed it to the doctor. He thought no more of it, until he got a copy of the program later, and saw himself down for "My Unusual Case."

He had not bothered to go himself, or try to bring Cayce, because he felt the medical profession—and the lay public—was not prepared to accept what he had to say. And could he have had second thoughts, he would probably have withdrawn his paper. As it was, it was read by Henry E. Harrower, M.D., of Chicago, a frequent contributor to the *Journal of the American Medical Association*, and fully reported in a subsequent issue of the *New York Times*. The *Times* considered it pertinent to mention Dr. Ketchum's own credentials. "It is well enough to add that Dr. Wesley H. Ketchum is a reputable physician of high standing and successful practice in the homeopathic school of medicine. He possesses a classical education, is by nature of a scientific turn, and is a graduate of one of the leading medical institutions of the country. He is vouched for by orthodox physicians in both Kentucky and Ohio, in both of which states he is well known. In Hopkinsville, no physician of any school stands higher, though he is still a young man."

The assembly of physicians listened with mingled reactions as Dr. Harrower read off the paper for the absent Ketchum. It spelled out Ketchum, almost as much as it did Cayce. "About four years ago," it went, "I made the acquaintance of a young man twenty-eight years old who had the reputation of being a 'freak.' They said he told wonderful truths while he was asleep. I, being interested, immediately began to investigate, and as I was from Missouri, I had to be shown. And truly, when it comes to anything psychical, every layman is a disbeliever from the start, and most of our chosen profession will not accept anything of a psychic nature, hypnotism, mesmerism, or what not, unless vouched for by some M.D. away up in the profession and one whose orthodox standing is unquestioned."

Ketchum then mentioned how he put Cayce into trance. "While in this sleep, which to all intents and purposes is a natural sleep, his objective mind is completely inactive and only his subjective is working. By suggestion he becomes unconscious to pain of any sort, and strange to say, his best work is done when he is seemingly 'dead to the world.' "

He stressed Cayce's clinical detail and his accurate terminology. "His psychological terms and description of the nervous anatomy would do credit to any professor of nervous anatomy. There is no faltering in his speech and all his statements are clear and concise. He handles the most complex jawbreakers with as much ease as any Boston physician, which to me is quite wonderful, in view of the fact that while in his normal state he is an illiterate man, especially along the line of medicine, surgery or pharmacy, of which he knows nothing. He is awakened by the suggestion that he will see this person no more, and in a few minutes will be awake. Upon questioning him, he knows absolutely nothing that he said, or whose case he was talking about."

He had never known Cayce to err in diagnosis, though he did once describe the wrong person living in the same house as the one wanted. "The cases I have used him in have, in the main, been the rounds before coming to my attention, and in six important cases which had been diagnosed as strictly surgical he stated that no such condition existed, and outlined treatment which was followed with gratifying results in every case."

Conventionally schooled himself, Ketchum boldly anticipated the reaction to his remarks. "The regular profession scoff at anything reliable coming from this source, because the majority of them are in the rut and have never taken to anything not strictly orthodox. You may ask why has a man with such powers not been before the public and received the indorsement of the profession, one and all, without fear or favor? I can truly answer that they are not ready as yet. Even Christ himself was rejected. 'Unless they see signs and wonders they will not believe.' "

Not long after the Boston report, which brought a descent of curious newspapermen on ordinarily drowsy Hopkinsville, the organized medical groups in Christian County decided the time was at hand to take action against an upstart who seemed to encourage unlicensed quackery at the expense of the conventionally licensed profession. A special meeting, of which Ketchum had not been apprised, was held in the Hopkinsville Courthouse. Practically every licensed M.D. in Christian County was there, crying for Ketchum's scalp. "You and your Freak were both cussed and discussed," a friendly doctor advised Ketchum later, "and the outcome was that they're sending a committee to the state capital to have your license revoked, because no physician of judgment would take up with such a crazy thing."

In due course, Ketchum was formally notified of a second meeting, in which charges were to be made publicly against him. The resourceful Ketchum considered his course of action carefully. There were forty or forty-five doctors in the county, and they would be solidly arraigned against him. He could not expect one supporting word, not to mention one vote. On the morning of the meeting—a Tuesday—he went down to the First National Bank of Hopkinsville, where he kept his account, and announced to a surprised cashier, "I want a thousand dollars in two separate packs, five hundred each. New money." Later, that day, he put the two stacks into his pocket, and sauntered off to the courthouse, picking out a seat in the back row of the trial room. Dr. Frank Steitz, located directly across the street from Ketchum, called the meeting to order. The minutes from the last meeting rehashed the complaint, and named the committee chosen to go to Frankfort, the state capital, to strike Ketchum from the list of licensed practitioners. It was pointed out that he was dealing openly with the freak Cayce, a well-known faker, and thus reflected discredit on the entire medical community. The sooner he was eliminated, the better.

There was no comment on the minutes, and it was Ketchum's turn to speak for himself. He stood up, a tall and commanding presence, and with all eyes on him, strode down to the front of the courtroom, taking his place next to Steitz. The wily young doctor had his strategy well planned. He began evenly enough, placatingly, much as Mark Antony had done with the conspirators in his memorable address burying Caesar. "Gentlemen," he said in a conciliatory voice, "I am very sorry to have brought this on the doctors of Christian County. You were born and raised here, the majority of you. I was not. I was raised north of the river [the Ohio], and I came here a few years ago at the encouragement of a number of your leading citizens, and one of these, Professor Dietrich, the father of your wonderful school system, told me about this boy Cayce. All I did was to investigate him, and that's all I'm still doing now."

In the same silky voice, he appealed to them for help in deciding whether Cayce was a fake or not. "I have a suggestion," he said. "I'd like you to appoint six men, each to choose his most complex case, and then have Cayce diagnose each of the six cases, with two stenographers taking it all down verbatim."

He looked around the room with a face full of nothing but good will. The doctors were following him raptly. Dramatically, he reached into his pocket and slapped two stacks of fresh bills on the table before him. "Here's a thousand dollars of good American money," he said. "Now after the diagnoses have been made, and the patients have been examined, if the diagnoses are not absolutely correct, I will turn this money over to any charity you name in Christian County, deducting, of course, the money paid out for your examinations."

There was a stunned silence. Ketchum's eyes traveled around the room, relishing every moment of drama, every bit of the consternation that his bold thrust had engendered. Then as he surveyed the faces of his accusers, Ketchum's manner abruptly changed; all the righteous wrath of the injured lion burst forth. "Here's my thousand dollars," he snapped, smacking the two piles on the table. "Now either put up or shut up."

It was so quiet that Ketchum could hear the breathing of the doctors in the first few rows. And then a voice broke the long silence, saying with a humor lost on everybody but Ketchum, "Mister Chairman, I make a motion that the subject be laid on the table."

Ketchum chuckled to himself. Cayce would have appreciated that touch. In fact, he might have absent-mindedly sidled onto the table and fallen into trance.

That was the last Ketchum was to hear from organized medicine in Christian County. However, what the doctors had not dared, the lawyers did. Months after the abortive medical meeting, Ketchum produced Cayce for banqueting lawyers from three states—Kentucky, Tennessee, and Indiana. The guest of honor was the Attorney General of Kentucky. It was a simple demonstration of Cayce's power of universal knowledge. Several lawyers wrote out questions of a personal nature, and Cayce answered them, shocking each and every one with his intimate knowledge of their private affairs. The incredulous looks on their faces reflected his accuracy.

The State's highest legal authority had watched with special interest, knowing of the action against Ketchum that had almost landed on his desk. Ketchum looked at the Attorney General sharply, and liked what he saw. "What do you think of it, sir?" he asked, nodding at Cayce who was now standing around, busily disavowing knowledge of anything he had said in his sleep.

The Attorney General stared at the doctor for a moment, raised his eyes heavenward, and observed, "It's not very far, you know, from Here to What's Over There, and Cayce falls through somehow."

Ketchum kept repeating the Attorney General's phrase to himself. Cayce did fall through, into a completely different sphere, of which the ordinary mortal could only speculate at the most.

The problem again with Cayce was that just as Ketchum had to be convinced, so did others, and Cayce, troubled by his own gift, was a little weary of being a "freak." Mistrust and skepticism wore on him, just as it affected one who worked greater miracles two thousand years before. Even when he performed wonders of diagnosis and treatment, there were medical men to scoff that chicanery was obvious. For what he was doing was impossible, even though Christ had once said that others could heal like himself given the faith in the Father. And certainly Cayce had that.

Ketchum's faith was also put on trial. But his was a far different personality than the introverted Bible-reader, with his constant misgivings about himself and his power.

Ketchum was the hyperadrenalin type, an extrovert, who slugged back when slugged.

And he believed in Cayce.

Cayce had closed his photographic studio in Bowling Green, the year before Ketchum's big blast, and was working as a photographer in Alabama when the doctor persuaded him to return to Hopkinsville, setting him up in a studio of his own, and arranging for him to give daily readings, as a Psychic Diagnostician. The enterprise was co-sponsored by hotel man Albert Noe. And for the first time Cayce was to work professionally as a psychic, and receive a fee.

The new firm did a flourishing business. Sacks of mail arrived daily, asking for readings, enclosing various sums of money. Along with the mail arrived Ketchum's father, a Pittsburgh horse trader. He had seen his son's picture in the paper, next to The Freak's, and wondered what he was getting into after all that expensive education doctoring. Ketchum was his usual dramatic self as he tried to reassure his father. He pointed to the daily mailbag of forty or fifty pounds. "I'll show you this boy isn't a fake," he said. "Reach down to the bottom of the sack and pull out a letter, any letter."

The elder Ketchum brought out an envelope postmarked Cincinnati. He tore it open. Inside was a twenty-dollar bill, with the note: *"Dear Doctor Ketchum: We have read of you and your Wonderful Man in Hopkinsville, Kentucky. Please find enclosed twenty dollars and send me a diagnosis."* The name and address were all that was given. There was no description of the condition, since the *Times* article had said that Cayce required only a written request to diagnose and treat.

Ketchum turned to his father. "Is there anything in this letter that would tend to tell you what the trouble is with this man?"

The older man shook his head. "No, not a thing."

Cayce was in his studio down the street. He quickly responded to a call. Ketchum senior was not particularly impressed by the gangling, bespectacled young man, but on the other hand he was pleasantly surprised that he at least didn't look the freak. He watched with some misgivings as Cayce loosened his collar and cuffs, slipped off his shoes, and stretched out comfortably on the couch in Ketchum's office. The doctor simply gave the man's name and address, and asked what could be done for him. After he lay there a while, breathing evenly, Cayce said, with his eyes closed, "Oh, yes, we have him here. The trouble with this man is all with his eyes. The central axis cylinder of his eyes is blank. He can only see out of the sides of his eyes, through the filaments around the edges. The optic nerve seems to be only active around the edges. The central part of his optic nerve is dead."

He then briefly gave the man's medical history, saying that he had been to a number of doctors and clinics without getting any help whatsoever.

"Will you suggest treatment?" Ketchum asked.

As a stenographer busily raced over her shorthand pad, the sleeping seer gave a detailed description of what should be done.

"Very well," Ketchum said, taking Cayce out of his trance, "you will wake up and see him no more."

As the elder Ketchum sat around, unconvinced, the secretary typed off the reading, and a copy was sent off to the subject in Cincinnati.

Anxious to demonstrate that he was not in anything shady, Ketchum invited a local eye specialist, who had just returned from three years of European study, to join him and his father for lunch. "I think he's the right man to review this particular diagnosis."

After the luncheon dishes were cleared away, Ketchum brought out a copy of the Cayce diagnosis. Dr. Edwards read it through carefully, re-read it even more carefully, and then turned to Ketchum's father. "Now listen closely, Mister Ketchum. Your son has only been here a relatively short time. He has good ordinary judgment. He's had thorough training in medicine and hospital work. So the sooner he forgets about this damn thing, the better it's going to be for him! It's the biggest farce that I ever heard of. And to think he believes in it, is beyond my comprehension."

Ketchum *père* was convinced, but not the way the son had planned. When they got back to the office, he blurted out angrily, "Just as I expected! I don't believe any of it, either."

Ketchum junior smiled rather bleakly. "Wait and see, we haven't heard from the patient yet."

On the third day, thereafter, there was a discreet knock on the Ketchum door. It was a man the doctor had never seen before. His head was averted, as though he was trying to see out of the corners of his eyes. "You're from Cincinnati, aren't you?" Ketchum said.

Ketchum had guessed right again. The man was too excited to write or phone, he had to express himself in person. He had set out almost as soon as he had received the reading in the mail. "This is the most wonderful thing," he said. "I have been suffering from eye trouble, but no one ever diagnosed my case before."

Dr. Edwards was summoned. He agreed to examine the visitor. Two hours later his examination was completed. This time he called to say that lunch would be on him. The group met again, with the patient present. Edwards turned to Ketchum with an apologetic smile. "I want to take back everything I said. I didn't know that such a condition could possibly exist. The central portion of the optic nerve is dead, as you said."

Ketchum took his win in stride. "But he can see out of the sides of his eyes."

"Of course he can. But not through the center. Every word Cayce said is absolutely true." He held out his hand to the damyankee from across the wide Ohio. "If any of the doctors raise any objection to you trying to demonstrate this boy, send them to me, and I'll tell them what I think of them."

There was not much for the patient, since there wasn't much that could be done. But one person was immeasurably helped: that was Ketchum's father. He went back to Pittsburgh, convinced that he hadn't produced a fool, after all.

During this period, with Ketchum, the fact that Cayce was making money on his readings for the first time continually bothered him. But somebody would be helped by a reading, and this again convinced Cayce they were worth doing. Meanwhile, his fame was spreading. In October 1911 Ketchum was persuaded to address the American Association for Clinical Research, in Boston. The doctors wanted to hear more about Cayce. Working with Cayce every day, Ketchum had tried to figure out how The Work worked. "As fixed laws seem to govern all phenomena in nature," he told the assembly, "it is but natural to infer that this is true of the workings of the psychic. In the course of my investigations I have discovered only one thing that seems to be absolute; that is that the patient should in some way solicit help in his or her particular case. Otherwise results are meager. In several instances where my Unusual Case tried to help patients who had no previous knowledge that such was being done for them, he only gave a rambling talk, hitting the subject only in high places, so to speak."

In a sense, Ketchum was years ahead of his time, not only in accepting a phenomenon that he didn't understand, but in comprehending that Cayce somehow represented a principle of nature, which like electricity, or flying, was part of a broad universal pattern that people could apply when they were ready. "After experimenting with my subject for several years," he said, "I can compare parapsychology only with aviation, which is just now commanding the attention of the mechanical experts of the world; and there can only be one outcome, success eventually. The same is true in the psychic. Conditions in nature have always been as now for aviation, but men said, 'It is impossible,' and of course nothing happened. Heretofore, the medical profession has assumed the same attitude. They could scarcely reconcile themselves to the teachings of those who belonged to different schools of medicine; so it naturally follows, since they did not even believe in each other, that they surely would place little confidence in anything of a psychic nature."

In time the relationship with Ketchum and Noe ended. Cayce, overly concerned perhaps that he was becoming a money-making machine, temporarily broke off the readings, turning back to photography. He had suffered recurring headaches during this period, as when he visited Chicago to demonstrate for a newspaper there. He had to be his own master, doing things his own way, or not function at all. Ketchum eventually left Hopkinsville, took a refresher course at Harvard, and then went out to Hawaii to practice. He had a long, productive career, before retiring in California.

Though he sent people to osteopaths, chiropractors, and physiotherapists, Cayce actually didn't favor any of these over the medical men. He just felt that they, too, had a place in the healing art. He himself was treated by all at various times. In fact, his favorite therapist was the dean of Virginia Beach medical doctors, Robert Woodhouse, who is hale and hearty today at eighty-three. He remembers Cayce as an intelligent patient, who professed to know little or nothing about medicine in the waking state. He had enjoyed their chats together during consultations, and had seen nothing ironic about the man who went to sleep for others coming to him with his own personal health problems. "We have a saying in the profession," the wise old doctor observed with a smile, "that a man who treats himself, has an idiot for a patient, and a fool for a doctor."

Chapter Eight

TWENTY YEARS LATER

In March 1966, as I sat listening to the moving theme music for "Nehru and India" on CBS television, I could not help thinking that but for Edgar Cayce millions would have been denied this musical thrill. Dead now more than twenty years, Edgar Cayce was still saving people, and the prolific, talented American composer-conductor Alan Hovhaness was gratefully one of them. Half-crippled, disabled, debilitated, suffering from hemorrhoids, the musical wonder had about given up. Then, one day on the radio, listening with his wife, he heard the mystic's son mention to interviewer Long John Nebel that his father still lived in the healers using his remedies to help people. "Here in New York," Hugh Lynn said, "physiotherapist Harold J. Reilly is using the same kind of treatments my father once sent people to him for."

At this Nara Hovhaness' eyes brightened, and she turned eagerly to her husband. "Alan," she said, "maybe he can help you."

The composer gave her a wan smile. He was considerably older than his wife—in his mid-fifties—and not as impressionable. He looked at his hands and shook his head tolerantly. It was an effort just to make that movement, and he winced. His body was racked with bursitis and arthritis, and the crippling stiffness was edging down his arms, foreshadowing an end to his career. He had tried one specialist after another for years, and had not been helped.

His wife looked at him appealingly. "Mr. Cayce said there were special exercises recommended by his father that Reilly had given for years with great results."

The composer shrugged. "I don't have to go to Reilly to exercise," he said.

So that summer of 1964, Alan Hovhaness compromised, trying to please his wife by swimming at a midtown Manhattan pool. But it was a dismal failure. "He didn't have enough strength in his arms to hold on to the edge of the pool and tread water," she recalled.

Five months later, the composer was desperate. He had to stop his conducting because he could no longer lift his arms above his waist. He could lie on only one side at night, and even this was painful. Even finger movement was restricted, composition was a strain, and soon an impossibility.

"Alan," his wife said, "there was a reason for us to be tuned in that night; let me make an appointment with Reilly."

By this time, it was apparent there was nothing to lose. The composer sighed, "As you will."

A few weeks later, Alan Hovhaness was a new person. He could raise his arms to the ceiling, he could rest comfortably for the first time in years, and he was beginning to get an idea of what it meant to feel well.

What miracle had the seventy-year-old Reilly wrought?

Actually, nothing that he hadn't been doing for some forty years. "It was all very simple," the youthful septuagenarian said. "I made a few adjustments of the vertebrae and limbs, taking the pressure off nerves; gave him massage to stimulate blood, lymph, and glands; pine oil fume baths and colonics to eliminate toxics; and a few simple exercises."

It was hard to believe that a cure could have been so easily effected.

Reilly shrugged. "He had to keep at it for months, but he's now functioning all over the lot, and he enjoys the exercises."

I had dropped by Reilly's office to discuss the Cayce work, generally, only to become interested specifically in Hovhaness.

During Cayce's lifetime, Reilly had treated scores of patients sent by Cayce, the first arriving in 1931 before Reilly had even heard of Cayce, and, for that matter, before the waking Cayce had heard of Reilly. They had arrived with slips in their hands, describing the treatment, and Reilly had given it. He knew of no case where the treatment was followed that the patient didn't improve or get well. Now with Cayce gone, he gave what was indicated for obvious disorders, already accurately diagnosed, since he was no diagnostician, and Cayce was gone. But it wasn't hard to figure Hovhaness, a simple case of rack and ruin.

I anticipated meeting the composer whose work I had long admired.

Reilly consulted his watch. "He should be here any minute, and you can see for yourself."

In a few moments, the composer bustled through the door. His step was springy, his eye alert, his arms were swinging loosely at his sides. He had the look of a man who got a kick out of life. He shook first Reilly's hand and then mine. His grip was strong and firm.

"I'm so pleased about the way I feel," he said, "that I don't care who knows about it." He smiled. "It's a miracle, thanks to Mr. Reilly, and Cayce."

A year had passed since his first visit to Reilly. In that time he had been to Russia for the State Department, observing the music of that country, and had traveled extensively as a guest conductor. He had returned just the day before from leading a symphony orchestra in Rochester, New York, and was off the next day for Seattle, Washington, to lead another. He was working ten, twelve hours a day at the composition that made him the country's most versatile and prolific composer.

How had Reilly managed it?

The physiotherapist had retired to an inner office to finish with a patient, and we were alone. "He manipulated and massaged me," Hovhaness said, "but apparently what helped most was the bending and stretching. It brought new life to my arms and legs." His exercise routine was elementary. He had done the neck rolls, a simple Yoga exercise, often recommended by Cayce; he had bent forward down, allowing his arms to swing back and forth like a pendulum, a specific for bursitis, and he had stretched toward the ceiling, visualizing the sky. The pendulum and the manipulations, bringing fresh blood into his arms, had given him the flexibility to get his arms above his waist—and from there progress was rapid.

He had not been able to do much at first. The manipulations and fume baths had helped to ease his stiffness, the colonics had detoxified him. For a few minutes each day, he exercised on a massage table, bending his arms and legs, reaching behind his head and for his toes, bringing his legs up to his chin and over his head. Each day he did a little more, straining to the point of tension but never fatigue. His muscles and joints began to open up and live again, the blood coursed to every part of the anatomy. He began to get over the idea that he was an invalid, becoming imbued with his body's capacities, not its limitations. Each exercise became a revelation of unaccustomed movement. The first gingerish approaches were replaced by sure, confident thrusts. Everything seemed possible now. He was on his way.

Though normally shy and retiring, Hovhaness was not at all backward about discussing his transformation. "I'm so eternally grateful that I'm for helping anybody who wants to help himself." He still exercised faithfully.

"I wouldn't miss the exercises for the world. In Rochester the other day, I had an hour between rehearsal and performance, so I hurried back to my hotel room and exercised."

"Which exercises seem to help the most?" I asked.

He plopped down on the floor, his feet planted firmly against the floor molding, and straightened out as though about to do pushups. Instead, supported by his arms, he started rotating his body with his hips, first one way and then the other. "That not only makes me feel better generally, strengthening my shoulders, but got rid of the hemorrhoids which the doctors have been wanting to operate on for twenty years." The composer laughed easily. "The stretching helped the upper part of me, the torso twist the lower part."

He scrambled to his feet with the grace and ease of a much younger man. "I have new confidence in my powers to get well and stay well. As Reilly—and Cayce—stress, the body is a self-healing organism. All it needs is a starter, plus proper stimulation, assimilation, and circulation." He was talking like a Cayce reading.

I saw the composer two or three times thereafter, and was impressed, above all, by his robust attitude toward life. He was fifty-seven, but his outlook was that of a boy, eager, expectant, nourishing each new experience as part of the great adventure. "I feel as though Edgar Cayce just reached out and guided me to the man who could help me, even though it took me a while to listen."

As a Cayce practitioner Reilly has been the agency, posthumously, of many Cayce cures. One of the most remarkable concerned a wealthy Connecticut woman, who had read about Cayce in my book, *The Door to the Future,* and had hunted up doctors who knew anything about the Cayce method. Her search finally led her to her own Fairfield County, where a physician, who had once researched the Cayce readings, confirmed that she was suffering from a vaginal tumor, and recalled that Cayce had successfully prescribed high-frequency ultraviolet in similar cases. He sent her to the physiotherapist, Reilly, noting that the ultraviolet appliance would have to be carefully inserted. "She apparently required a pelvic operation and had learned about the Edgar Cayce material," the doctor reported. "She wanted some treatment in accordance with the readings. Apparently, several physicians refused to do this and this is how she came to me. I outlined a course of treatment for her, according to the Cayce data, which she will obtain at the Reilly institute in New York City."

The patient was of a distinguished family, represented in the Franklin D. Roosevelt wartime cabinet. She had consulted many doctors without being helped, and so was in the mood to get help from a dead psychic. Reilly proceeded as Cayce had indicated. After a few treatments, the tumor began to noticeably dwindle. And in a few weeks, it had vanished completely. Gratefully, the patient gave a grant for medical research into the Cayce readings.

Harold Reilly had studied Cayce well. "After a while," he said, "I got the idea that all a healer had to do was start the body healing itself. Once blood, lymph, and nerve impulses were flowing through the system, once circulation, assimilation and elimination were normal, then the body would counterattack wherever its defenses had been breached."

As reflecting the Cayce concepts, I quoted Reilly one day to Mrs. Louise Ansberry, a former Washington society woman and public relations counsel. Mrs. Ansberry seemed more than casually interested. "I wonder," she said, "if he could help my daughter."

Ten-year-old Hale Ansberry, it developed, was suffering from a little-known skin affliction, and had been to three New York specialists. The dermatologists had heard of only two or three cases like it. They identified it as lichen sclerosis, and pronounced it incurable.

The disorder was beginning to affect the child's personality, as well as health. She was a pupil at the Spence School, and she had become acutely sensitive to the stares of classmates and their innocent references to the infection, which had cracked the skin of her legs, leaving them scaly and chalk-like. The child's body was similarly marked, as were her arms. She was not exactly a basket-case, but she was a comely girl, on the edge of puberty, and a chronic infection of this sort could very well distort her personality. She already was growing morose, and kept to herself, a distinct change from the laughing extroverted little girl I had enjoyed.

As the child sidled in, curtsied, and quietly went off to bed, Mrs. Ansberry's eyes followed her with a worried frown. "Certainly," she said, "Reilly could do no harm."

That weekend we all drove to Reilly's place in the country. Reilly gave Hale a friendly smile, and took her into a treatment room equipped with shortwave diathermy, steam cabinet, and massage table. They came out together about forty-five minutes later. The child was ruddy of face and looked fresh and alive, but a little sheepish. She had never been on a massage table before.

Reilly turned to the mother, "You might bring her back for a couple more treatments."

Five or six weeks passed. Mrs. Ansberry traveled to Japan and India, and phoned me on her return. "How is your daughter?" I asked.

Her voice rose in excitement. "Didn't I tell you," she said, "her skin has practically cleared up. There are only a few faint red marks, and they seem to be vanishing."

I called Reilly to find out what miracle he had performed.

"I can't even remember what I did," he said, "I keep no records in the country. Why not bring her up again? It'll refresh my memory."

I scanned Hale's legs and arms before we started. The cracks in the skin, and the chalkiness, had completely disappeared. If she hadn't called a few pale pink spots to my attention, I would never have noticed them. Hale was her "old" self, relaxed, friendly, trading quips as though I was her age.

We had a pleasant ride, the two of us, and Reilly was waiting. "I remember now," he said, leading Hale to the treatment room, "I adjusted her spine."

He placed the child on the massage table, ran his hands expertly over her vertebrae, and told her to relax on her stomach. "She's still a bit out of adjustment," he said, as his strong hands flexed her spine tenderly. "There could very easily have been some pressure or nerve impingement, which threw off the normal vibration of the body." His hands moved up and down her spine. There were three distinct pops in the dorsal (midback) and lumbar (lower back) area. Reilly grunted in satisfaction. "That ought to do it," he said.

Two weeks later, the last signs of the rare skin disorder had apparently vanished, and we were ready for the post-script. Mrs. Ansberry called to say that she had reported the cure to one of the dermatologists, mentioning that the condition had cleared completely after two spinal adjustments.

"That's impossible," said the learned M.D., whose office fee had been seventy-five dollars. "The condition is incurable."

"But it's gone," the mother protested.

The specialist's voice turned cool. "Then the diagnosis was false."

"But the other doctors agreed," she reminded him, "and you removed patches of the child's skin and tested them."

"The condition," he repeated, with a note of finality, "is incurable."

The mother then phoned the original diagnostician. His reaction was not quite as arbitrary. "It could have been a spontaneous remission," he said, "these things happen."

Mrs. Ansberry's conversations with the doctors were conveyed to healer Reilly. A broad grin brightened his face. "It's a curious thing," he said, "these spontaneous cures always happen with somebody else's cases, never theirs."

Although many of his Cayce-patients staged dramatic recoveries, there was none more remarkable than one reviewed before his very eyes at a meeting at the old McAlpin Hotel in New York City. Reilly had shared the speaker's rostrum with the osteopath, Frank Dobbins of Staten Island; Cayce's old friend, David Kahn, and Cayce himself, when Kahn, a Kentucky-born businessman, whose whole life had been influenced by the Cayce readings, got up to tell of a miracle Cayce had performed for a man who had been in a mental institution. Because of Cayce, Kahn said, that man was now free, and Cayce had correctly diagnosed and prescribed for him without knowing more than his name and plight. He had never seen him, nor consulted any of the diagnoses of his condition. As a matter of fact, the man in question was still in the institution when Cayce read for him in Virginia Beach. It was all documented. Through a nurse, who had once worked for David Kahn, had come the appeal for Cayce aid. Her sister was married to the victim, who was forty-seven, the father of three, and a post office foreman.

"I have a very worthwhile case that I would like you to assist me with," Kahn wrote. "This man had a nervous breakdown while in the postal service, from overwork, or so the doctors stated. They tell us he will now be dismissed in two weeks from a State Hospital and will return to New York. The problem of the family is whether he will be able to assume the new duties, or what they should do under the circumstances?" The troubled wife and children had a number of questions:

Will it be best for the patient to return to work in the Post Office Department immediately upon his leaving the sanitarium?

Are there any dangers of the pains in his head returning?

Is there any adjustment necessary in the home for his wife and children to know about so that they can make whatever changes are necessary upon the father's return?

In what way can his illness be discussed so that he will not develop an inferiority complex?

What will enable him to regain his health physically?

How long will it take for him to regain his normal equilibrium?

Can he be entirely cured?

The man had already been in the asylum for three years, and as he well knew, his return was probationary, since he would be scrutinized closely for signs of any relapse.

With Kahn's letter came a written request for a reading from the wife. "My husband is in Rockland State Hospital, Orangeburg, New York, in Building X, Ward Z, which is on the ground floor of the building. He is not confined to one room, but is around the ward."

As usual, Gertrude Cayce put the hypnotic suggestion to her husband and Gladys Davis was there to take down whatever Cayce said. The suggestion by Gertrude was the usual: "Now you will have before you the body of . . . who is at Orangeburg, New York. You will go over this body carefully, examine it thoroughly, and tell me the conditions you find at the present time, giving the cause of the existing conditions, also the treatment for the cure and relief of this body. You will speak distinctly at a normal rate of speech, answering the questions as I ask them."

As Cayce fell into the shallow trance that preceded his deeper slumber, Gertrude repeated the suggestion in a soft undertone. With his face impassive, and his lips moving precisely, Cayce responded in clear-cut tones. "Yes, we have the body," he said, as he had said so many times before. And now, from what Cayce was to say, it became apparent that the whole diagnosis of the complex causes of the man's condition had been erroneous, either that, or Cayce was wrong. For, immediately, warning that there could be a recurrence, unless the cause was treated, Cayce pointed directly to a physical source as the cause of the mental disorder. "Unless there are other applications to keep this coordination, or to supply the activities to the nerve energies of the system, we find that with the realization that there is an improbability of being restored to active service [at the Post Office] the condition would become very much disturbed again."

And now he came to the immediate cause, though he would only later relate, remarkably, what the instigator of this immediate cause was. The trouble had begun in an area at the base of the spine. "For through pressures upon nerve energies in the coccyx area and the ilium plexus, as well as that pressure upon the lumbar axis, there has been a deflection [derangement] of coordination between the sympathetic and the cerebrospinal nervous system. Thus we find impulses for activities become very much exaggerated. While the hypnotic that has been administered, and the sedatives have allayed the conditions and created rather a submissiveness in the impulses through added suggestions to the body, and the activities in which it had been engaged." In other words, the condition had only been masked.

Cayce then recommended spinal adjustments in the coccyx and lumbar centers, and application through low electrical vibration of gold to "revivify the energies through the creating in the glandular forces of the body the elements necessary for the replenishing of the impulses, so there may be a restoring of the mental forces and a better coordination."

Cayce was nothing if not specific. The spinal adjustments would be made each day for ten days, and then every third day. Chloride of gold would be administered, via a wet cell appliance, three grains to each ounce of distilled water, a half-hour daily, with the solution changed at least every fifteen days. He even specified how the appliance should be attached to the body. "The small anode or plate would be attached first to the fourth lumbar, while the larger plate, through which the gold solution passes, would be attached last, to the umbilicus and lacteal duct plexus, or four fingers from the umbilicus center toward the right in a straight line."

Not even the most formidable pathologist or anatomist could have more precisely employed this technical terminology. A sympathetic physician would be required for both the adjustments and the gold application, which meant some osteopath, since almost any medical doctor would have laughed the reading away at this time.

Additional questions were then put to Cayce, which made his reading all the more incredible.

Q. What was the original cause, or what produced this condition?

A. A fall on the ice, injuring the coccyx end of the spine.

Q. What caused the original pains in head?

A. Reflexes from those injuries to the pressures made upon the pineal center.

Q. What doctor in New York will be best able to aid this man to get his mental equilibrium?

A. Anyone in sympathy with the conditions to be applied. But the adjustments should be made by the same.

Q. How long will it be before he will be able to return to work after leaving the institution?

A. It would require at least sixty to ninety days.

Q. Should he be told that he has been put on the retired list of the Post Office Department and will have to apply for reinstatement to active work, or what should be done considering his mental condition at present?

A. To give the body the impression that it has been entirely left out, without there being some adjustments and some reconstruction, will make for a greater derangement through the mental incapacities of the body, and will cause violence.

As Cayce saw it, it would be necessary to gradually build up the body to gain the equilibrium needed for active service in Post Office work.

He was then asked: "What kind of body-building exercise would be best?"

"Keep in the open as much as practical, but *never* alone, until there is at least the opportunity for better equilibrium to be gained by the releasing of the pressures and the building up to the glandular forces and to the activities from the electrical forces through the gold chloride in the system."

Thereafter, in accordance with the Cayce reading, the man was treated by Dr. Dobbins, with the treatment getting under way on March 26, 1938. By this time, the man was out of the asylum, and confronted with the task of bringing together the threads of his life. Kahn met him at Dobbins' office, and reflected sadly on the man's institutionalization. "I wish you could see what a fine upstanding figure of a man this is," he wrote Cayce, who had already seen through him with his X-ray eyes. "He stands over six feet tall and is as broad and handsome a man as I have ever seen anywhere, and his mind seems to function even more normally than mine. Yet, the doctors up here put him in an insane asylum and he had a terrible time getting out, when, according to the reading an adjustment in the base of the spine would make him perfectly normal. It certainly is remarkable, and the pity of it is that so few people can know the wonder of it."

Without having been shown the reading the postal foreman was asked if he had ever suffered a bad fall on the ice. He recalled one such spill; it bothered his lower spine for a few days, then seemed to go away. Cayce had seen it all. All this was now eight or nine months in the past and Kahn was happy to announce to the McAlpin audience that the man, given the case number 1513 to protect his identity, was happily rejoined to his family and job.

At this point, as Kahn moved to introduce Cayce, a tall, square-shouldered man got up from a back seat and began lumbering down the aisle to the speakers' platform. His eyes seemed intent not on Kahn, who was watching him closely, but on Cayce sitting nearby, ready to take the platform himself.

There was a hush, as the audience sensed the determination in the stride of the man nearing the rostrum. Finally, he came to the front of the hall, and in a quiet, choked voice, turned to face the audience, and said, "Every word Mr. Kahn has spoken is true, and I came tonight to shake the hand of the man who gave me back my life."

It was the postal foreman. With tears in his eyes, he turned and offered his outstretched hand to the equally affected Cayce. There was hardly a dry eye in the auditorium, including the normally phlegmatic Reilly. Awkwardly, Cayce rose to acknowledge the help he had given. "I feel like exhibit A," he said, "I myself have done nothing. I am but a channel of this great gift, and I feel that I am more helpful to you asleep than when I'm awake."

Over the years, Reilly had become a portable repository of practical Cayce therapy. He wasn't always sure how the Cayce treatment worked, but was content that it did. During Cayce's lifetime, everyone coming to Reilly, even for a simple massage or colonic, had their treatment spelled out in detail. Massage varied according to the physical problem. For epilepsy, for instance, peanut oil and olive oil were recommended as a rub, with precise particulars: "Extend massage from base of brain to end of spine. Massage in circular motion either side of spine. Give this regularly, once a week, during the castor oil packs treatment."

The massage for the diabetic, with peanut oil exclusively, was somewhat different. "Massage across small of back, sacral, hips, even along sciatic area." There was a brief reference to the cause. "Unbalanced circulation by lack of proper reaction through pancreas. Excess sugar." A patient with severe anemia had more rigorous massage, with peanut oil. "Each morning upon arising, all body will absorb. Once a week massage into abdomen and over stomach area, whole spine, across sacral." For psoriasis, there were explicit directions. "Take colonic after the first cabinet sweat. Osteopathic adjustments. Fume baths [pine oil or wintergreen]. Massage. Diet." Again, a reference to cause. "Poisons in lymph blood arising from lack of coordination in eliminations. A form of strep that brings pus-forming activities even to the surface."

Perhaps the most unusual of Cayce's purifying baths which included Epsom salts for stiff, arthritic joints, was one of hot coffee. "Bathe feet when there is tiredness with hot coffee made from old coffee grounds to stimulate better circulation and aid eliminations through entire system. Rub bursae of feet and limbs well and the acid will aid in circulation." Reflecting his own belief in the essential unity of the body, Cayce advised: "This will eliminate heaviness in throat and head disturbances."

Even the type of massage was important. A well-known advertising tycoon, for instance, had come to Reilly with a prescription for a gentle, soothing massage. "Otherwise," the reading said, "he will disintegrate." The subject was an obvious case of high-blood pressure, and Reilly would not have permitted a brisk or deep massage in any event. However, the executive, a millionaire used to his own way, balked at the massage. "I like the kind of rub I can feel," he said.

Reilly insisted on following the reading, and the man went elsewhere, getting what he wanted. "Less than a month later," Reilly recalled, "he was dead. He disintegrated."

As he worked with the various oils that Cayce recommended, Reilly noticed that some, like peanut and camphorated oil, seemed to have remarkable healing powers, indicating that they were being absorbed through the skin, and were not mere emulsions. After Cayce's death, Reilly's study brought him to Virginia Beach to pore through the readings, and discuss Cayce's therapy with others who had used it.

In Virginia Beach, as I soon discovered, he was as celebrated for his rehabilitating work with Cayce remedies, as he was in New York City.

Still, with it all, I couldn't help but feel a twinge that Cayce's psychic contribution had been lost when he himself passed on. "It's too bad so much of this is lost," I remarked one day to Marjorie Bonney, a Virginia Beach matron, who was the mother of two.

Mrs. Bonney, an attractive woman in her mid-forties, gave me a searching look. "The important thing," she said, "is that so much of it remains."

I regarded her enquiringly.

"You know Harold Reilly?"

I nodded.

She hesitated. "It's a rather personal story, but I suppose they all are, or we wouldn't be talking about them."

I waited quietly.

"It concerns my daughter, and it goes back a while, though Cayce was already dead then, and you could hardly have expected any help from him. We were in a terrible automobile accident, my daughter and I; this was back in 1948. Emily was three years old. We were both taken to the hospital. After weeks of hospitalization, Emily's face and body were terribly scarred, and one of her legs seemed to have lost its development. It became like a stick, and her foot wobbled as she walked. Even with surgery, the wobbliness persisted. It was apparent the condition would only persist and grow worse with time."

At this stage of the girl's infirmity, Reilly was visiting in Virginia Beach, and happened to be around near A. R. E.

headquarters, watching some children at play. He noticed, particularly, a small girl limping after a ball. His eyes ran professionally down the skimpy little leg. Frowning, he turned to an attractive woman standing nearby. It was Marjorie Bonney, though he did not know her at the time.

"Do you know whose child that is?" he asked.

Marjorie nodded. "She's mine."

"Well, if something isn't done about that leg pretty soon," he said, "the muscles will atrophy completely, and she'll be crippled for life."

Marjorie Bonney felt sick inside. "We've been to the best doctors, and there's nothing that even the surgeons can do now," she said.

Reilly regarded her kindly. "Why don't you talk to Gladys Davis, Edgar Cayce's secretary," he suggested, "she may remember two or three readings that applied to wasted muscles?"

Familiar with Cayce, Mrs. Bonney promptly conferred with the secretary. Three or four readings dealing with apparently similar afflictions of an arm or leg were dug out. They recommended massage with peanut oil and camphorated oil, applied on alternate days, the muscles to be rubbed from the toe toward calf, thigh, and groin.

Each night before bed little Emily got her massage. "One night I would massage her leg for a half-hour, the next night my husband would." The two oils had an added purpose. They would rub some on their daughter's hands, and then have her rub her scarred face with it. The readings had said that the peanut oil stimulated the growth of new tissue. The massages continued for two years. Improvement was gradual during the first year. The muscles expanded and developed until both calves were the same size and shape, the ankle became firmly attached to the foot, the wobble stopped, and with it the limp. At the same time the facial scars began to disappear, both small and large. Edgar Cayce had again reached out from the dead to help. His dearest supplicant—a small child.

Marjorie Bonney didn't see it quite that way, though her daughter, now Mrs. E. F. Friedrich of Buffalo, New York, grew up normally and happily. "I just don't think," Mrs. Bonney said, "that Edgar Cayce ever left us."

Although he now talks freely about Cayce, there was a time, when Cayce lived, that Reilly seldom mentioned the work he was doing with Cayce patients. "I felt foolish telling people that a sleeping Yehudi, as I thought of Cayce then, was telling me how to run my business. They would only have laughed, and nobody likes being laughed at."

Today, Reilly no longer cares what anybody thinks, so long as the treatments work. "I know more about Cayce now for I understand the concept behind his work. You get everything working right, body and mind, and illness hasn't got a chance."

Even now as he thinks back on it, Reilly is amazed by the sequence of strange events that brought Edgar Cayce and his patients into his life. He had never heard of Cayce, and the waking Cayce, as noted, had never heard of Reilly. Yet, one day, a middle-aged man, looking a bit under the weather, walked into the Reilly health center, then located in New York on 63rd Street and Broadway, and handed him a slip of paper. The handsome Irishman looked at it curiously. It didn't seem too different from a lot of other prescriptions that came his way from physicians, osteopaths, and naturopaths. On it was a diagnosis of a gall bladder condition, and a recommendation for a certain type of bath and manipulation. As his establishment specialized in hydrotherapy, electrotherapy, manipulative therapy, Reilly didn't give the reading another thought. He figured Cayce might be an osteopath that he hadn't heard of.

The number of people coming in with Cayce readings continued, and Reilly grew even more curious. This "Dr." Cayce seemed to know his stuff. Whatever it was he recommended, whether the patients had bursitis, arthritis, nervous tension, asthma, or whatever—the results were the same. They improved and got well.

One day, Reilly called one of the patients aside and asked about Dr. Cayce. The patient shook his head. He had never seen the "doctor." Reilly looked at him as though he were deranged. The man explained. "My wife sent in a request that he read for me, saying what was wrong. We had been to all kinds of doctors and they hadn't helped."

It was difficult for the reading process to get through Reilly's practical mind. But he finally accepted that he wasn't being the butt of any joke. Still, there were other obvious mysteries. How did Cayce get his, Reilly's, name? How did he know of the types of treatment Reilly was giving? Where did he get his understanding of the therapies for differently ailing individuals? With all Reilly's experience, it was impossible to improve on Cayce's suggestions. It seemed incredible that Cayce could merely go into a trance and get the information he did. Even after two years, receiving streams of Cayce patients, Reilly had no clue as to the method of the man who was throwing all this business his way. "I can't understand," he told friends, "how a man can go to sleep and give as good, or better, advice than I can, wide awake, in my own special field."

So Reilly decided to get acquainted with the wizard. He made arrangements for a meeting on Cayce's next trip to New York, and had another surprise in store for him. He had envisioned a person of commanding appearance with piercing eyes and majestic gestures, with perhaps a turban draped around his head. But the only mystic he saw was a tall, slightly-stooped scholarly-looking man with a mild eye, gentle mien, and soft-spoken drawl. "He reminded me of a minister of some quiet country church," Reilly said later.

They chatted and had lunch together, the canny Reilly watching every move by the mystic. When Cayce ordered his meal, carelessly giving his request to a waiter, Reilly observed that his guest did not pay much attention to the rules of diet, for one so stringent with the diets of others. Noticing the inordinate amount of fattening starches on the Cayce platter, Reilly mentioned the apparent health discrepancy. Cayce replied that in his everyday waking life he had no special knowledge of diet or any other health measures, nor was he greatly concerned about his health. Still, in his trancelike state, as Reilly had already discovered, the wisdom of the ages came through him. On one hand, he had suggested remedies thousands of years old; on the other, some so up-to-date they hadn't been packaged yet. As the two men sat together, Reilly found himself reviewing the treatments that Cayce had sent him—all forms of drugless healing, invoking the use of baths, oils, heat, light, colonic irrigations, massage and other forms of manipulative therapy, diet and exercise. To Reilly, it was obvious that the Cayce health readings not only helped to overcome sickness and disability, but would as a broad principle tend to prevent illness.

As lunch drew out, Reilly peppering his guest with questions, and Cayce chain-smoking to Reilly's consternation, it became evident to the physiotherapist that Cayce's physical therapy resolved itself into four broad patterns: increased cir-

culation, elimination, assimilation, plus a proper approach to
eating. "It was better not to eat at all, than to eat when
upset," Reilly learned. "Long before anybody else suspected
it, Cayce was saying that the mind, not the stomach, induced
stomach ulcers."

The waking Cayce didn't seem to know any more about
his treatments than Reilly did. And so, after their meeting,
Reilly went back to analyzing the cases that had walked into
his place, and classifying them, so that today, some thirty
years later, he is able to effectively apply Cayce's physical
therapy approach. Elimination, à la Cayce, was a complete
process, through stepped-up action of kidneys, intestines,
skin, lungs. "To stimulate kidneys and skin, for toxic people,
generally the rheumatic or arthritic," Reilly observed, "Cayce
recommended warm pack treatments, chiefly with castor oil."
A swathe of flannel eight inches wide was soaked in the
warmed oil, and placed over the gall bladder, liver, or kidneys, wherever the seat of trouble was. Packs of hot Epsom
salts were applied across hips and back, in lumbago. Packs of
Glyco-Thymoline, little known until advocated by Cayce,
were also prescribed in some cases, increased stimulation
through the skin taking the burden off overworked kidneys.

The readings recommended fume baths and occasional
friction rubs. The fume bath, opening the pores, also toned
up elimination through the respiratory tract. Reilly used the
soothing vapors of the balsam, eucalyptus, pine, Atomidine
(another Cayce nostrum). Formulas varied for the individual
malfunctions but, generally, Reilly used about one-half to one
teaspoonful of the solution or oil, in one to two quarts of
steaming water. "If the person is not able to go to an institution for a fume bath, it is quite simple to fix one for himself." He issued instructions. "Sew together four blankets, or
take a large piece of canvas and sew it together with an opening for the head, and an overlap at this opening—flexible,
non-flammable plastic might be better. Next, take a stool and
place it over an electric stove with a steaming pot on it. Fold
towels on the seat of the stool and hang a towel in front of
the stool to protect legs from the heat. The hotter the water,
the more quickly the steaming takes effect. Then sit on the
stool, wrap the covering close across shoulders and fasten it
around the neck, after, of course, removing the clothing. A
person with a cold can clear nasal or bronchial congestion, by
leaving a small opening in the front where he can put his head

down to inhale, closing off the opening when the inhalation becomes too strong."

Reilly stressed exercise, having maintained gymnasiums for forty-five years, and Cayce's simple therapeutic exercises caught his interest. He noted that the mystic, while seldom exercising himself, recommended sitting-up exercises from a vertical position in the morning, floor exercises later in the day. "In this way," Reilly explained, "Cayce changed the flow of the lymphatic and blood circulation, getting the person who had been lying down all night on his feet to start the day." He also got him breathing deeply, preferably before an open window to eliminate stale lung air and oxygenate the body, giving it a full head of steam to open the day.

"Cayce," Reilly pointed out, "specifically mentioned a Yoga breathing exercise, the alternate breathing." Mouth closed, the individual started off by breathing in through the left nostril, the thumb closing off the right, to the count of four, retaining the breath to eight, then exhaling through the right nostril to a similar eight count, closing off the opposite nostril. The breath was then taken in through right nostril, and the exercise repeated three or four times.

Demonstrating the Cayce floor exercises, the supple septuagenarian promptly got down on all fours and started moving his muscular body forward like a big cat. "This is the cat crawl," he announced. "You take five strides forward, five back, stretching every muscle in the body and bringing the vital hinge and rotary joints into play."

As he finished his crawl, Reilly sat up with a smile. His face was red from the reversal of normal posture, but his blue eyes sparkled. "Getting back to nature drains the sinuses. It wasn't so many millions of years ago that man got around that way normally."

Next was the Cayce roll-over. Sitting on the floor, knees hunched up, Reilly began to rock sidewise, from one half-reclining elbow to another. "This stretches the side muscles along the ribs, flexes the hip joints, trims the thighs." He shook his head. "Amazing that a man who didn't know about exercise, consciously, should have hit on this simple yet effective movement."

Reilly then slipped into a Cayce old-timer, the buttocks walk. Sitting up, legs stretched out, arms toward the ceiling, the septuagenarian started to move forward by first lifting one buttock and then the other. "Many a woman's hips I've slimmed with that one," he said, negotiating the width of the room on the seat of his pants. "I call it the beam-shrinker."

From pushup position, Reilly then repeated the torso twist that Hovhaness had earlier demonstrated, his hips forming a circle, in first one direction and then the other.

The bear walk, similar in posture to the cat crawl, was next. Reilly, again on all fours, walked flat-footed, his knees stiff, hips high in the air, heels and palms of hands flat on the floor.

And how was this different from the cat crawl?

"A stiffer walk," Reilly explained. "It stretches the leg tendons, the hamstring muscle, and the area of the sciatic nerve, while also developing the arms and shoulders."

Still demonstrating, Reilly slid into the morning exercise routine. After taking a few deep breaths, and practicing the alternate breathing, he began swinging one arm forward five or six times like a sidewheel on a Mississippi riverboat, and then reversed, repeating with the other arm. "The individual," he stressed, "is better stimulated, vertically, after a night of horizontal inactivity."

After the arm swing, Reilly rotated first the left and then the right foot from the hip, in a brief circular motion, repeating five or six times in each direction. He then did a standup stretch, up on toes, arms high over head, meanwhile tightening the buttocks and then bending the hands to the floor, keeping the knees stiff. "That's the exercise," he said, "that helped Hovhaness with his hemorrhoids, that and the torso twist."

The demonstration continued. Arms again stretched overhead, Reilly lowered his head slowly to his chest, and then slowly pulled it back over his shoulders. It was the beginning of the head-and-neck exercise. Still stretching up on his toes, he circled the head slowly three or four times in each direction, and then, relaxing, started to rub his head. I suddenly noticed a new fuzzy growth of silver gray on the front of his scalp, where there had been no hair before. He noted my surprise .

"I don't know what's doing it," he smiled, "but I've been growing hair on the bald spots for the last few weeks. It's either the Cayce head-and-neck exercise, which I've been doing recently, or the castor oil I've been rubbing on my scalp. Nothing else has certainly changed after seventy."

Some of the Cayce readings providing relief via drugless

therapy were given long before physiotherapy was practiced generally, when there was no opportunity for Cayce to have become familiar with such physiotherapy. Yet he gave readings advising electrotherapy, short wave and ultra-short wave. "Strange as it may seem," Reilly recalls, "the machine for this special type of therapy had just been perfected and the Reilly Health Service had obtained it just three weeks before it was mentioned in the readings."

Chapter Nine

THE DOCTORS CATCH ON

"One striking concept has come out of the Cayce health readings," Dr. William O. McGarey said, "the concept that each cell has a consciousness of its own. Apparently, Cayce was able to identify clairvoyantly with the consciousness of these cells, to look at every gland, organ, blood vessel, nerve, and tissue from inside the body. His unconscious seemed to communicate with the autonomic nervous system, traveling through the sympathetic and parasympathetic systems, which it controlled, into each and every cell."

The doctor's lean, sensitive face lit up with interest as he held out a slim finger. "An uncomfortable cell in this finger might tell Cayce's unconscious there was pressure on it, and the unconscious would recommend an oil that would soothe and comfort it. All through the body, cells were apparently conveying their message to this remarkable unconsciousness—for even as there are wars between nations, cells war among themselves." And in this conflict, there was dis-ease or illness.

Like many doctors who had studied the Cayce readings, Dr. McGarey had begun to apply them to patients and was gratified at the results. "It requires an almost intuitive knowledge, at times," he observed, "for the practitioner to sense when some of these measures may be most effective." But many remedies seemed broadly applicable.

McGarey knew Cayce only through reading about him. He

was considered a solid practitioner, operating a clinic in Phoenix, Arizona with his wife, Gladys, also an M.D. Like other physicians, McGarey was vexed and saddened when the orthodox didn't work, left with a sense of helplessness. There was so much about therapy that was a mystery. Recognizing his own shortcomings, the doctor brought into his assault on disease a certain humility. He did not discount what he had learned at the Cincinnati medical school, or in the training years that followed, but his mind was open. And so as his interest developed in Cayce, he did something about it. He pored over some of the Cayce health readings, studying their results, and out of the health readings of the unschooled mystic, came successful adaptation of some Cayce treatments. McGarey's greatest luck has been with castor oil packs which have helped reduce sundry abdominal complaints: stomach ulcers, appendicitis, colitis, gall bladder. Conventionally trained, he applied the packs only after more conventional cures failed. His most remarkable recovery, à la Cayce, was an eighty-year-old woman with an intestinal obstruction. Because of an irritated bowel, he was afraid of gangrene. Surgery was inadvisable because of the patient's condition. So, as a last resort, he began applying the packs to the abdominal area, which was noticeably distended and sore. Within twenty-four hours, magically, the obstruction had cleared up; within a few days, the patient's stomach was as flat as a teenager's, distention and stress clearly removed for the first time in years.

As Cayce had suggested, in cases of hypertension and high blood pressure, he found the packs had a quieting effect in some instances on the autonomic nervous system. "Apparently by speeding up the lymphatic flow," he observed, "the packs relieved stress on the sympathetic system, which directly reacts when people get excited or angry, what doctors call the fright-flight symptom."

Cayce's treatment usually embraced the whole system, not only specific local areas. After the packs, olive oil was given to clear out the gall bladder and stimulate the liver, stirring an apparent outflow of toxicity via liver, kidneys, skin, lungs. Apparently, the castor oil reduced local toxicity, soothing stiffened arthritic joints and modifying local abcesses.

McGarey's theory of how the packs worked has been elaborated on elsewhere. Dr. George O'Malley of Galien, Michigan, practicing successfully from the readings, suggested that the castor oil packs beneficially stimulate the lacteals, tiny lymphatic vessels in the small intestines. "Some authorities," he said, "suggest that the vital life force of the human organism begins in these cells."

O'Malley, an osteopath, has been applying the remedies Cayce dredged out of his dreams, since the time a friend impishly gave him a copy of Tom Sugrue's book, *There Is a River*, which features the Cayce cures. Intrigued, O'Malley obtained files of Cayce readings on diseases particularly difficult to treat. He noticed that castor oil packs were commonly recommended, as was Atomidine, an iodine derivative. Where an eye specialist had failed, O'Malley reported relieving a corneal ulcer with two drops of Atomidine daily, just as Cayce had recommended. But his most outstanding successes came with castor oil packs. In one notable case, even as surgeons were planning to operate on a fifty-four-year-old patient for an abdominal obstruction, O'Malley kept faithfully applying his castor oil packs. When an electrical storm held up the operation, the packs were additionally continued, and then an hour before the rescheduled surgery, the obstruction dramatically cleared up, and the surgery became unnecessary. O'Malley has reported similar success with chronically inflamed gall bladder, chronic stomach disorders, ulcerative colitis, chronic appendicitis, even swelling of feet—all as susceptible to the packs as the obstructions.

From the Cayce readings O'Malley concluded that castor oil packs, absorbed through the skin, served to relieve abdominal congestion due to sluggishness of the lymphatic circulation. Widely used as a laxative internally, castor oil is sometimes known as Palma Christus—the hand of Christ. "The action of the castor oil on the skin is twofold," the doctor found. "It directly stimulates the lymphatic flow through the superficial and deep lymphatic vessels, and strengthens some deep organs of the abdomen."

O'Malley applied the packs just as Cayce had outlined. "Three thicknesses of soft flannel soaked in hot castor oil were applied over the abdomen in the area of the liver and gall bladder, extending down over the caecum [right lower quadrant of the abdomen] and appendix. A heating pad or heat lamp was used to retain the heat, with the packs applied three consecutive days each week, for one and a half to three hours per day. They were followed by olive oil taken internally for the next three days. "Apparently," the doctor theorized, "the olive oil stimulates the increased production of lymph, which acts to decrease the circulatory stasis [stoppage] in most abdominal disfunctions. At the same time, it stimulates the production of lymphocytes, a forerunner in the body-defense mechanism."

Whatever happened, the relief of ailments which had been troubling people for years was often miraculous.

One day, O'Malley made an emergency call on a middle-aged school teacher, stricken with an apparent heart attack at the dinner table. He soon discovered that she had a history of chonic pain aggravated by injudicious, fatty foods. X-rays revealed an inflamed, nonfunctional gall bladder. Her heart was sound. She was anxious to get back to her classes, as only two weeks of the semester remained. "Doctor," she said, "it would please me and my class to finish the year together."

Castor oil packs were relatively new in the O'Malley armory at this time. He told the teacher about them, and she agreed to give it a try. "She was instructed to report any adverse symptom at once," the doctor said, "and keep us up on her progress." A week later the husband phoned to report his wife better than in years. The deceptive heaviness in the chest had virtually disappeared. She was to continue the packs for another week. The next report, weeks later, came from the local superintendent of schools, as he mentioned how well the teacher looked as the new term opened. In three months there was no recurrence.

Ulcerative colitis was like a plague to most doctors, difficult to diagnose, difficult to treat. An elderly woman, sixty-six, injured in an auto accident, entered a clinic; the diagnosis was ulcerative colitis, due to trauma and shock. Treated six months, she lost considerable weight, as she was afraid to eat, since it immediately irritated her bowel. When she complained of palpitations, the family feared a heart condition and called in O'Malley. He immediately prescribed castor oil packs. "With the first treatment," he noted, "she began to respond. After three weeks, all the pain had subsided in her abdomen. She began sleeping without medication."

One of the more rewarding cures, so unexpected, came in treating an eight-year-old girl for a recurring abdominal pain, dating back to a siege of measles. She was operated on for chronic appendicitis, and surgery revealed an old appendix rupture, complicated by an acute abscess. Due to adhesions, the removal of the appendix was difficult, and the child's condition critical. There was abdominal bloating, vomiting, high temperature. Antibiotics were not effective. Finally, castor oil packs were used, for an hour at a time, three times a day. "There was slight improvement during the first twenty-four hours," O'Malley observed, "but by the third day, the bloating began to subside, and the temperature dropped." The packs were continued for twelve days of convalescence. "It is my conviction," the doctor recorded, "that the castor oil packs stimulated the body's defense mechanism, and with the improved circulation, the medication helped to restore homeostasis [equilibrium between cells]. It was of interest to note that an anemia, which the patient had picked up, appeared to respond much better to iron therapy while the castor oil packs were being applied to the abdomen."

As they relieved congestion, the castor oil packs were helpful also in reducing excrescences such as moles, warts, and cysts, and in psoriasis, gout, and kidney stones. Like McGarey, O'Malley not only profited from treatment of specific cases, but gained a broader concept of what some ailments were all about. The castor oil packs seemed helpful in maladies where a lack of lymphatic circulation resulted in improper removal of "toxins of the body or of the disease." This seemed to offer the possibility that the packs might have even broader application. "In tabulated cases of psoriasis, cancer, and arthritis," O'Malley observed, "the readings refer to lack of absorption of lymph circulation through the alimentary canal."

Many healers have pored over Cayce's remedies for such mystifying ailments as arthritis and cancer, looking for clues that would be therapeutically helpful in their treatment. Many "cures" for arthritis are recorded in the Cayce files, with testimonials years later from those who got well. Cayce approached arthritis on a broad front, understanding what many doctors have only recently come to accept: that arthritis is the body's—and mind's—reaction to multiple wrongs and abuses. Scores of readings on this crippling disorder were closely examined by Dr. Henry George III of Wilmington, Delaware, descendant of the noted economist. In forty-nine of fifty-nine cases under study, Cayce recommended olive oil or peanut oil massage, general osteopathy with special stress to adjustments in the cervical (neck) and low dorsal area in thirty-eight cases. Gold chloride or Atomidine was used in combination with these therapies eleven times; colonic irrigations, cleansing the system some fourteen times. In nine cases, he urged the subjects to improve their mental and spiritual attitude. He was strong on diet, banning large quantities of meat in half the cases and *pork* in virtually every case. Many were told to avoid white bread, potatoes, fatty foods and grease, encouraged to eat root vegetables.

The progress reports were interesting. Twenty-three were cured or improved, eleven found the diversified treatment too complex to follow, two died before they could start the treatment, and the balance couldn't be located for a report-back.

It was rather absorbing to follow the question and answer process by which Cayce arrived at a dramatic cure. In one pertinent case, the subject was a middle-aged nurse, who had made the rounds of doctors and finally turned to Cayce.

She got right to the point. "What," she asked, "is causing the hard places or knots to form on or around the joints of my fingers?"

"The lack of the proper eliminations through the general system," Cayce said, "and the stimulating of the circulation in the upper dorsal and through the cervical areas [through osteopathic adjustments] should set up better eliminations through the general alimentary canal." A diet suggestion: "Add to the diet a great deal of watercress and beet tops."

Nurselike, she was persistent. "Should anything specific be done for the hard place on the joint of my little finger which is now sore?"

"Application of an Epsom salts pack will bring relief to this area, but the better eliminations set up in the order as indicated [colonics every ten days] will relieve the conditions through the general system."

There was a war on, and she was an enterprising soul. "Would it be safe—not harmful to my health—for me to donate blood to the Red Cross?"

"Not harmful under the present conditions."

She threw in still another digressive question.

"What is the best treatment for a bedsore—I ask this for my patient?"

Cayce obviously didn't mind two subjects for the price of one. "The best application as a general condition for such is the use of ichthyol ointment."

The nurse followed the treatments faithfully, and they worked. The adjustments were made by Dr. André Aillaud, an osteopath, of Charlottesville, Virginia, and the patient did the rest. Some ten years later, in November 1952, she reported back enthusiastically, both for herself, and the auxiliary patient, with bedsores. "The knots on my fingers cleared up; I gave blood six times during the war years. The bedsore remedy was wonderful; my patient never had any more trouble from sores." In December 1965, when last checked, the patient was approaching seventy. She was described as "the picture of health."

Philosophically, Cayce often intrigues the scientists who use him. "I could give twenty or thirty case histories of arthritis treated by the readings," reported M. L. Hotten, an osteopath, of Arvin, California, "and indicate good results. But when one starts to use these readings, one cannot help but ask questions about some of the gaps in the information. There is a challenge to the material which we cannot easily ignore. We can scarcely accept health readings, for instance, and ignore the spiritual and psychological overtones. We must not simply use what we want and throw the rest aside."

Hotten observed the same clinical attitude toward the Cayce readings that he did in determining the best treatment for a patient; he suggested that other practitioners do likewise. Many of the Cayce readings dealt with arthritis, and a survey of the recommended treatment revealed enough similarities for Hotten to arrive at a therapeutic pattern. "A simplification," he pointed out, "shows four major steps:

1. Improved circulation through salt packs and baths.
2. Specific massage with certain oils and resinous extracts such as myrrh and peanut oil.
3. Dietary alteration to change the chemical balance and reduce intake of certain minerals.
4. Osteopathic manipulation of the third cervical, the ninth dorsal, and the fourth lumbars; these latter three areas are most often mentioned."

Like McGarey, he had become convinced that the body was acutely conscious of its own state. "We know there is a 'consciousness' innate in the entity, which is usually termed the subconscious or unconscious. This is usually related to mental activity, but there may be still another type of consciousness at a still deeper level which is sensitive to the state of balance existing in the sympathetic and parasympathetic nervous systems."

Because nobody else could apparently explore this consciousness, the Cayce readings, together with the underlying philosophy, became doubly important. And so Dr. Hotten delved eagerly into Cayce's conception of the cause of disease, and of healing. "Is it possible," Cayce was once asked, "to give information through psychic readings, which will lead to the cure of diseases now known as incurable?"

He replied: "We find that all conditions existent in physical bodies are produced by that which may be met. There are in truth no incurable conditions. For each ailment is the result of the breaking of a law. Healing will of necessity come when there is compliance with other laws which meet the needs. No healing is perfected without some psychic force exerted. In regard to healing of any kind, the counteracting force, whether operative or medicinal, or self-producing, is nothing more nor less than the active force exerted in psychic force."

Apparently, this was one reason why Cayce preferred a request from an individual for a health reading. He wanted subjects whose minds were already prepared for help.

Just as many skeptics have been converted through exposure to the Cayce readings, Hotten feels that science might learn more about healing if it would but consider ideas foreign to orthodox medical concepts. "It is really unscientific and dogmatic," he observed, "to indict any treatment, concept or idea because one *thinks* it has no value." As the arthritic have been helped, so may the cancer-ridden. And just as peanut oil was helpful in arthritis, that was the function of almonds, frequently mentioned by Cayce in cancer therapy. Cayce often emphasized the vibrations of various substances, and Hotten questioned: "Is it the vibration of peanut oil, applied once or twice a week, which helps prevent arthritis? What is the vibratory nature of almonds that could alter the physiology of the body so that, for one individual at least, one or two almonds a day would help prevent cancer?"

Hotten was not saying that almonds would prevent or cure cancer. He was just suggesting that the possibility be scientifically explored. "Now that cancer cells can be grown on synthetic culture media, perhaps the chemical components of almonds could become a subject for such research. Or," he added with delicate irony, "perhaps this is too simple an idea to appeal to men who are searching for a drug to cure disease, rather than considering the delicate chemical balance probably essential for prevention of disordered physiology."

The doorway on apparently universal knowledge was not

closed to those with open minds. "One man in our time, Edgar Cayce, with deep inner desire and perfected vehicle, was able to be the perfect channel, while in hypnotic trance. Let us not close the door on that channel."

It is easy to see why even the most open-minded doctors were baffled by Cayce. His knowledge of the anatomy, disease and drugs was encyclopedic. He was an authority on diet, down to the last calorie and vitamin, and gave minute lists of meals for his subjects. He not only prescribed the drugs, but told how they should be made, just as he once said how a glass of orange juice should be ten minutes in the drinking. His treatments were many-sided. Not only diet and drugs, but massage and manipulation and therapeutic baths, all for the same patient; whatever would help. A fully documented report on one of his most outstanding cases was a marvel of detail. Reading it, one wondered how even the most erudite physician could have been so explicit in diagnosis and treatment, not to mention one who had never progressed beyond grade school.

To the sleeping Cayce, the body was a connecting network of blood, muscle, nerves, and bone, and when any of these were out of order, the whole entity, as he described the individual, was out of order. In one instance, the subject was suffering from paralysis of the limbs, and had consulted many doctors without success. He was a man of thirty-five, doomed to invalidism. Cayce, reading for this man three hundred miles away, whom he had never seen, said the patient was suffering a disturbance in the lower lumbar plexus, affecting coordination of the sympathetic and cerebrospinal nervous systems. With great detail he advised adjustments of the spine, specifying the dorsal and cervical vertebrae, and declaring that the resultingly restored vibration of the body would help step up the blood supply and hasten the healing process. As a supplementary aid, he recommended a concoction of herbs and told how it should be put together. Nobody could have consciously memorized it:

"First, we would take eight ounces of distilled water. To this add garden sage one-half ounce, ambrosia leaves, not much stems, but leaves—one-quarter ounce." Then: "Prickly ash and dog fennel, one-quarter ounce, and wild ginseng, one-half ounce." The directions continued: "Reduce this by simmering, not boiling too strong, to one-half the quantity. Strain, and while warm, add one and a half ounce 85 proof alcohol, with one dram of balsam of tolu cut in same. Then add three minims tincture of capsici. The dose would be half a teaspoonful four times each day, taken about fifteen to twenty minutes before the meals."

He then minutely described each meal. Breakfast would consist principally of citrus fruits, though gruels might be added, "especially those of the whole wheat, of the oat, or of those where both the gluten from rice and wheat are conbined." He even directed how the patient should be handled. "Positive suggestion, in a gentle, quiet, easy way and manner. Blustering will only irritate. To scold, or to be too much of the commanding nature, is to destroy that which may be built up in the body." There was even a moral, years ahead of its time: "Teach or train the body not only to be good, but to be good for something."

The first reading for the paralytic occurred in September 1930. To make sure treatments were properly administered, the patient was moved to the then functioning Cayce Hospital on October 6. He remained a patient there until October 24, and then, showing marked progress, was returned to his home to continue the treatment. The person who had sent him to Cayce noted with satisfaction, "Doctors have admitted their inability to help, and yet his cure will now be a comparatively fast one."

His appetite was picking up, he was gaining weight, and beginning to move his limbs, and take a few halting steps. In November, he was walking. He sent the Cayce Foundation a grateful letter on November 17. "I am glad to tell you that I am still gaining. I weigh 170 [a gain of thirty pounds]. I can walk about a mile in a day, but of course I get awfully tired."

His care was supervised by Dr. Theodore J. Berger, a New York osteopath. On December 1, he had another reading, and the treatment modified because of his improvement. Cayce stressed massage for the reviving circulation. "We would change now to one general osteopathic treatment each week, and one massage with balsam of sulphur in the lumbar and sacral regions, rubbing thoroughly along the limbs to the knees and ankles, following the course of the muscles rather than the nerves. Greater strength will be gained by the body through this application." It could be done by any masseur, or by somebody at home, if thorough. The balsam of sulphur, not too dry, was to be massaged thoroughly "into the lumbar and sacral regions, and along the muscular portions of the limbs, to the feet, ankles, and on to the upper portion of the body, to the hips." The general diet was to be maintained, along with outdoor exercise. And then Cayce predicted, "It will be found that earlier than expected the body will be able to return to daily labors."

An interesting sidelight developed, when the subject asked if he should stop smoking.

"If in moderation," Cayce replied, "does not become harmful to the body."

In February of 1931, a few months after the first reading, the patient was so much better that he asked for a life reading, feeling that if Cayce was so right about the physical he most likely was right about everything else.

Cayce kept to the physical at first. He altered the diet, since the patient was now too heavy. "Leave off too much starches for the next thirty to forty days. The only character of meat being either kid or lamb; nerve-building meats, no sweets, no butter; taking all foods in as near its natural state as possible, without sugar. No potatoes of any kind." The drug intake was tapered off. "When it's to be filled again, leave off. Decrease in quantity until this is gone." Then some job advice: return to work at once, in congenial surroundings.

"What kind of work?" the convalescent asked.

"That which has been followed, or found to be more in keeping with the nature or tendencies of the body."

There was one last question. "Any advice regarding mental or spiritual body?"

He was pleasantly reassured. In the discipline of getting well he had also developed spirit and mind. "As the body has built in the mental force, this recuperation has begun. Keep an ideal and work toward it."

In May of 1931, the patient was reported fully recovered. The A.R.E. record revealed a letter of gratitude to Cayce from his sister-in-law. "It took a great responsibility off our shoulders. He is fine, working every day and always talking about you." Six months later, the patient added his own testimonial. His name was not used, but was available, together with this accolade: "I am writing this letter in appreciation of all you did for me. When I went under your care, I could not use my hands to write, and my legs were partially paralyzed and I could not straighten them out at all. I only weighed 140 pounds. I had been in this condition for six months previous and was gradually getting worse. I was not at the Cayce Hospital one week before I wrote letters home and straightened my legs out and have gradually gained ever since. I now weigh 184 pounds. Also medical doctors had as much as told me there was no help for my condition. I was able to go to work May 5, 1931, eight months after I started your treatment and have not laid off one day since. When I got home everyone was more than surprised to see me walking as good as ever again. I cannot word this letter to show my appreciation and thank you enough. As you know, when people first hear about a reading they cannot believe in it. I did not at first and I hope others who are sick will let you help them before waiting too long."

The Cayce concoctions amazed the pharmacists, who had seen nothing like them before. As a young druggist fresh from college in Richmond, Virginia, Milton H. Snyder had knit his brow over the prescriptions of herbs and roots that Cayce had sent into the Virginia Beach pharmacy where he worked. In one prescription, for instance, the man who had never looked at a medical book or pharmaceutical journal ordered for a patient two ounces of strained honey, brought to a boil in four ounces of distilled water, and then—before it had cooled entirely, but after it had stopped steaming— added: Essence from wild ginseng, tincture of stillingia, essence of wild turnip, essence of wild ginger (made from the herb itself); essence of cinchona bark." The directions were explicit: "Shake the solution before the dose is taken, which would be half a teaspoonful twice each day, preferably before the morning meal and before the time for retiring in the evening. Take the whole quantity."

In time, Snyder moved from the drug to the jewelry business, operating a shop in Portsmouth, Virginia. However, his thoughts often turned to the eccentric Cayce. Nobody, he recalled, could have shown more concern for a patient, including an inordinate interest in the mixtures he had specified in his readings, which he referred to constantly. "He would stand over me in the beginning," Snyder recalled, "and make sure that I boiled a preparation in an enamel pot rather than metal, so that there would be no danger of contamination." There had been no potions like Cayce's since the Middle Age alchemists, Snyder reckoned, but the roots and herbs were certainly harmless, if not helpful, and he had no compunction about filling them. "There was no question of Cayce's sincerity," he drawled, "he wanted everything just the way it was ordered."

Had Snyder ever had a reading?

He could recall having one, back in January of 1931, not long before the Cayce hospital closed. He was bothered by a bladder problem and bad headaches, and his employer, S. J. Benstock, had made an appointment for him. Snyder had not been impressed. "I don't think he helped me," he said reflectively, "but he was a nice man, quite unusual."

"I had understood," I said, "that his treatments helped practically everybody who did exactly what he said."

"Well, I don't remember now what he told me," Snyder said, "it was quite a time ago, but I finally went over to Charlottesville and some medical doctor fixed me up."

"May I check through your reading?" I asked.

Snyder laughed. "I'd be right curious myself to see what there was."

It was no problem finding the reading. Snyder had been twenty-four years old at the time. In the file, there was no complaint, no hint of his ailment, just the request for a physical reading.

The Cayce reading was rather brief. By and large, Cayce said, the subject was in good shape, organically sound though functioning improperly. He blamed some of his difficulties on the digestive and nervous system, causing at times headaches, as well as problems with eyes and throat.

At any rate, Cayce had the headaches right.

Additionally, the reading continued, these conditions distributed toxins throughout the system, and produced pressures in various parts of the body. Cayce's remedy was rather simple, too simple perhaps. He recommended a diet that would combat the "acid forces in the body" and osteopathic adjustments in the cervical and dorsal area, so that the nerve impulses, now under impairing pressure, would function normally.

That was all for the reading, but Snyder had some questions. "What causes the specific ailment?"

"By the creating of a balance in the digestive and assimilating system," Cayce replied, "we will overcome these disorders. Also those pressures that exist in the lower portion of the system, for these are as of a filling up of the glands themselves."

I remembered Snyder telling me of a urination problem.

"Are the kidneys in good condition?" That question soon followed.

"These are in sympathetic disorder, from the over amount of the pressure produced from the poisons [toxics]. Remove the pressures that produce same, and we will bring the condition to normalcy."

Snyder asked how often the spinal adjustments should be made.

"At least twice each week, until the muscular forces and nerve centers are aligned through the cerebrospinal system."

Snyder, who had been consulting a doctor, now asked, "Is treatment now being given correct?"

Cayce replied drily, "If it had been, we wouldn't have changed it."

Reviewing the reading, it appeared to me that Cayce had been half-right anyway. His diagnosis had been correct, headaches and pressure trouble in the lower areas were certainly applicable to the kidneys. How had he missed?

I got back to Snyder again. He was as affable as before.

A sudden thought had struck me. "What did the osteopath do for you?" I asked.

"What osteopath?" Snyder said.

"For the adjustments Cayce ordered."

Snyder's voice came back pleasantly. "I never went along much with that sort of thing."

"Well," I said, "that's what Cayce suggested."

"Is that right—well, I remember something like that now. I didn't put much store by it."

"Then, you didn't follow the treatment?"

"I guess not, because I didn't go to an osteopath, and I didn't get any adjustments. I just couldn't see anything like that then."

Snyder's voice became almost wistful. "I'd like to know now what one of those osteopaths would say about what Cayce got for me—let me know if you find out?"

A week later, I checked the Snyder reading with Harold J. Reilly. He gave it an expert eye. "The adjustment that Cayce described," he said, "could very easily have relieved pressure on the kidneys. That was the area directly affected."

Cayce's Universal Mind explored public as well as individual health. In view of current controversy on fluoridation, it

seems noteworthy that Cayce opposed indiscriminate fluoridation of the public reservoirs, warning that fluorine could com-
bine dangerously with minerals already there.

Cayce first considered the problem in September 1943,
when a research dentist asked, "Is it true, as thought, that the
intake of certain form and percentage of fluorine in drinking
water causes mottled enamel of the teeth?"

"This, to be sure, is true," Cayce replied. "But this is also
untrue, unless there is considered the other properties with
which such is associated in drinking water." His sleep voice
elaborated, "If there are certain percents of fluorine with free
limestone, we will find it beneficial. If there are certain percents with indications of magnesium, sulphur and the like, we
will have, one, mottling; another, decaying at the gum."

The dentist asked, "Does too much fluorine cause decay of
teeth, and where is the borderline?"

"Read what has just been indicated," Cayce said. "It depends upon the combinations, more than it does upon the
quantity of fluorine itself." Still, an over-supply of fluorine
could bring on an adverse chemical reaction within the body,
manifested chiefly in the teeth. "But, to be sure, too much
fluorine in the water would not make so much in the teeth, as
it would in other elements of activities which may be
reflected in teeth; not as the cause of same but producing a
disturbance that may contribute to the condition."

Cayce repeated his admonition about magnesium and sulphur in combination with fluorine, adding another warning
about excessive iron deposits. "Where there is iron or sulphur
or magnesium, be careful!"

In a rather remarkable passage, considering he had no conscious knowledge of the fluoridation problem, Cayce briefly
reviewed the natural appearance of fluorine in water, pointing out that in its beneficial state it could serve as a safety
control in artificially fluoridating drinking water. "There are
areas within the United States," he said, "as in some portions
of Texas, portions in Arizona, others in Wyoming, where the
teeth are seldom decayed. [And where fluorine safely occurred.] Study the water there, the lack of iron or sulphur or
the proportions of sulphur."

Cayce stressed that the success of any fluoridation experiment hinged completely on the properties of the water to
which the fluorine was to be added. "There are many sections

where fluorine added to the water, with many other chemicals, would be most beneficial. There are others where even a small quantity added would be very detrimental. Hence it cannot be said positively that this or that quantity should be added save in a certain degree of other chemicals (forming a beneficial combination) being combined with same in the drinking water." He picked out spots in central Texas, northwestern Arizona, and around Cheyenne, Wyoming, where fluorine combined with other natural elements to offset tooth decay. However, supplementary water pumped in from other areas could alter this natural therapy. "Where there have been contributions from other supplies of water, there will be found variations in the supply of magnesium and other chemicals—as arsenic and such—and these cause destruction of the teeth."

Asked the best way of protecting teeth, Cayce said iron balance was of primary importance. "Keeping the best physical health of the body and protecting it from iron or iron products that may become a part of the body-physical in one manner or another. These (iron deposits) are needed, but when their proportions are varied from normal, the teeth do not show the proper relationships, when you lose that quantity of iron needed."

"What other factors are there," the dentist inquired, "that control and have an effect on mottled enamel and decay of teeth?"

The empirical Cayce replied, "The general health of the body and the chemical processes that are a part of the digestive system, the process of digestion, the chemical processes through same, and the blood stream."

The dentist went back to fluoridation. "Should drinking water in certain localities be prepared with a percentage of fluorine for prevention of decay and for preventing mottled enamel in the teeth? If so, how and where?"

Again Cayce stressed that the value of fluoridation depended entirely on the type of water fluoridated. "This would have to be tested in the various districts themselves, much as has been indicated. There's scarcely an individual place in Ohio that wouldn't be helpful, for it will get rid of and add to that condition to cause a better activity in the thyroid glands; while, for general use, in such a district as Illinois (say in the extreme northern portion) it would be harmful.

These [possible fluoridation] would necessarily require testing, according to the quantities of other conditions or minerals or elements in the water."

As remarkable as Cayce was, not all Cayce patients were satisfied. Indeed I had met one, a psychic researcher, who was downright unhappy about the treatment he had received. Even now, twenty-five years later, he argued that Cayce was a fake. "The treatment nearly killed me," he told me, with fire in his eyes. "Cayce didn't know what he was doing."

As I had already talked to numbers of people miraculously helped by Cayce, I suggested that something may have inadvertently misfired. "Perhaps," I said, "you didn't do everything you were supposed to do."

My dyspeptic friend had been a victim of ulcers. "I did what it said I should," he growled. "Cayce sent me to a chiropractor with my ulcers, and he practically killed me."

"Maybe," I suggested, "the chiropractor didn't do what he was supposed to do." The directions were often complex and an error conceivable. It had happened more than once. Besides that, there was always an allowable margin of error, the claim being that Cayce was right at least 97 percent of the time on his physical readings, a remarkable average if it checked out.

The researcher eyed me darkly. "Don't buy that tommyrot," he said. "If it hadn't been for the doctors I wouldn't be here today."

Subsequently, I saw where my friend had chosen to criticize Cayce to a reporter, who had added a criticism of her own, about the fees exacted by the Cayce people. The last attack was patently absurd, since there is no charge for treatment at the Cayce Foundation today, and no treatment!

In view of the charge, I decided to check back on the questioned reading. It was all in the A.R.E. files in Virginia Beach. The original reading was given on November 2, 1938. Cayce found that the researcher, then forty, had "a great deal of disturbance through the stomach, duodenum and throughout the intestinal system." The subject didn't have ulcers yet, but was apparently on the verge. That was pretty good diagnosis, I thought, since Cayce only had a name and address. "There has not been produced as yet lacerations or ulcerations in the pyloric end of the stomach," Cayce said ominously, "but there is more of a catarrhal condition in the duodenum and the pylorus."

He recommended a balanced diet: "Not too much white bread, not too much of meats, and never fried foods." My friend, like myself, was of a choleric temperament, a researcher's syndrome, it seems, and Cayce suggested, "Whenever there is great anxiety or stress, do not eat, especially raw apples nor bananas nor fruits of that nature which are acid-producing." Additionally, he recommended hydrotherapy, a colonic irrigation, and electrotherapy treatment, "for stimulation to the system especially across the stomach, the diaphragm and the centers in the cerebrospinal system from which the organs of assimilation and digestion receive their impulse."

I kept checking through the file. Four days after the first reading, my friend, duly grateful, had written Cayce that the reading "was remarkable and agreed in every way with the diagnosis of my physician." He commented, "I have suffered great pain for some weeks, as you reported, due to partial closing of pylorus valve under nervous tensions." He approached treatment hopefully. A month later, I noted, poring over the file, that he still didn't report much relief. There was a request for a check reading, with Cayce asked to be more specific: "How much electrotherapy—what kind?"

On December 23, 1938, Cayce gave a second reading, pointing out that "there is still some regurgitation from the duodenum to the stomach through the pylorus." He recommended more hydrotherapy, but cautioned against the electrotherapy. "Not too strong with the electrical forces that have been applied. These have been somewhat severe. Use the same kind, but not so high, so much." Three weeks later, on January 17, 1939, my friend wrote Cayce, asking for another check reading. "You certainly are being grand and most helpful to me." He asked: "Is former suggested treatment advisable at this time?"

Cayce, disapproving of the electrotherapy as it was being given, ordered its discontinuance. "The reactions that cause almost an extra flow of blood, or hemorrhage," he said, "arises from too great a quantity of the electrical forces." However, he suggested osteopathic adjustments, and a new therapist.

My friend was again impressed. Cayce, rather remarkably, had correctly visualized what had happened, though at no time did he meet the patient, who was in New York City all through this exchange.

"Your check reading was excellent," my friend confirmed. "I had a hemorrhage about two weeks ago, and apparently another one before that while on the table taking a too drastic electrical treatment." He had now returned to his own doctor, who was sympathetic to the readings and wanted a test reading himself.

"Your own readings," my friend continued, "have been amazingly accurate and to the point—above all frank—even to censuring certain well-intentioned treatments given. They have also been most helpful."

My friend now asked for a life reading, and an appointment was made. Two weeks later, he again reported on his condition. "I'm feeling much better. Had a series of X-rays which confirmed report in your readings. Also confirmed your statement that hemorrhage was caused by too severe electrical treatment." My friend was bitterly critical of the therapist, but had only praise for Cayce. "The ulcerated condition [another confirmation] was present, but with proper treatment a hemorrhage could have been averted, as your readings indicated."

There was an exchange of friendly letters the next few years between my friend and the Cayces, and then in 1952, seven years after the mystic's death, came the first indication of criticism. "I did not blame Edgar Cayce at the time," he wrote. "I blamed myself for having blindly followed the reading without double-checking."

If anything had gone wrong—which it obviously had—it seemed clear it had gone wrong in the application of the therapy, always a possibility, at any clinic, hospital or health service, where human frailty must be considered.

The criticism, where there once had been only praise, intrigued me.

"Do you know my friend?" I inquired of a Cayce intimate. He nodded. "Yes, and I like him."

"Do you remember his case?"

He hesitated a moment. "It is my recollection that Cayce recommended electrotherapy, and the therapist may have been more severe than he should have been." He looked up with a smile. "But I hadn't thought he blamed Cayce, since he wanted very much to do a book about Cayce later, but Tom Sugrue got to do it instead."

Chapter Ten

THE INCURABLE DISEASES

The Cayce file on cancer has been well-thumbed, and the various therapies purifying the system given considerable attention. However, one method of treatment advanced by Cayce made even the faithful wonder. For Cayce, of all things, advocated the use of a serum prepared from the blood of the rabbit. True, this was done in only five cases out of the seventy-eight that he diagnosed as cancer, but it was still rather bizarre. He apparently recommended the rabbit in instances of glandular cancer, of the thyroid, the breast. In two or three cases, he suggested that the rabbit be freshly skinned, and the raw side, still warm with the blood of the animal, be placed against the affected area, in this case the breast of a woman.

In one reading, back in 1926, for a cancer patient in New York, he was quite explicit about the use of the rabbit, both for external and internal application. He had been asked, "Should the fur be put on with the raw side next to the body?" and he answered, "With the fur side *out*, for the animal heat will add."

And then he gave a description of how an anti-cancer serum should be produced, "or there may be prepared a serum from the infusion from the pus from this body, injected into the rabbit between the shoulder, and when this brings the infection, this injected or placed on the sore will heal. Or the culture of same may be made and injected in the blood of this body."

Four years later, he read for a cancerous woman, recommended the rabbit serum, and gave directions for its manufacture. In the question period immediately following the main reading, he was asked, "Through whom may this serum be obtained?"

And he replied, "Hasn't been made yet."

"How can this be made?"

Answering, he added cattle to the rabbit as a potential vaccine source. "This should be drawn off—that is the wolve [or wolf of the rabbit]—punctured by a hypodermic. This drawn off, and then a culture made into the flesh of the same animal from which it's drawn, whether beef or hare. Then the culture applied to the human body, or blood drawn and a culture made for the human body and then applied to the body. There must necessarily be experimentations, with the proper heat, the proper precautions taken as to the character of cell as is destroyed in the culture made, and in the activity of the animal as well as human when being used. But for this character of the condition [apparent breast cancer], this would be most effective in at least fifty percent of such ills."

Cayce was dead more than twenty years when a startling announcement was carried on the front pages in April of 1966: A team of doctors at Wayne State University in Detroit reported an apparent cure for cancer, a serum formed from the blood of rabbits and the patient's own cancer cells.

It was apparently just what Cayce had anticipated; particularly noteworthy was his warning of "proper precautions taken as to the character of cell."

Only twenty patients had been treated with the rabbit serum, so the American Cancer Society wisely warned against raising false hopes. Those treated with the new technique were all terminal cases. Still, the research team headed by Drs. Paul L. Wolf and Norbert Czajkowski, reported two complete recoveries, and "stabilization or retardation of tumor growth" for eight. The remaining ten died. Total regression came in a case of breast cancer and of cancer of the skin of the jaw. Arrested were cancer of the skin, lung, and pancreas.

The Detroit doctors had begun their research project four years before. "The technique," the *New York Times* reported, "is one of tricking the cancer patient's body into rec-

ognizing his cancer as foreign matter, and thereby triggering
the immune-system to fight it off." The process was akin to
that described by Cayce. "The patient's tumor is removed.
The tumor cells are then chemically linked to a foreign protein, gamma globulin, from the blood serum of the rabbits.
The gamma globulin-tumor cell combination is injected into
the patient at intervals of several weeks."

The *New York Herald Tribune* reported that "Dr. Wolf set
about attaching the patient's own cancer cells to a derivative
of rabbit blood. He [Wolf] got the cancer by cutting away
some of the patient's own disease and breaking it up into individual cells. After treating the cells with the rabbit blood
and a linking chemical, he injected the complex mixture back
into the patient." And so Cayce had indicated.

In the blood of the patients so treated, the medical team
detected antibodies against the particular cancer. "Dr. Wolf
hoped that if he could produce an allergy to cancer, that is,
antibodies against the cancer, as the body sometimes does
against penicillin, he might have a chance of killing off the
cancer. He knew, too, that it was possible to stimulate anti-
body production to an 'innocent' chemical by attaching that
chemical to a protein totally foreign to the body."

One of the problems, as Cayce had pointed out in other
cancer readings, was that the cancer cell was an uncontrolled
growth of normal-like cells; it hoodwinked the body's immune system into thinking they had a right to be there. "In
these patients," the *Times* reported, "the body's immune system does not recognize the tumor tissue as foreign and does
not produce antibodies against it."

With heightened interest I turned to the Cayce file on cancer. What else did Cayce recommend, and how far-fetched did
it seem? Would science take another twenty, thirty to fifty
years to painstakingly discover what he only had to go to
sleep to learn?

On the cancer file was a warning that the extracts "are not
to be used as a prescription for the treatment of a disease" by
the layman. However, the information was available to licensed physicians, if any wanted to use it.

Some of Cayce's readings on cancer were given fifty years
ago, the last more than twenty years ago, when relatively little was known of the consuming disorder. In all, Cayce gave
360 readings on cancer, for 78 sufferers, and since his own
death these have been consolidated to present an over-all pic-

ture of the deadly malady. Cayce said there were many kinds of cancer, nineteen variations, externally and internally, arising from glandular or organic disturbance, or from infectious forces arising from bruises.

Long before the modern concept of cancer, he described the difference between benign and malignant growths. "Ulcer is rather that of flesh being proud or infectious, while cancer is that which lives upon the cellular force by the growth itself." The dread sarcoma, he said, was "caused by breaking of tissue internally which was not covered sufficiently by the leukocyte [germ-killing white corpuscles] due to the low vitality in the system." Not necessarily hereditary, tendencies were passed on and blood descendants should build up their blood plasma.

In some cancer, he recommended mercury-type ultraviolet ray, refracted through green glass; often combined with a substance known as Animated Ash, taken in water. He urged also two ounces of beet juice, the beets cooked in patapar paper so that the salts and juices were retained.

With his therapy Cayce expounded a whole broad concept of cancer origin, linked to toxics overloading the system. The ultraviolet, applied from the upper dorsal to the lower spine, "will produce in the blood stream that which is as the strainer, or eliminator, of the dregs of used tissue."

He explained what he meant by used tissue: "Each portion of the system uses so much vitality; this [becomes] as used tissue, just as the corpuscles in the blood stream become used." Normally, there were accumulations of such tissue in bruised areas, but it was either eliminated or so walled in by white blood cells as to contain any potential damage to the body.

Many have found interesting what he had to say about X-ray therapy. He found the ultraviolet through green-glass preferable because "green is the healing vibration," more effective even than the penetrating X-ray that "destroys tissue, but not being enabled to eliminate that destroyed tends to come back upon itself after certain radiations." In other words, destroyed tissue, too, became noxious "used tissue."

Cayce was a chronic pioneer. In 1929, the Animated Ash-Carbon Ash was first suggested for a woman with cancer. A friend, seeking information on how to make it, was told: "Where carbon is used in a near vacuum, if the residue produced by combustion [in a mercury quartz arc lamp] were to be saved, it would prove to be a product which, taken internally, would be more valuable than water treated by radium." The friend experimented with the ash, manufacturing it until his death ten years later. "The product," he reported, "is secured by taking bamboo fiber and passing a powerful electric current through it to secure partial combustion. The value of the resulting power lies evidently in a vibration in a manner similar to the activated foods being produced by German scientists."

Vibrations were generally electrical vibrations; they reflected the health and vitality of the individual. And Cayce again was decades ahead of his time, learned professors only recently finding the human body one big magnetic field. "Life in its expression in a human body," he said, "is of an electrical nature. The vibrations from low electrical forces, rather than the high vibrations [which have destroyed tissue in this case] produce life-flowing effects."

For both sarcoma and melanoma tumors, he advised special purifying foods, in keeping with his concept of cancer as a by-product of cumulative waste. "Live mostly for a while," he told one victim, "on watermelon, carrots, beets, having these almost daily." He explained, "The watermelon is for the activity of the liver and kidney, the beets and carrots for the purifying of the blood, as combined with plantain tea and ointment."

Both the tea and the ointment were to be made from the tender top leaves of the plantain plant, the ointment drying up "warts or moles that become infected and sore, and run," the tea purifying internally.

An ounce of prevention was clearly worth a pound of cure. Cayce frequently cited the almond as a preventive. "A form of vitamin may be obtained from certain nuts—as the almond—that would be helpful as a preventive." Elsewhere he was more specific. "And if an almond is taken each day, and kept up, you'll never have accumulations of tumors or such conditions through the body. An almond a day is much more in accord with keeping the doctor away, especially certain types of doctors, than apples." The almond moved him to poetry: "For the apple was the fall, not the almond; the almond blossomed when everything else died."

Almonds were a recurring theme. Somebody once asked if he should resume peanut oil rubs. Cayce replied: "Nothing better. They supply energy to the body. And just as a person who eats two or three almonds each day need never fear cancer, those who take a peanut oil rub each week need never fear arthritis." Another gem was similarly tucked away: "Also there may be obtained from the turtle egg those influences for longevity that may be created in certain cellular forces in the body."

Since Cayce's diagnoses were often unconfirmed, medically, skeptics argued that his cancer "cures" might have been for anything from hysteria to hiccoughs. However, authenticated "cancers" did come to him from doctors, and were helped, according to follow-throughs made over the years by the A.R.E. One such patient, a middle-aged woman, had been referred by a woman doctor, who thought that massive surgery, recommended by other doctors, would be disastrous. As usual, Cayce gave his reading without seeing the subject, in December 1937. "While the conditions are very well understood, the causes, and that which would counteract, are not." He identified the cancer, and its nature. "This we find is a sarcoma, an insidious condition, that is feeding upon the lymph and the blood circulation." He described a sort of tug-of-war between the cancer and the system's natural resistance. "Yet there is in the system that which has at times gained upon the rebuilding and replenishing system, and at other times the disturbing factors or humor in the cellular destruction, which in its distribution [through the body] have gained upon the physical forces of the body."

He traced the origin of this particular cancer. "They [the cancer] arose first, primarily, from too much of meats that carried an infectious force and that, working with the mammary glands, produced, through irritation, and through the breaking down of cellular forces, the beginning or hardening in those glands in the breast." From there, as he explained it, the cancer drained into the system, with various nodules, or little lumps arising in the breakdown of certain cellular forces in the lymph, in turn affecting the blood stream. With all this, there was a weakening of the organs.

Cayce recommended for this particular cancer a course of treatment stimulating the natural resistance forces of the lymph, and improving both circulation and elimination. "Stimulate those centers in the cerebrospinal system, that make for the drainages from the lymph through the eliminating systems." This was to be done through electrical therapy, of a low vibratory force. Then: "At least once a week give a maximum amount of atropine, giving it through the electrical anodes [wet cells] attached to the ninth dorsal plexus and to the lacteal duct (where the lymph forms) and umbilicus center (the navel). The current should not pass through the area for more than a minute in the beginning. The atropine taken vibratorially in this manner will stimulate the resistances in the lymph, *from which arises* [the stress was Cayce's] that producing the breaking of cells in the body, thus destroying their effective activity within themselves." There was a delicacy of treatment. "The maximum amount of the atropine, though it may be begun with the mimimum amount in the anodes. Take the vibration, not injections, for the age or conditions would prevent the injections from working with the lymph." The disorder was attacked on other fronts. Cayce suggested a purifying, low-carbohydrate diet, which the most recent physician had already prescribed. Again he stressed the importance of elimination. "This should bring much nearer normal conditions, and with proper precautions, without infectious forces or cold or congestion or other conditions arising, should bring relief." In other words, cancer was an affliction connected with the body's general condition.

"When may improvement begin?" he was asked.

"During the first cycle, within twenty-seven days."

A week later Cayce expressed the humility he felt about his gift in a letter to the referring doctor. "There is little use in trying to comment on the information," the waking Cayce said. "It speaks for itself. Hope you will find it in some ways at least in keeping with good judgment."

In six weeks, the sleeping giant received a report from the treating doctor. "As soon as I could get the machine working [the wet cell appliance], I carried out the instructions. The patient felt almost immediately that the treatment was helpful. We really feel that the case is progressing exceedingly well and I am hopeful of a complete cure." She added a grateful footnote. "I am most happy in feeling that I am, in a sense, working with you."

Six months after the initial reading the patient asked for a check reading. Miraculously, she felt better than she had in years. "At the present time," she wrote, "I am feeling far better and am grateful for your suggestions to the doctor, to whom enough praise and credit cannot be given for her faithful and untiring efforts in bringing about a most marvelous cure in a potentially incurable case."

She had a number of questions for Cayce: "How much of the cancer condition is left in bloodstream at the present time? Are further injections of atropine advisable? Has the malady affected any organs or internal parts? If so, what course of treatment is advised? Will there be a recurrence of the disease at any future time? If so, how will it manifest itself?"

Cayce's check reading was to the point. "There are great improvements in the general physical forces of the body. The infectious forces have been eliminated. However, there are still inclinations or tendencies. The system in combating same will need more of the vibratory forces that have assisted in eliminating those causes of disturbance." Treatments with the electrical appliance could be gradually eased, then eliminated. The atropine could be discontinued, unless there was a feeling of irritation in the lymphatic circulation. But until the patient felt fully recovered, she was not to extend herself physically or expose herself to mental strain.

Cayce had not specifically commented on the question regarding a recurrence. It was put to him again. His reply was rather conditional. "This depends altogether upon the amount of irritation, or how well the elminating is completed before there is a resuscitation of the condition." The tendency lingered, but once the condition was knocked out, and the health forces built up, so that there was a normal balance in the system, the patient would be over the hurdle. It all seemed to work. Four years later, the cancer had not reappeared, and the patient, apparently fully recovered, had moved to sunny California.

Repeatedly, Cayce stressed there was nothing incurable, provided one got to the primary cause. There was no point to treating symptoms. I had discussed Cayce's healing philosophy with a dear friend in Los Angeles, a voice teacher, who had suffered from the disfiguring skin disorder of psoriasis most of his life. The disorder had marred his personality, giving him an inferiority complex with accompanying defensiveness and insecurity. Sometimes, he wore long sleeve shirts even in the warmest weather to hide the angry red scales on his arms; other times—when his resentments got the better of him—he wore clothing which displayed the inflamed sores to their greatest disadvantage. It was a way of showing he didn't really care. But one way or the other, it was obvious he was never very far emotionally from his affliction. "It doesn't really matter," he told me once sardonically. "I am a fat old man, and nobody would love me anyway."

Psoriasis was one of the first things I looked for in the Cayce readings. I had stumbled through a thin file on the skin disorder, when somebody mentioned that a local osteopath had been treating psoriasis successfully from the dead psychic's readings.

I made plans to see the osteopath, Dr. Olis M. Wakefield, a respected practitioner, who had relieved my own sciatica three years before with a series of simple adjustments.

Meanwhile, I turned back to Cayce on psoriasis. One reading was for a twenty-five-year-old woman, bothered with the disorder for years. Her mother, a naturopathic physician, had asked Cayce: "What is the cause of psoriasis? What remedies will cure it, or what kind of treatments will do the work? How long will it take until complete cure [of daughter] is effected?"

The mother came to the obvious conclusion: "If you can give this reading, it will not only help our daughter but many others afflicted with the same condition, for which medical science apparently has not found a cure."

As usual in health readings, Cayce got quickly to the point, picking out conditions of a complex nature leading to incoordination in the eliminating system. "While there is the thinning of the walls of the small intestines and there are poisons absorbed through the system that find expression in the attempt to eliminate through superficial circulation, we find that there are pressures also existing in the areas of the sixth, seventh dorsal that upset the coordination of circulation through the kidneys and liver. These contribute to the condition causing the abrasions which occur as red splotches or spots at times."

He suggested osteopathic adjustments, twice a week, for three weeks, and then gradually spread out. "There should only be required about twelve adjustments, if properly made, coordinating the muscular forces in areas where the sympathetic and cerebrospinal systems coordinate in the greater measure."

After six osteopathic treatments, he recommended a compound prepared with equal tablespoons of sulphur, Rochelle salts, cream of tartar. "Take a teaspoonful every morning, either in water or dry on tongue, until the whole quantity has been taken." Other recommendations followed: "Then begin with yellow saffron tea, a pinch in a cup of boiling water, allow to stand for thirty minutes, strain and drink each evening when ready to retire. Occasionally, about two or three times a week, drink elm water, a pinch of ground elm [between thumb and forefinger] in a cup, filled with warm water [not boiling water]. Stir thoroughly and let set for thirty minutes. Drink this preferably in morning rather than at the period when the saffron is taken." There was some diet advice. "Eliminate fats, sweets, and pastries. Do have a great deal of fruits and vegetables."

The mother inquired if psoriasis always had the same origin.

"No," Cayce replied, "more often from the lack of proper coordination in the eliminating systems. At times, the pressures may be in those areas disturbing the equilibrium between the heart and liver, or between heart and lungs. But it is always caused by a condition of lack of lymph circulation through alimentary canal and by absorption of such activities through the body."

The reading was given in April 1944, and I read along rapidly to see how the patient fared. Unfortunately, the girl never followed the treatment. Years later, the mother reported in response to a followup query, "The reading was never carried out. She went to two osteopaths, and they both made fun of it, so she quit."

Cayce had better luck with his second psoriasis patient, a woman, twenty-eight. The diagnosis was similar. "The conditions that exist through the thinning of the walls of the intestines allow the poisons to find expression in the lymph circulation, producing the irritation to and through the epidermis itself. Through the warm weather these show the tendency for greater activity in the perspiratory system, causing greater irritations."

Again Cayce prescribed the yellow saffron tea, but alternated this with mullein tea, gathered fresh. "Use an ounce of the flower and leaf of the mullein to a quart of boiling water. Let this steep as ordinary tea, and it may be kept for a period of a week, provided it is put in the ice-box or kept very cold." He also recommended treatments externally. "In the evenings when the bath is taken, we would apply Cuticura ointment followed by Resinol, both applied, you see, one following the other. Apply these especially over the areas of the abrasions. Do not apply it in the hair, but around the edges, and on all other portions of the body where the skin is irritated."

His dietary advice was a little more complex than before as there was an obesity complication. "Cut down on the foods that give the great quantity of calories, increasing those that give the greater vitamin content, especially B-1 and B-4, as in all foods that are yellow in color. Yellow corn meal made in bread, cakes, mush or the like; carrots both raw and cooked; yellow peaches, let these be practically the only sweets taken." He advised repeated use of grape juice, prohibited carbonated beverages and sugar. After the saffron and mullein teas had been used for three weeks, he suggested holding an ultraviolet ray rod applicator in each hand for about three minutes at a time, to step up electrical vibrations. With all this went "patience, persistence, and right thinking also."

The woman began the treatment at once. In a week, she responded with a happy testimonial. "I just can't tell you how much better I feel, body and mind. The places on my body are fading away and I have lost seven pounds in six days." There was a progress report five months later: "The psoriasis condition cleared up completely, except in places of scalp; there was some flareup, when careless of diet."

I was now ready for Dr. Wakefield. I recalled Wakefield as a down-to-earth practitioner, with one of the busiest practices on the Virginia cape. He was a tall, spare, yet ruggedly built man, reminding one of a middle-aged Gary Cooper. He had just returned from a Rotary Club meeting, and was preoccupied with detail work as president of the Virginia Osteopathic Medical Association.

He soon made clear his own views. "If something helps a patient, even if the treatment is not medically authenticated, I am for it. After all, my chief concern is helping people, not establishing the superiority of one concept of medicine over another."

Recently, he had had some luck with psoriasis, clearing up the scales of a twenty-two-year-old college student, son of a prominent Virginia Beach attorney, who had vainly consulted specialists around the country. The treatment had come out of the Cayce readings, and in a strange way, as Wakefield recollected. In April 1962, a patient walked in with angry red scales on his knees and elbow. It was a clear-cut case of psoriasis, as to both location and appearance. The patient was Lewis Love, an engineer. Dr. Wakefield told him he was suffering from psoriasis, adjusted his spine, and prescribed a mercury ointment. Spinal adjustments were helpful, but provided only temporary relief. In all his experience, Wakefield had never before cured a case of psoriasis. Love left, and he heard no more from him. Eight months later, in January 1963, the patient returned to the office, this time for treatment for a shoulder dislocation. As he examined him, gently probing his body, Wakefield looked up with a start. Love's knees and elbow, he suddenly realized, were completely clear. There was not a mark of any kind on him. "What happened to your psoriasis?" the doctor asked.

Love smiled enigmatically. "It's cured."

Wakefield fairly beamed. "You mean the treatment did that?"

Love shook his head. "I never tried your treatment."

Instead, knowing now what he had, he had gone to the A.R.E. library and studied the readings on psoriasis. He had then used the Cuticura soap and the Resinol on his skin, and taken the yellow saffron and mullein teas. Almost immediately, the scales had begun to disappear.

The next day, the open-minded osteopath was running through the Cayce psoriasis file himself. And soon, with startling results, he began to apply the Cayce treatment. Where patients followed the treatment faithfully, relief was nearly always immediate and total.

The osteopathic adjustments helped, the osteopath meanwhile noting that Cayce's recommended adjustments so often named the third cervical and the ninth dorsal, at which point the spinal nerves branched off to major glands. "Apparently," Wakefield said, "stimulation of the glands was vital to the Cayce therapy."

It was four years later now, and I wondered how the Cayce therapy had stood up. And so I phoned the Love home. His wife answered. "Oh, yes," she said, "Lewis isn't troubled anymore, except for an occasional flareup, when he gets in a swivet. I suppose what happens then is that he builds up an overload of toxics, and they permeate through the thin walls of the intestines, like Cayce said, and show up on his skin, where his weakness obviously lies." She laughed. "But he keeps calm, since he knows what's good for him."

What had Cayce said? Right-thinking. That appeared to be the antidote for a variety of human ailments.

Though he never came up with anything like a Salk vaccine (so far as anybody knows), Cayce was also ahead on poliomyelitis, advancing the fortified-blood concept of gamma globulin, as well as recuperative manipulation and massage.

In May 1934, he gave an emergency reading for a ten-year-old girl at Mount Sinai Hospital in New York. Without being told anything of her condition, he diagnosed it as infantile paralysis, discussing the "wasting of those centers of bulb gland or plexus forces along the spine, attacking principally the locomotory centers." As part of the therapy, he recommended a "transfusion from a body that has been cured or relieved of that known as infantile paralysis." In other words, years before its introduction, he was advocating gamma globulin to step up the body's resistance to the infection.

Because of the girl's critical state, he sent a telegram listing the treatment. There was internal as well as external medication. "Give three to five drops Atomidine thrice daily," he advised. "Begin immediately massaging not too briskly but to redden skin from base brain downward on, not upward, even on lower limbs with compound as follows, adding ingredients in order named: Russian White Oil, two ounces, oil of cedar wood one-half ounce, oil of mustard twenty minims [drops], tincture of benzoin one ounce, oil of sassafras three minims."

His directions were explicit: "Shake well each time, massaging what will absorb once daily or oftener if suffering continues." If a fever continued, he recommended the transfusion of the built-up blood.

The doctors in New York had meanwhile diagnosed the child's ailment as spinal meningitis, whose symptoms are often similar to polio. Cayce's recommendations were resisted, though the child lay dying, without any other help forthcoming.

The end with all its pathos was related by a family friend, who had handled the request for a reading. Ironically, a transfusion was effected, but of normal blood. "I got to the hospital at 3 P.M." the friend reported. "It took me until 8 P.M. to get the doctors to give the Atomidine, and to allow the rubbing, but only a transfusion of 'pure blood' was given. She passed away at 9:15 P.M., one hour later. I was sorry that you didn't get the reading for the little girl sooner. She was beautiful; ten years old, sick nine weeks, and looked just like

Alice in Wonderland. They [the family] all appreciated your [Cayce's] willingness and aid, but it's almost impossible where doctors are so arbitrary."

Actually, the child had little chance, as Cayce had said it would take from twenty-four to thirty-six hours to respond to his treatment. Too little, too late, a familiar story.

Of late, Cayce has been getting more attention from the doctors than he did when alive. Quietly, many physicians have delved into his readings, searching for clues to conditions which resist orthodox therapy. Only recently an enterprising young physician affiliated with the Harvard University faculty studied extracts from the Cayce record on such incurables as epilepsy, leukemia, and multiple sclerosis, and summarized the Cayce-given etiological or causative factors and treatment program. His abstracts in no way implied approval of the Cayce approach, but were an effort to see whether a pattern could be worked out which would lend itself to large-scale medical research.

The doctor reviewed ninety-five cases of epilepsy. In a majority, he found lesions (impairing injuries) of the lacteal duct (supplying the lymphatic vessels) and the spine given as the basic cause. "The lesions in the spinal segments and the lacteal duct lesion," he observed, "produced what was described as an incoordination between the cerebrospinal and the autonomic nervous system. From this data, it can be implied that there was a type of reciprocal action between lesions in the spinal segments and the lacteal duct."

The endocrine or ductless glands were involved in some twenty-five percent of the cases. "Because of the disturbances in the lacteal duct area and the spinal segments, the adrenals and the gonads would be affected. These glands in turn would cause a response in the pineal and pituitary glands in the brain. The end result of these disturbances was an overflow of neuronal (nerve cell) discharge via the central nervous system in the case of grand mal seizure, or the temporary loss of consciousness in a petit mal seizure." The medical investigator stressed the explanation was incomplete, unverified by present medical knowledge. "The readings were more concerned with treatment than cause," he observed, "and usually only gave as much theory as was necessary to understand and carry out the treatments." Nevertheless, the Cayce readings tended to dissipate the notion that epilepsy was inevitably tied up with a malfunction of the brain. The doctor briefly quoted from one reading:

Q. Do you find any condition existing in the brain, or is it reflex?

A. The accumulations that have been there are rather reflex, produced by the condition in the lacteal duct [abdominal] area.

Q. Of what nature was the injury that brought about this condition in the lacteal area?

A. This was a pressure, or a licking.

In another diagnosis, Cayce was considerably more explicit in tracing the background: "The causes arise from an injury received some years ago, in the coccyx area [base of spine], and then contributory causes later above the lumbar axis of the spine. These caused a slowing circulation through the lacteal duct area, producing a cold area there that has produced a partial adherence of tissue. When there is the lack of proper eliminations through the alimentary canal, coordination between the sympathetic and cerebrospinal system is affected, governing impulses to the brain, or a form of spasmodic reaction that might be called epileptic in nature." He warned that ordinary treatment would only make things worse, increasing the attacks that "occur from this deflection of impulse."

Asked the nature of the original accident, his Universal Mind promptly replied: "Striking the end of the spine on a banister."

In a minority of cases, brain damage was listed as a cause; even fewer were involved with mental retardation. Where incoordination between the autonomic and cerebrospinal nervous systems was mentioned as a definite factor, the doctor found that Cayce usually recommended castor oil packs, together with additional therapy. "In order to break up the lesions and adhesions in the lacteal duct area," the physician noted, "a combination of hot castor oil packs, massage, olive oil taken internally and manipulations of the spine were employed. In addition, proper elimination and diet also were supposed to have their effect upon the lacteal area. The hot castor oil packs were usually given in a three-day series, and were kept on from one to three hours over the entire right abdomen." The doctor, school trained for half a lifetime, was as technical as the unschooled Cayce in describing how the pack was applied: "Both anterior and posterior from the right costal margin to the crest of the ileum and covering the area of the caecum and the umbilicus." He explained how it presumably worked: "These hot packs were described as being able to start the breakup of the lacteal lesions and adhesions. The heat alone would tend to increase the circulation to the area. It was also implied that castor oil itself would have a beneficial effect by absorption through the skin. In some cases, kneading of the right side of the abdomen was advised immediately after the removal of the packs, to help in the breakup of the lesions and adhesions. This massage was done with either peanut oil, or a mixture of olive oil and myrrh, and sometimes a combination of all three."

The doctor summarized the balance of the treatment, so effective in some cases: "The olive oil which was given internally [usually two tablespoonfuls] was to be taken at bedtime on the last day of the series of packs. The olive oil as a fat would be absorbed through the lacteal ducts and might help to increase the flow through them. Osteopathic massage and manipulation on and around the spine followed the day after the series of castor oil packs was finished. The manipulative treatment was supposed not only to correct any mechanical abnormalities in spinal segments, but also to stimulate the autonomic nervous system to help overcome the imbalance between the autonomic and the cerebrospinal nervous system, by an increase in circulation and a relief of nervous tension. The hot packs seem to be an essential preliminary step, so that the manipulations would have their maximum effect."

Cayce's treatment extended to diet, elimination, herbs, exercise. Olive oil was described as a natural laxative. Colonics were recommended for those with a difficult problem. The diet was designed to be easily digestible, aiding eliminations. "The diet was low fat in nature," the Harvard man reported, "with definite prohibitions of fried foods, pork, fat meats, and sweet milk. Alkaline forming foods and vegetables were recommended but most tuberous vegetables were excluded. Acid-producing foods such as meats, sugars, starches, and condiments were discouraged." In one respect, the treatment was exotic. Cayce recommended a boiled concentrate of the Passion Flower to replace the use of normal sedatives. "Although in various places the readings approved the temporary continuance of sedatives such as Dilantin or Phenobarbitol," the doctor observed, "the ultimate goal of successful treatment was the elimination of the need for such drugs which acted as poisons in the system." He had a word about the Passion Flower. "This fusion was described as a nonhabit-forming herb compound and not a sedative itself, though it was supposed to have a calming action on the nervous system and to aid the eliminations, as well as to help retard muscular contractions."

Outdoor exercise was recommended both as an outlet for excess energy and obtaining the fullest relaxation during rest. He quoted Cayce, "The body should take as much physical exercise, in the open, as is practical each day, but not to be overstrenuous. Calisthenics or anything which has to do with the general movement of the body in the open is well. Walking is one of the best of exercises, swimming, tennis, handball, badminton, any of these activities."

The aim of the treatments, the doctor noted, was complete cure. "Therefore, all traces of the underlying difficulties had to be eliminated, as well as factors which would set up new tendencies. In most cases the treatment recommended was at least six months."

The cure was not easy—but neither was epilepsy.

Leukemia was one of the more intriguing studies tackled by the Harvard doctor. There were only eleven authenticated blood cancer cases in the Cayce readings, and many of these were terminal, but Cayce did indicate a cause and suggested treatment. "The cause of leukemia was not given in a detailed way," the doctor observed, "but a disturbance in body catabolism [normal breakdown of tissue to waste] was noted along with loss of the energies of anabolism [normal food change to living tissue]. Infection through the spleen was linked with an excess of destructive forces of the lymph." The spleen has the function of modifying the structure of the blood, and this is perhaps the first time it has been pinpointed as the culprit in leukemia. "It is a medical fact," the doctor pointed out, "that the red cell count decreases and the white blood cell count mounts in leukemia. In the readings this destructive process chiefly of red blood cells was linked to an overactivity and infection of the spleen."

Oddly, the doctor noted, in one of the four cases of Hodgkin's disease in the readings (confirmed by autopsy), the described cause and treatment was similar to that in the leukemia readings. "These similarities," the doctor suggested, "hint that perhaps there are some similar underlying biochemical mechanisms having to do with the endocrine glands and the spleen in various diseases of the blood."

The sufferers invariably turned to Cayce too late—if they could have been helped at all. Treatment, quite complex, was summarized: Ultraviolet light (mercury quartz lamp) was to be used forty inches from the body with a green stained glass plate (at least ten by twelve inches) suspended between the source of the light and the body. The light was to focus for not more than one to one and a half minutes in any one spot with special emphasis on the spleen and rib area, and not more than an all-over total of five minutes. Infrared light (thirty to forty minutes) was to be applied every other day to the cerebrospinal area, particularly along the rib zone. Also recommended was massage, osteopathic manipulations, iodine trichloride (Atomidine), supplementary diet of beef juice, rare calves liver, massive intake of fresh orange juice. The treatment was at least geared to where Cayce said the cause lay. "The whole process of the disease," the doctor indicated, "was said to be caused by a glandular disturbance from unbalanced chemical reactions in the body. This could point toward a biochemical cause of the disease. One reading specifically mentions iodine deficiency. This could be the reason for Cayce's advising iodine trichloride as a gland stimulant. In one case the thyroid gland was mentioned in particular. A lack of proper activity of the structural portions of the body could refer to the red blood cell producing capacity of the marrow, especially the ribs [which are mentioned specifically]. These portions of the body could in turn be affected by the glands. Mention was also made of the activity having become static in the cerebrospinal system centers which control the marrow production from the ribs. Apparently an attempt was made to stimulate these centers through ultraviolet and infrared light, as well as manual massage."

The same distinguished medical authority researched Cayce's treatment of multiple sclerosis. However, he made the same reservations as with other abstracts, in proposing controlled clinical trial. "The summary of treatment is not to be taken as an endorsement," he warned, "the validity of the data can only be decided by careful research in the form of controlled experiments by qualified physicians. The etiological [causative] mechanisms described are meant to be considered as theories to be proved."

The doctor pondered one hundred readings for sixty-nine subjects, but was particularly impressed by one reading made at the request of a physician, Dr. Charles Goodman Taylor, since this could be scientifically validated as a case of multiple sclerosis. In postulating how the disease formed, he integrated the material from other readings with this specific reading. "The basic biochemical mechanism stated in the reading was that multiple sclerosis was a result of a lack of gold which caused a glandular imbalance which in turn resulted in a hormonal deficiency or imbalance. This hormone was said to be necessary for proper functioning of the nerves."

The normal balance of metals in the system was out of equilibrium due to a lack of gold primarily. In forty cases, gold was mentioned as a factor which needed to be added to the system. "The reason for the lack of gold," the doctor commented, "was tied to a defect in the assimilating system [by this was probably meant the digestive system] which in turn was kept in proper working order by the proper hormonal balance from the glands." It was all part of a delicate relationship on which the well-being of the body depended. "Because the glands were in turn dependent upon the proper amount of gold in the system, this would apparently lead to a circular feedback relationship between gold, the glands and the assimilating system. Though not explicitly stated, it could be assumed that the disease was not caused from simply a lack of gold in the diet, but perhaps from a lack of the capacity of the digestive system to assimilate gold or perhaps inability of the body to use the gold assimilated. In this reading, a genetic factor was suggested as the underlying cause of the imbalance between these three factors: gold, glands, and assimilation." There was a way of checking this out. "A connection of the normal balance of metals in the system could be discovered in the male by a lack of sperm [i.e. some degree of sterility]. However, it was not clear whether this was simply a decreased sperm count or a lack of potency of the sperm due to a lack of metals, most notably gold, in the sperm." The doctor then observed, "There is no medical data to confirm the theory that sterility is a result of multiple sclerosis." However, as he pointed out, impotency has been reported.

Some type of glandular disturbance was mentioned in numerous cases. In this case, in response to the question "Which glands are involved?" the Cayce reply was:

"Those about the liver and gall duct."

The liver was repeatedly described as the direct link to the malfunctioning of the nervous system in multiple sclerosis. There was a hormone deficiency but the lacking hormone was not named. This missing substance from the glands was supposed to be a nutrient to nervous tissue, and the nerves were repeatedly said to lack proper balance of nervous energy or stamina. Some of the apparent pathology was then noted. "The reading stated that this lack of nervous energy caused a poison to form in certain nerve cells, and then other surrounding cells were poisoned. A description was given of the pulling apart and elongation of originally round cells. Perhaps this was the same process referred to in one case in which the hormonal lack was said to cause a breakdown of the cellular forces in the nerve walls and led to an inflammation and irritation via an action on the nerve plexuses and ganglia between the central and the autonomic nervous systems." This was analogous to what medicine has since learned about the disorder. "This breakdown of nerve walls coupled with wasting away or dissolving of the nerves could be taken as a description of the pathological loss of myelin sheath or white matter in multiple sclerosis. Pathologically, there is damage to both the 'white' myelin sheath and the 'gray' axone in this disease." Cayce remarkably mentioned a lack of "gray" matter.

The doctor analyzed three treatment approaches: addition of the atomic effect of gold through a wet cell battery, massage and diet. "The atomic effect of gold was said to be necessary for the glandular production of the hormone which maintained the proper structural condition and functioning of the nerves. However, gold was not to be added directly to the system by ingestion or injection, but vibratorily through the use of the wet cell battery." The wet cell was a weak battery composed of two poles, with a wire from one pole suspended in a solution of gold chloride and then attached to the body. The readings indicated that the vibration given from the gold in solution would be electrically transmitted into the body and have the [needed] glandular effect. The vibration did not act directly but only enabled other elements [perhaps gold already in the body in an inactive form] to become active and have the desired effect. The wet cell was to be recharged [new solutions added] every thirty days and to be used each day, preferably before retiring, for thirty to sixty minutes.

Massage with nourishing oils was an important part of the Cayce treatment. Curiously, years after the first Cayce readings, massage became current medical treatment (as supportive therapy) for multiple sclerosis. As the doctor pointed out: "It certainly helps to maintain the tone of muscles which have lost their normal innervation [active nerve network], the advantage being that when and if function returns, the muscle will not have atrophied and shortened."

However, there was a basic difference between the medical and Cayce concept of the function of the oils. Where medicine attributes chiefly a lubricating effect to the oils, Cayce said the oils nourished weakened tissue, as borne out in his own cases, and by Hotten in California, McGarey in Arizona, Reilly in New York.

There were two basic blends. "The simple mixture," the doctor noted, "was usually a combination of equal parts of olive oil and peanut oil plus melted lanolin in this ratio: two ounces of olive oil, two ounces of peanut oil, one-quarter ounce of lanolin. The complex mixture had an olive oil base plus peanut oil, various combinations of Russian white oil, oil of cedarwood, oil of sassafras root, oil of pine needles, lanolin, oil of wintergreen, tincture of benzoin, tincture of myrrh, spirits of camphor, spirits of turpentine, mutton suet and/or oil of mustard."

The directions varied. "In the majority of cases, it was suggested to massage from the spine to the distal [farthest] portions of the extremities, but in some from the tips of the extremities to the spine. Although the spine and extremities were mentioned most, the chest and abdomen were also suggested. A circular motion for the massage was recommended."

With Cayce dead, of course, it was not quite clear what treatments, even if generally effective, should be applied to a specific case. As Dr. McGarey had said, commenting on his own research, it entailed an almost intuitive rapport with Cayce's subconscious to know when to do what to whom, à la Cayce.

The recommended diet was consistent with Cayce's normal diet for the ailing, or well, for that matter, low-fat, non-constipating. "Foods containing B vitamins were stressed," the doctor found, "and sometimes brewers yeast or wheat germ was advised. Seafood, liver, wild game and fowl were recommended as the meats, but broiled and not fried. The bones of chicken and fish were to be chewed. Fried foods were generally prohibited. Raw vegetables such as watercress, carrots, celery, beets, and salads with gelatin were stressed. Vegetables, fruits and cereals were to be eaten much more than meat. None of the emphasized foods were designated as providing gold in any form. Seafood was explicitly mentioned as being especially important because of its iodine content—the Cayce readings stating that iodine has an effect on all the endocrine glands, not only the thyroid."

The experienced Cayce reader had something to learn from the fact that gold was not mentioned. Obviously, the problem was not so much a lack of gold intake, but of activation of this gold, and this apparently was provided by the wet cell's vibratory influence. The Harvard researcher pointed out that Cayce's treatment was connected, the massage immediately following the wet cell treatment, when the body was extremely susceptible to external impulses. But, scientifically, he added, almost regretfully, the Cayce readings could "only hope to give hints and point the direction for further research which perhaps may unravel some of the present unknown in the etiology and treatment of multiple sclerosis."

After all, it only worked.

Chapter Eleven

CAYCE'S HOME REMEDIES

One Sunday I was having dinner with friends in New Jersey, about an hour's ride from New York City.

There were several people at the table, and somebody had been talking of making a trip to Europe.

"Be sure to take a bottle of Cayce's seasick drops," a middle-aged man said. His wife nodded her emphasis. "We never travel without them," she said. "They are even more useful than Cayce suggested. In New Orleans recently, Al"—here she turned to her husband—"Al felt some distress after overeating, and the thought of getting on the plane made him want to cancel out. He took the drops, and the nausea disappeared."

I looked up politely. "Where do you get these drops?"

"We make them ourselves, from the Cayce formula," Barbara Anton said. "We've given them to twenty of our friends." She laughed. "The kind of people who turn green just looking at a boat have found an end to all their dread about ocean travel, and the same with air or car sickness."

The drops were a first-aid must. But there was still another substance they wouldn't travel without. This was a mild antiseptic known as Glyco-Thymoline. Cayce had recommended this for all sorts of packs, douches, and gargles. The husband, Al Anton, a jeweler, rubbed his hands over his eyes. "Sometimes, I've felt as if my eyes were coming out of their sockets. Three parts of distilled water with one part of Glyco-Thymoline, in cotton pads applied to the eyes for five to ten minutes, and all the ache, sting, and smart goes out. It's amazing."

The rest of the company had looked up with interest. A man sitting down the table from me put in, "And don't forget the witch hazel for athlete's foot. There's nothing better; Cayce certainly knew what he was talking about."

How could so many home remedies be put to practical application so long after Cayce's death?

"That's the easiest part of it," our host spoke up. "Haven't you heard of the famous black book? It's all there, clarified, collated, and indexed, for anybody that wants it."

The black book consisted of extracts from diverse readings. Everything from baldness to stuttering was represented, with tips on how these conditions could be helped. The book was brought out, and I dutifully leafed through it, turning to Glyco-Thymoline, and its various uses.

"What should be done to relieve my eyes?" somebody had asked thirty years before.

And Cayce had replied, "Bathe them with a weak Glyco-Thymoline solution. Use an eye-cup, two parts of distilled water preferably, to one part of Glyco-Thymoline. This irritation is a part of the kidney disturbance that has come from the upsetting in the digestive forces."

The conversation had become general, and another woman looked up with a sheepish grin. "I don't know if I should mention this in mixed company," she said, "but a little Coca-Cola after the menstrual period does a lot toward getting me feeling better."

I suddenly remembered. "But I thought Cayce disapproved of carbonated beverages."

She smiled. "The Coca-Cola syrup is mixed with water."

I thumbed through the big black book, to good old Coke. Cayce had recommended the drink for both men and women, for purifying the body. Apparently, it helped clear the system of toxics. "Do take Coca-Cola occasionally as a drink, for the activity of the kidneys," he told a twenty-nine-year-old woman, "but not with carbonated water. Buy or have the syrup prepared and add plain water to this. Take about one half-ounce or one ounce of the syrup and add plain water. This to be taken about every other day, with or without ice. This will aid in purifying the kidney activity and bladder and will be better for the body."

Cayce hadn't exactly recommended Coke as a steady diet.

By now, of course, nearly everybody was recalling some miraculous way that someone had been helped. "This man I knew," a woman said, "threw away his glasses after doing the head and neck exercise."

There were exclamations of interest, and she continued. "He was suffering from eye-strain, and somebody mentioned doing this simple neck-rolling exercise a few times a day. His vision improved to a point where the headaches left him and he threw his glasses away in a week."

It had all happened two years before, twenty years after Cayce's death.

I remembered now Gladys Davis telling me how a few simple neck rolls, advised in a reading, had helped her as a young woman to get rid of her reading glasses, not to return to glasses until she was fifty, though constantly doing close work.

Again I skimmed through the black book.

"How can I improve my vision?" a fifty-four-year-old woman had asked Cayce.

"The head and neck exercise will be most helpful," he said. "Take this regularly, each morning and each evening for six months, and we will see a great deal of difference."

He then described what seemed a simple Yoga exercise to an old Yogi like myself.

"Sitting erect, bend the head forward three times, to the back three times, to the right side three times, to the left side three times, and then circle the head each way three times. Don't hurry through with it, but take the time to do it. We will get results."

For some, I noticed Cayce suggested a variation of this exercise, along with a brisk walk. "Do the head and neck exercise in the open, as you walk for twenty to thirty minutes each morning. Now do not undertake it one morning and then say, 'It rained and I couldn't get out,' or 'I've got to go somewhere else.' "

I put the book aside. Between the conversation and the food, the table was heavily freighted. My hosts were health faddists and I had half-surmised they were vegetarians, organic vegetables at that. But, pleasantly, a thick, sizzling steak was brought on, set off with a variety of vegetables. As the meal ended, I mentioned my surprise that they were meat-eaters.

My host laughed. "Actually," he said, "we follow what

might be called the Cayce normal diet. Pork was about the only meat he was dead set against. He was for a little of everything in moderation, favoring a well-balanced diet full of natural vitamins. He didn't believe much in the synthetics. He was full of surprises. For instance, he felt that coffee, without milk or cream, was a food and not necessarily harmful. With milk, it formed a leathery substance inside the stomach, he said, and it was better taken alone than with a meal."

He reached for the black book, and turned to coffee. "Coffee," Cayce said, "is a stimulant to the nerve system. The dross from coffee is caffeine which is not digestible in the system. When caffeine is allowed to remain in the colon, poisons are thrown off from it. If it is eliminated, as it is in this individual, coffee is a food and is preferable to many stimulants."

My host had made a study of Cayce's dietary advice. "It wasn't only what he prescribed, but the way he felt foods should be consumed. The person should always be relaxed at the table, or the meal would become almost immediately toxic. As a digestive aid, he recommended a glass of warm water on rising. Not so hot that it is objectionable, not so tepid that it makes for sickening, but this will clarify the system of poisons. Occasionally, a pinch of salt should be added to this draught of water."

It seemed to me that we were getting a little afield. What was the perfect diet?

My host shrugged. "Even Cayce varied it for the individual and his individual needs. He was great for the shellfish with their natural iodines, as he felt they toned up the thyroid, and he recommended the lighter meats, fish, fowl, lamb, fresh vegetables, and fruits." This was not at all unusual in the current nutrition-conscious period, but Cayce had been advocating this fifty years ago, when hogs, hominy, and grits made pellagra epidemic in the South.

At times, Cayce outlined an ideal diet, as he did for a six-year-old girl. "Mornings: whole grain cereals, or citrus fruits, but these never taken at the same meal; rather alternate these, using one on one day and the other the next. Any form of rice cakes or the like, the yolk of eggs. Noons: some fresh raw vegetable salad. Soups with brown bread, broths or such. Evenings: a well-coordinated vegetable diet, with three vegetables above the ground to one below the ground. Seafood, fowl, or lamb; not other types of meat. Gelatin may be prepared with any of the vegetables, as in the salads for the noon meal, or with milk and cream dishes."

Cayce ruled out fried foods, preferring the roasted, broiled, or boiled. He didn't vary the normal diet much for adults, but stressed the seafoods twice a week, particularly clams, oysters, shrimp, or lobster. "The oyster or clam should be taken raw if possible, while having the others prepared through roasting or boiling with the use of butter." He advocated "foods of the blood-building type once or twice a week—pig's knuckles, tripe, and calves liver, or those meats of brains and the like." He was definitely no vegetarian, for specifying certain vegetables and fruits, he stressed, "These foods with the occasional eating of sufficient meat for strength, would bring a well-balanced diet."

I found the diet business rather tedious, but my host observed, "Cayce never believed that you are only what you eat, but rather what your body does with what you eat, and what you do with your body and mind."

My host, on the portly side, had tried one of Cayce's special diets, raw apples, for reducing. After three days of all the apples he wanted, he had dropped twelve pounds, and was well on his way to pruning off a desired twenty pounds. "There's something about the apples that pulls the water out of the system," he said. His diet had been topped off each night with a couple of tablespoonfuls of olive oil, for cleansing.

I wondered what kind of apples he had eaten.

"Golden, red, purple, McIntosh, Delicious, Baldwin, Northern Spy. I kept mixing them up, but they were still apples."

Hadn't he gotten weak or hungry?

"All I had to do was eat another apple."

Cayce was the answer to the cigarette manufacturer's current nightmare over cancer. He said that moderate cigarette-smoking—five or six cigarettes a day—never hurt anybody, and he was an inveterate smoker himself. They relaxed him.

He saw no harm in an occasional drink, but said wine was the only alcoholic drink actually helpful. "Wine is good for all, if taken alone, or with black or brown bread. Not with meat so much as with just bread. This may be taken between meals, or as a meal, but not too much, and just once a day. Red wine only."

Eventually, the dinner party broke up, all agreeing that Cayce was affecting more people's well-being today than he had even while alive.

As the others drifted off, I retired to my room with the precious black book. I thumbed through the index, stopping at asthma. A dear friend had a child suffering from this affliction. What could Cayce do for it?

Here was a girl, thirteen, whose mother had written, "The asthma has bothered her two and a half years."

Cayce was as specific as gravity. "For the asthmatic condition," he said, "have those properties made into an inhalant. To four ounces of pure grain alcohol (not 85%, but pure grain, 190 proof) add: oil of eucalyptus, twenty drops; benzol, ten drops; oil of turpentine, five drops; tolu in solution, forty drops; tincture of benzoin, five drops. Keep in a container at least twice the size, or an eight ounce bottle with a glass cork. Shake solution together and inhale deep into the lungs and bronchi, two or three times a day."

Under attitudes and emotions, to which I next turned, Cayce translated a whole course in psychosomatic medicine into a few simple paragraphs. My host, a well-known healer himself, had marked the margin, "Here is the root of nearly all illness—Cayce was a generation ahead of his time."

I read where Cayce told a man whose simmering resentments had affected his health: "Attitudes oft influence the physical conditions of the body. No one can hate his neighbor and not have stomach or liver trouble. No one can be jealous and allow the anger of same and not have upset digestion or heart disorder. Neither of these disorders is present here, and yet those attitudes have much to do with the accumulations which have come gradually, tendencies towards neuritic-arthritic reactions." It was all part of an emotional backwash, hindering the healthy flow of glands, blood, lymph, and nerves. "Stiffness at times is indicated in the locomotories; a nausea, or upsetting of the digestive system; headaches seem to arise from a disturbance between liver and the kidneys themselves, though usually the setting up of better eliminations causes these to be eased." All these were symptoms, not cause. Then came the crux of all Cayce healing, "There is within self all healing that may be accomplished for the body. For all healing must come from the Divine. For who healeth thy diseases? The source of the universal supply." He put it all on the individual and his outlook. "How well do you wish to be? Are you willing to coordinate with the Divine influences which may work in and through you by stimulating the centers latent with nature's activities? For all of these forces must come from the one source, and the applications are merely to stimulate the atoms of the body. For each cell is as a representative of a universe in itself."

From my own Yoga, I knew pretty well what Cayce was saying. With Yoga had come a new positive state of mind, a freedom from illness, a reliance on strength. Pains, aches, colds disappeared. The head and neck rolls, similar to those advocated by Cayce, had dissolved an arthritic stiffness in my neck resulting from a whiplash injury. In my new tranquillity, I was more tolerant, less critical, more productive and energetic. Nearing fifty, I was keenly aware of a well-being I had never known before. Each cell of my being seemed proudly confident of its ability to maintain its integrity. A Virginia Beach physician, viewing a brief Yoga demonstration, had observed, "You can stave off the inevitable but eventually you will need a doctor." And the Yogi had replied with equal conviction, "Only for the death certificate." He was sure of his health, for he drew on the universal supply.

Still skimming through the black book, I came upon the heading baldness. It appeared to me that if Cayce could have cured baldness, he could have named his own price and never gone without. Yet, there were some who insisted the readings had halted premature loss of hair. Cayce's advice on hairgrooming had chiefly helped those whose hair loss was sudden, indicating some striking deficiency in body chemistry. A twenty-six-year-old youth had turned desperately to Cayce. "Is there any chance of restoring my hair? I am the only one of six brothers who is going bald."

"Yes," Cayce replied. "There is a lack of activity of the glands in the thyroid areas. This causes a weakness in the activities to nails and hair over the body." The treatment was sweeping. "We would take small dose of Atomidine to purify the thyroid activity. Take one drop each morning for five days in succession. Then leave off for five days. During that period give the scalp a thorough massage with crude oil, using the electrically driven vibrator with suction applicator. This should be done very thoroughly, not hurriedly and should require at least thirty to forty minutes for the massage with the crude oil and then the application of white Vaseline and the vibrator again. Then begin the first of the next week with the Atomidine, one drop each morning for five days. During the next five days (now the middle of the week) give another crude oil shampoo following with the white Vaseline and the vibrator treatment. Leave these off then for two weeks. Then have another complete series, but between each two series allow two weeks to elapse. Doing these, we will find that in six or eight months, it will begin to stimulate the activities for the growth of hair over the scalp and the body.

"Use the diets that carry iodine in their natural forms. Use only kelp salt or deep sea salt, plenty of seafoods. Not too much sweets. The egg yolk but not the white of egg should be taken. These will bring better conditions to the body."

For another person with a dry scalp, losing his hair prematurely, he advised massaging the scalp once every twelve days with hog lard, allowing it to soak twenty minutes before washing it out with tepid water and a dandruff remover. He had several diet recommendations: "Eat the soup from the peelings of Irish potatoes, take raw vegetables such as lettuce, celery, watercress, radishes, onions, mustard greens and all of those that may be prepared as salad and the like. Carrots will make better conditions in combination with these for the sparkle of the eye and the general vision."

"What will thicken the hair?" somebody else asked.

"Massage the scalp with crude oil," he replied, "cleansing it with a twenty percent solution of grain alcohol. This will thicken the hair and bring better conditions to the scalp."

Cayce never completely lost his sense of humor.

"What should the individual now do," he was asked, "to cause the hair to grow in the front of the forehead?"

"You won't have much brains there, and hair, too," he replied drily, but added seriously, "This may be assisted, though, by using any vapor rub, or the use of Listerine will keep the hair in a healthy normal condition."

The same person asked again, "What causes the scalp to itch?"

"Irritation, produced by the accumulations in the system. The digestion is bad, and the nerves on edge. Use the Listerine twice a week on the hair."

I had gone through much of the black book when my host dropped in for a good-night chat. "I don't want to run this into the ground," he said, "but if there had been more Cayces around, a lot of doctors would be out of business. Take the common cold; nothing causes more misery and disruption than colds and flu, yet I haven't had a cold in thirty years."

I surveyed his robust figure appraisingly. "Maybe your resistance is better than most."

He laughed. "Naturally, but I avoid the situations Cayce told me to avoid, and I keep alkaline. Cayce once suggested that people give themselves a litmus paper test. If they turned blue, they were all right. Pink, and they had an acid condition, usual forerunner of a cold." He picked up the black book, turning to Common Cold. His finger stopped at "susceptibility."

"A body," he read, "is more susceptible to a cold with an excess of acidity. An alkalizing effect is destructive to the cold germ. An extra depletion of the vital energies produces a tendency for excess acidity. At such periods, if an individual comes in contact with one sneezing or suffering with cold, it is more easily contracted."

The whole mechanics of cold causation were explored. Cayce went into drafts, sharp changes in temperature, unusual changes in clothing, wet feet. "All of these affect the circulation by the depletion of the body-balance, body-temperature, or body-equilibrium. Then if the body is tired, worn, overacid—or more rarely, overalkaline—it is more susceptible to a cold, as, too, from being in a warm room, overheated. When overheated there is less oxygen, which weakens the circulation of the life-giving forces that are destructive to any germ or contagion."

My host looked up pertly. "I always keep my rooms cool, stay away from drafts, dress lightly during the winter, and don't do any heavy eating or drinking that would turn my stomach acid. And no sweets—they're the worst."

I couldn't help but smile. "You don't have time to think of much else."

He growled. "I don't have time to be sick."

His mood changed. "You know, I knew Cayce quite well. He read for me a number of times. Generally, he would give me a life reading or advise me on business problems. I was seldom under the weather because I did maintain the hygiene he recommended."

As we chatted, I recalled a learned doctor friend expounding on a recent theory that equalization of body temperature was important in forestalling colds. And yet here was Cayce saying a generation or so before: "Much may also depend upon the body's becoming immune to sudden temperature changes, by the use of clothing to equalize the pressure over the body. One that is often in the open and dresses according to general conditions, or the temperatures, will be less susceptible than one who bundles up too much."

Vitamins, he said, could be used judiciously during the cold season, as a preventive, not after the infection had taken hold. "For that which may be helpful may also be harmful, if misapplied, whether by the conscious activity in a body or by an unconscious activity in the assimilating forces of the system."

Analyzing body resistance, Cayce stressed that the system functioned as a unit, drawing on one area to shore up another; therefore it helped to have a natural reservoir of vitamins and minerals to tap in emergency.

My host explained, "So often people get over their colds only to come down with a secondary infection, because they depleted themselves. That's why Cayce stressed rest in the first days of a cold." To show how body repair works, Cayce used this analogy: "If there is a bone fracture, the body of itself creates that element needed to knit this fracture or broken area. Yet it does not supply or build as much of such an element during the periods when the fracture does not exist. Hence when it exists, unless there is an abundant supply of that which is needed by or from that which is assimilated, other portions of the body will suffer."

In treating a cold, there should be an over-all approach. "One may get one's feet wet and yet have a cold in the head. One may also get the head wet and still have a cold in the head."

Cayce's cold therapy would be generally accepted today. "Do not attempt to go on, but rest. For there is the indication of an exhaustion somewhere, else the body would not have been susceptible." The victim's vulnerability to secondary infection was explored. "Then, too, the inflammation of the mucous membranes tends to weaken the body, so that there is the greater susceptibility in the weakened portions of the body throughout the special areas of influences of the lymph and the head, throat, lungs, intestinal system. If there has been an injury in any of the structural portions of the body, causing a weakness in those directions, there is a susceptibility for harmful effects from such a cold."

Different colds were treated differently. "In correcting a cold, determine where the weakness lies. Is it from lack of eliminations, which causes many ailments? Hence quantities of water, as well as an alkalizer, as well as a booster to assimilating forces, are beneficial toward producing a balance, so that the cold and its consequences may be the more readily eradicated."

Cayce really hadn't contributed much on colds that a sensible doctor wouldn't.

My host smiled. "Cayce only knew the cures, when there was a cure. The system with a cold was a system run down; the cold, sniffles, sore throat, or what have you, was only the symptom, generally a warning signal."

"You mean Cayce was like the doctor who let a cold develop into pneumonia so he could cure it?"

"Oh, Cayce could knock out a cold quickly, when the basic resistance was strong." He turned to a reading Cayce gave for a man with a heavy cold thirty years before. The subject was a New York industrialist, who didn't give in easily to anything. His secretary had requested the reading, saying her boss was so choked up he couldn't speak above a whisper.

Cayce got right to the remedy. "Take first an eliminant, or about eighteen hundred drops [two bottles of Castoria] but not at once. Take it in very small doses, a half teaspoonful every half hour. After the first bottle has been taken in these proportions, then take the Turkish bath; first the sweats, then the salt rubs, then the alcohol rub after the oil rubs. Keep more of an alkaline diet. No white bread. Principally use fruit juices, and citrus fruit juices at that. A little coffee without cream may be taken as a stimulant or a little whiskey and soda later in the evening. The body should feel physically fit by morning."

Apparently it worked. For here was the subject's report tacked on to the reading. "I felt miserable, but after taking the day's rest and the bottle of Castoria, and the rubs, I could talk the next morning and was at work all day."

The rubs had concentrated on the lower dorsal and lumbar area, though the cold manifested itself in the nose and throat. It was all the same body.

My host skimmed through the black book. "Cayce told

them how to look pretty, grow hair, clear up their kidneys, get rid of their migraines. But people hate to do anything about themselves. Women, for instance, just want to sit down in a chair and let somebody coat them with cosmetics, when essentially, real beauty stems out of good health."

One brief passage illustrated Cayce's attitude toward vanity.

"How can people avoid aging in appearance?" he was asked.

"The mind," he replied drily.

The questioner, a thirty-two-year-old woman, persisted, "How can sagging facial muscles be avoided? How corrected?"

Cayce relented. "By massage and the use of those creams as indicated [Black and White Genuine] over the chin and throat, around the eyes and such conditions of sagging. Occasionally, the use of the Boncilla or mud packs would be very good." He elaborated for a thirty-year-old woman, "About twice a month the mud packs, face and neck, across the shoulders and upper portions about the neck; especially extending over the area of the thyroids, as an astringent and as a stimulation for better circulation throughout the system."

Cayce had a special preparation for the girlish complexion and told a thirty-two-year-old woman, whose skin was beginning to dry, how to use it. The treatment amused my host. "I know a dozen women who look ten years younger because of the preparation, and the exercise they get rubbing it into their skin," he said with a chuckle.

"For a good complexion for the skin, the hands and arms and body as well," Cayce said, "prepare a compound to use as a massage by self, at least once or twice a week. To six ounces of peanut oil, add olive oil, two ounces; rose water, two ounces; dissolved lanolin, one tablespoonful. This would be used after a tepid bath in which the body has remained for at least fifteen to twenty minutes, giving the body then, during the bath, a thorough rub with any good soap, to stimulate the body forces. Sweetheart, or any good Castile soap, or Ivory, may be used.

"Afterwards, after shaking it well, massage with this solution, which will be sufficient for many times. Pour some in an open saucer, dipping fingers in same. Begin with the face, neck, shoulders, arms, and then the whole body would be massaged thoroughly with the solution, especially in the area

of the limbs, in the areas that are across the hips, across the
diaphragm. This will not only keep a stimulating effect with
other treatments (hydrotherapy, and osteopathy) taken occasionally, and give the body a good base for the stimulating of
the superficial circulation, but the solution will aid in keeping
the body beautiful, as to being free from any blemish of any
nature."

Topping this off, the tissues of the face could be patted, an
act more beneficial, Cayce said, than any facial exercises.

My host handed back the black book. "Have you any
friends with halitosis?" he said lightly. "I got rid of mine with
Cayce."

As I turned to Halitosis, he finally bade me good-night.
"Don't sleep too late," he said cheerily. "Cayce said mind and
body develop from conscious stimulation of same."

I wondered what Cayce had to say about what-
best-friends-won't-tell-you. "The condition of halitosis," he
said, "is produced from the stomach and from the throat and
larynx. In the blood supply, in the lungs proper, the body
does not receive sufficient carbon. Hence the whole body is
under strain at times and this interferes with the blood supply
having sufficient properties to supply the organs in their functioning and in keeping coagulation effective in the system,
where organs use the force and energy in their functioning.
Hence, non-elimination often shows and through this same
condition brings much of the condition exhibited in the intestines and stomach of the catarrhal condition."

I had always thought of halitosis as something pertaining
simply to the mouth, and here was Cayce again insisting that
the body functioned as a unit, malfunctioning where outer
circumstances and inner conditions combined to provoke a
weakness.

The cure conformed with Cayce's belief of over-all tough-
ening. "First take that which will give an incentive for correction in the body through the digestive organs, as well as
through the mental reaction in the system." But there had to
be other incentives. "Unless the body desires to improve itself, it will continue to enjoy poor health." The subject was a
longtime hypochondriac.

Elsewhere, he was more specific. "Get rid of bad breath by
making better conditions in the eliminations. Take Glyco-
Thymoline as an intestinal antiseptic, two, three times a day
put six drops of Glyco-Thymoline in the drinking water.

"This is a condition of poisons being thrown off into the lungs [into the body forces] from the changing in cellular activity of lymph forces that become fecal."

Hypochondria was something Cayce dealt with constantly, but he didn't give out placebos or coddle anyone. And though some doctors, without knowing his work, insisted that many of his cures came through the power of suggestion, they themselves acknowledged they had rarely, if ever, cured anybody with similar suggestion.

To Cayce, there was no incurable ailment; the patient had to be ready, and the therapist knowledgeable. He was familiar with incurable migraine headaches, and where many thought these the result of a nervous, tense disposition, Cayce noted this was again only the symptom, not the cause.

But even a Cayce could do little with long-sufferers who clung desperately to their illnesses, fancied or otherwise. Earlier that very day I had a long talk with a friend of forty-five or so who had complained proudly, I suspected, of migraine headaches for years. Ever since I had known her, she had used them as an excuse for long periods of bedrest, with her telephone off the receiver, and a cluster of pillboxes on her night table.

Recovered periodically from an attack, she would close her eyes and sigh, "I don't see how I can ever go through another one." Then she would look up and say brightly, "They're incurable, don't you know, and nobody knows what causes them—nobody."

According to the black book, my migraine friend was wrong. Cayce seemed to know all about migraines, even to the sage advice, "In the activities mentally, keep optimistic, even when everything goes wrong."

There were several migraine cases, and all, I noted, stemmed not from pressures within the head, but the abdominal area. "Most migraine headaches, as in this case," Cayce said, "begin from congestions in the colon. These poisons cause toxic conditions which make pressures on the sympathetic nerve centers and on the cerebrospinal system. And these pressures cause the violent headaches, and almost irrational activities at times. These should respond to colonic irrigations. But first, we would X-ray the colon and find areas in the ascending and transverse colon where there are fecal forces that are as cakes."

I wondered if this was what was bothering my lady friend, and whether Cayce's remedy would help.

"There will be required several full colonic irrigations, using salt and soda as purifiers for the colon; and we will find that these conditions will be released. The first cleansing solution should have two level teaspoonfuls of salt and one level teaspoonful of soda to the gallon of water, body-temperature. Also in the rinse-water, body-temperature, have at least two tablespoonfuls of Glyco-Thymoline to the quart and a half of water."

Additionally, in his mass attack on dis-ease, Cayce recommended the use of a radioactive appliance, along with an hour of meditation for self-analysis. "Keep the attachment plates very clean, polishing them with the emery paper each time before attaching to the ankle and the wrist, and polishing them each time when taking them off."

He also recommended osteopathic adjustments to relax the neck area, and in the sixth dorsal, the midback; and in the lower back, the lumbar axis. "Do these," Cayce said, "and we should bring help for this body."

This particular migraine sufferer reminded me of my friend. She just wouldn't recognize the possibility of a cure.

"Is any of this trouble due to allergy?" she asked.

I could almost see Cayce shrug in his sleep. "Some of it is due to allergy, but what is allergy? These are the effects of the imagination upon any influences that may react upon the olfactory or the sympathetic nerves. If we will cleanse the system as we find, we should bring better conditions."

The subject apparently couldn't believe that those terrible racking pains in his head came from another part of the anatomy. "What mental factor," he persisted, "is responsible for the disturbance to the subject's head?"

Cayce was adamant. "Those pressures, as indicated, between sympathetic and cerebrospinal system, and these arise from condition in the colon. X-ray the colon, and you'll find it."

I made a mental note to Xerox the Migraine pages and present them to my friend the next time she proudly invoked her own incurable migraine. It might at least quiet her.

I was about to close the black book when a flipping page stopped me. Menstruation. As one twice-married, I had experienced the reflected agonies of woman's periodic cramps and headaches until I felt somehow guilty that I was not similarly oppressed. Therefore, I read with more than normal curiosity what Cayce had to say.

"Please explain fully the reason for cramps at menstruation?" a sufferer asked.

"Contraction of the uterus," the admirably concise Cayce replied. "And this is caused by the muscular forces that supply nourishment to the ovarian channels and the Fallopian tubes. Hence, have those osteopathic relaxations and the general body-building conditions indicated, that would be necessary for correction."

This didn't seem at all difficult, once the woman concerned took the vitamin and iron supplements needed to balance out a diet deficiency.

Now came the second of the monsters—menstrual headaches. How many hapless males had suffered through these!

"Why are there headaches at the time of my monthly period?" a forty-year-old female queried.

Cayce likened the cause to that of the migraines. "These are part of the clogging that is a part of the general eliminating system. There are channels or outlets for the elminating of poisons, that is, used energies, where there is the effect of the activity of circulation upon foreign forces taken in breath, taken in dust, taken in particles of food or those activities which come from such as these—from odors or the like. These all, by segregating of same in system, produce forces necessary to be eliminated. We eliminate principally through the activity of the lungs, of course, and the perspiratory system, the alimentary canal, and the kidneys. Then, as in the case of women, as here, we find that such periods of the menstrual flow cause congestion in certain areas until the flow is begun, or until there is the beginning of the let-up of same. This then, clogs some portions of the system. The headaches are the signs or warnings that eliminations are not being properly cared for. Most of this, in this body, comes from the alimentary canal and conditions that exist in portions of the colon itself, as to produce a pressure upon those centers affected from such periods. Hence the suggestion for the osteopathic corrections, which aid but which do not eliminate all of those conditions which are as accumulations through portions of the colon. Consequently, the colonic irrigations are necessary occasionally, as well as the general hydrotherapy and massage."

Cayce apparently felt his subject needed more than physical advice, for he counseled, "Keep the mental attitude of a useful, purposeful life, using the abilities to be helpful to others." In other words, stop complaining!

With some regret I put the black book away. But I did not forget it, not completely. A month later, my lady friend with the migraines phoned to complain about her inexplicable, incurable headaches. I suggested she would perhaps be interested in reading what Cayce had to say about migraine cure.

She had read about Cayce and had been duly impressed by the reports of his wizardry. But now she seemed strangely reserved and skeptical.

"Cayce," I pushed on, "said migraine could be cured if the sufferer cleaned himself out, got osteopathic adjustments of the spine, and improved general mental attitude. Would you care to see his report?"

The long-sufferer drew in her breath sharply.

"How ridiculous," she cried. "Nobody can cure migraine, nobody."

As she rang off, I recalled a line from the black book. What was it Cayce had said? Oh, yes, here it was: "For that builded, that held in the mental image of one, becomes the condition."

And so it was.

In Cayce-land, another way of saying Virginia Beach, Cayce home remedies were as common as saying hello. Even the Geologist, in the midst of his earth changes, was familiar with some. "Every time the kids get pinworms, my wife grates some raw cabbage and feeds it to them, for breakfast, lunch, and dinner. By bedtime, or the next morning, the pinworms are gone." The cabbage was all they took that day except for tea, also recommended.

"Cayce," the Geologist observed, "said that one cabbage leaf killed a hundred thousand pinworms."

Pokeweed was another great favorite of Cayce's, and it was used regularly by the faithful as a purifier. "Boil it up," a Cayce follower said, "and it tastes better than spinach and kale, while doing the work of sulphur and molasses." He laughed. "It's a funny thing, but at a meeting of the Virginia agricultural association recently, they told everybody how to grow more corn by killing the surrounding pokeweed, and the pokeweed will do you more good than the corn ever could."

Wherever I turned in Cayce-land somebody seemed to be following Cayce. In one household, I noticed that steamed leaf lettuce and sliced raw tomatoes were practically dinner staples. The tomatoes, a hostess advised, were the richest of vegetables in vitamins. Edgar Cayce had said so. As for the lettuce, it was served only in the evening for a very good reason. "The effect is so immediately sedative that my husband falls asleep at the table."

I was inclined to treat this lightly, until I read elsewhere that doctors abroad had just discovered that lettuce had a narcotic effect, taken in quantity.

Many householders in the Tidewater belt around Virginia Beach were familiar with Cayce table tips. "To lose weight, the easy way," a slimmed-down housewife reported, "merely take a half-glass of Welch's natural grape juice a half-hour before each meal. It satisfies the body's craving for sugar, and will break the habit of fattening desserts."

This housewife also fancied gelatin salads, with such raw vegetables as watercress, celery, lettuce, tomatoes, carrots. "The gelatin," she pointed out, "acts as a catalyst to increase natural absorption of vitamins in vegetables. Cayce said that with the Knox gelatin the vitamin intake from the vegetables was seven times what it would be ordinarily." Like my friends in New Jersey, the housewife thumbed through the Cayce black book for an explanation. "It isn't the vitamin content in the gelatin," Cayce explained, "but its ability to work with the activities of the glands, causing the glands to take from that which is absorbed or digested the vitamins that would not be active, if there were not sufficient gelatin in the body."

Oddly, even among oldsters who didn't look favorably to exercise, I found that the head and neck exercise had its converts. And the younger element had profited equally. Tom Hungerford, a middle-aged Chicago business executive, tried the simple exercise because of his dissatisfaction with bifocal glasses just prescribed. His experience was so transforming that he still marvels at it. "Though it seemed a bit odd that such an exercise could have any effect on the eyes," he said, "I decided I'd rather do anything than wear bifocals. So I took them off and started the exercise." There followed a six month period of hardly being able to see anything very well without his glasses, but Hungerford, believing in Cayce, persisted. "Then, gradually," as he continued the exercises twice daily, "came a clearing, and better sight than I'd had since my teens." His testimonial was glowing indeed. "This was all five years ago, and I have not worn any glasses since. I don't even have a restriction on my driver's license anymore."

In his enthusiasm, he has given the exercise to nearly a hundred people. "Some said it would not work [and it did not]; but it did work for an airline employee in Hawaii, and her mother. And it did work for a seventy-nine-year-old man in Las Vegas who was about to lose his driver's license, and who, on last report, could read the morning paper without his glasses." It not only helped vision, the enthusiastic Hungerford said, but cleared up the chronic sinus of one friend, and stopped the migraine headaches of another.

Like Cayce, latter-day disciple Hungerford has found that "that held in the mental image of one, becomes the condition." For ultimately, he concluded: "It seems to boil down to the fact that for those who believe in it and do it regularly, it works—for the eyes and for other things as well."

Chapter Twelve

THE DREAM WORLD

For many, the dream world is more revealing than the world of apparent reality. "In every man," Hugh Lynn Cayce once observed, "there exists a vast expanse, unfamiliar and unexplored, which sometimes appears in the guise of an angel, other times a monster. This is man's unconscious mind, and the language we call dreams."

Although little of Edgar Cayce's psychic power apparently has rubbed off on the son, Hugh Lynn, as directed by his sleeping father, has carried on diligently with the A. R. E. research effort, establishing a dream seminar at Virginia Beach, where psychiatrists and psychologists analyze dreams that the elder Cayce had casually interpreted in his sleep.

During his lifetime, Cayce gave six hundred psychic readings on dreams, some of the most notable his own. The Cayce dream readings dealt chiefly with the interpretations of individual dreams, but the symbols and suggestions he advanced for using one's own dreams to advantage still apply.

Studying his father's dream readings, Hugh Lynn concluded that dreams are not only a doorway to the unconscious, but can be readily opened by anyone who can recall his own dreams and wants to know what they mean.

From experience, the younger Cayce has discovered that this doorway is as available to the average person as a pencil and pad at his bedside table. At first, on waking, he may not remember a single fragmentary dream, but in time his unconscious will get a prod from the waiting pencil and pad, and will go to work for him, opening wide the possibilities of a whole new area of self-exploration. "Through his own dreams," Edgar Cayce stressed, "a person may gain more understanding of those forces that go to make the real existence—what it's all about and what it's good for—if the individual would but comprehend the conditions being manifested."

Dreams, of course, are a concomitant of sleep, and Cayce's description of sleep gives ample indication that this hiatus in the waking life of the individual is designed for more than mere rest of mind and muscle. In sleep, the subconscious mind, more powerful than the conscious, as hypnotism has shown, reviews whatever has passed through the conscious mind, and distills in dreams whatever warnings or messages it finds necessary.

"Sleep," observed the sleeping Cayce, "is that period when the soul takes stock of what it has acted upon, from one rest period to another; drawing comparisons, as it were, that make for harmony, peace, joy, love, long-suffering, patience, brotherly love, and kindness—fruits of the spirit; or hate, harsh words, unkind thoughts and oppressions which are fruits of Satan. The soul dreaming either abhors what it has passed through, or it enters into the joy of its Lord."

Edgar Cayce may very well have been the only living man who ever used his own subconscious consciously to interpret the dreams channeled through that subconscious. Through a desire to understand dreams of his own that remained vividly in his consciousness, he began to take interest in the dreams of others.

In some dreams he saw an immediate symbology, which antedated by years the symbology generally accepted by the psychiatric profession. Back in January 1925, in perhaps the earliest dream for which he sought an interpretation, Cayce visioned a close associate and himself standing together in a rocky area. There were many knots of people standing around, but they were separated from him and other groups by streams of running water. Incongruously, as dreams so often seem, Edgar Cayce at this point saw a fish jump out of the water. He tried to catch it, but in the attempt the fish was broken into fragments and he set about to put the pieces together.

All through that day and the next, the dream stayed with

Cayce. It vaguely troubled him, made him uneasy. But think of it as he would, it didn't seem to suggest anything that made sense. Finally, he went into trance, and the suggestion was put to him by his wife that he analyze and interpret the dream. The ever-present Gladys Davis was there to record the interpretation for posterity. Out of this dream came interpretations of symbols useful today to anyone with similar dream images.

As Cayce said: "In the dream of water, with the separating of the acquaintances and the body, we find the manifestation again of the subconscious forces, the water representing the life, the living way, that separates those of every walk of life and exists about each entity or group, building that which radiates in a spiritual sphere, the deeds done in the body."

His explanation, with symbology now generally accepted, continued: "In the fish is the representation of Him who became the Living Way, the Water of Life, given for the healing of the nations; in the breaking, in the separation there will yet be brought the force that will again make this the Living Way, the perfect representation of the force necessary to give life to all."

As Cayce saw it, this dream came under the heading of spiritual guidance. The fish, of course, symbolized Christ, an almost universal symbol, and water, life. Peace would yet come out of war—yet war would come.

The dreams fell into four general headings. Some dealt with the problems of the physical body, others with self-observation, psychic perception and spiritual guidance.

The most common dreams appear to stem from the body itself, the dream being the reaction to improper diet, lack of exercise, faulty regimen—the body registering its protest with the unconscious mind through the dream medium. One of these rather ordinary types of dreams was recorded on waking by one of two brothers who had been counseled by Cayce to study their dreams. He had the pencil and pad handy, and after writing the dream down, took it to Cayce.

"I dreamed my brother and I with our wives were out on a party with B. B. I fell asleep at the table. We got home very late. My brother left the car and walked home. He and I stopped to look at a bottle of milk that was marked 'undistilled milk.' "

To Cayce the message was plain. He interpreted it almost

literally. It was a warning to the dreamer, Cayce said, that his body was suffering from late hours (asleep at the table) and irregular diet—undistilled milk obviously referring to impure milk.

The brother was seen as more carefully disciplined—leaving the car and going on ahead, rather than taking the chance, apparently, of riding with somebody who had overly imbibed. Seeing the milk also was a warning to change the milk supply. For in reply to a specific question about the part dealing with the milk, Cayce had stated, "Change from the present supply, for this shows adulterations in same."

Many dreams, as Cayce pointed out, dealt with self-study. They included wish fulfilment dreams, suppressions, symbolic conflicts between good and evil in our natures, and work or family problems. Often these dreams had a prophetic quality, and were couched in horrible imagery to underline the gravity of the warning. Time after time, Cayce unraveled the tangled threads of dreams, psychically interpreting situations subsequently confirmed in ensuing developments.

One of the most provocative dreams was that of a businessman in Florida, disturbed by the vivid reality of the dream, and a guilty conscience.

He had heard of Cayce through a neighbor, whose health had been aided by one of Cayce's distant readings, and was delighted that he wouldn't have to lift an arm to get help—just send the dream in with a request for an interpretation.

With meticulous detail, the dreamer, a married man with two children, described a nightmarish dream: "I was standing in the backyard of my home—had my coat on. I felt something inside the cloth on the cuff of my left-hand sleeve. I worked it out, but it was fastened in the cloth and broke off as it came out, leaving part in. It proved to be a cocoon, and where broken a small black spider came out. The cocoon was black and left a great number of eggs—small ones—on my coat sleeve, which I began to pull off. The spider grew fast and ran away, speaking plain English as it ran, but what I do not remember, except that it was saying something about its mother. The next time I saw it, it was a large black spider which I seemed to know was the same one grown up, almost as large as my fist—had a red spot on it, otherwise was a deep black.

"At this time it had gotten into my house and had built a web all the way across the back inside the house and was comfortably watching me. I took a broom, knocked it down and out of the house, thinking I'd killed it, but it did more talking at that time. The next time I saw it, it had built a long web from the ground, on the outside of the house in the backyard, near where I first got it out of my sleeve—and it was running up toward the eave fast when it saw me. I couldn't reach it but threw my straw hat in front of it and cut the web and the spider fell to the ground, talking again, and that time I hacked it to pieces with my knife."

Perhaps because of a boyish loathing of spiders, I was fascinated with this dream. I had stumbled across it, shortly after my own introduction to the Cayce readings, and wondered what the psychoanalysts would make of it, and how it would tally with Cayce's interpretation.

I copied the dream, and took it to a distinguished psychoanalyst, who had studied with the first of the great dream merchants—Sigmund Freud. I told him none of the particulars of the dream. It might have been dreamed yesterday or the day before, for all he knew. I did not tell him that Cayce had already made an interpretation—in fact, made it some thirty-five years before.

The learned psychoanalyst studied the dream text carefully, and then gave his analysis. The dreamer, he said, was destructively obsessed with the thought of breaking up his home. His views of women, including his wife, had been formed from a childhood resentment of his mother, and this transference was behind the breakup—the web or cocoon being the nest or home, the spider the obvious home-breaker, himself.

After he finished, I showed him the Cayce reading. He had heard vaguely of Cayce, and he read the Cayce interpretation with interest, inasmuch as he accepted the psychic as having been scientifically established. "In my work with Dr. Freud," he said, "there were many examples of clairvoyant and precognitive dreams. It even made a believer of Freud."

Cayce's report, intriguingly, tallied with that of the psychoanalyst's, only Cayce's delved far more extensively—and prophetically—into the home situation. He clearly saw the dreamer straying from his marital vows and warned that continuation of a clandestine relationship would ruin both home and business.

Cayce's explanation of the dream was as explicit as the dream was cryptic: "In this dream, there is seen the symbolic conditions of those forces as are being enacted in the life of this body. And, as is seen, both the spider and the character of same are as warnings to the body as respecting the relations of others who would in this underhanded manner take away from the body those surroundings of the home—that are in the manner of being taken—unless such a stand is taken. For, as is seen, the conditions are of the nature emblematically shown by the relations of this body with this other body [the woman]; that its relations at first meant only the casual conditions that might be turned to an account of good, in a social and financial manner; yet, as has been seen, there has come the constant drain on the entity, not only in the pocket, but in the affections of the heart, and now such threaten the very foundations of the home; and, as seen, threaten to separate the body from the home and its surroundings; and unless the entity attacks this condition, cutting same out of the mind, the body, the relations, the conditions, there will come that condition as seen."

Cayce had no way of consciously knowing that the businessman had entangled himself in a financial way with his secretary, who had brought some shady backing into the business enterprise. Originally, as it developed, their relationship had been confined to business, but then had developed until he was, in fact, considering leaving his wife and family. At this point, as Cayce saw, there was still time to withdraw. And so Cayce viewed the dream as being of a warning nature, and so gave warning:

"Prepare self. Meet the conditions as a man, not as a weakling—and remember those duties that the body owes first to those to whom the sacred vows were given, and to whom the entity and body owes its position in every sense; as well as the duty that is obligatory to the body or those to whom the entity, the body, should act in the sense of the defender, rather than bringing through such relations those dark underhanded sayings, as are seen, as said by that one who would undermine, as well as are being said by those whom the body may feel such relations are hidden from; yet these have grown to such an extent as may present a menace to the very heart and soul of the body of this entity." In other words, the wife, too, was aware of the situation. The reading closed with an injunction rare for Cayce: "Beware! Beware!"

As might almost be expected of one who had gotten himself into this scrape, the businessman did not heed the warning. He kept on with his secretary, and lost wife, home, family, and business.

However, following a divorce, he did marry the other woman. He was now so impressed by Cayce's insight, that with his newfound wife he took himself to Virginia Beach to place himself at the disposal of the mystic. Cayce could give him no advice, except to profit by the mistakes of the first marriage. He started a new business in the North, consulted Cayce regularly, and managed maritally and business-wise, until his death recently.

Long before the psychoanalysts, Cayce had discovered a psychic content to dreams, similar in prophetic insight to the seven-fat-years-and-seven-lean interpretation given the Pharaoh's dream by Joseph and of the handwriting-on-the-wall clarification by the prophet Daniel.

The prophetic or precognitive dream might revolve around mundane things. As a matter of fact, Cayce, interpreting one such dream, warned the dreamer to get out of the stock market, and predicted an unprecedented stock market crash in a few months.

The forecast was made in April 1929; six months later— Black Friday, October 29, 1929, the market collapsed.

The dreamer, a Wall Street broker, had kept a daily record of his dreams, in accordance with an advisory from Cayce. Each morning, Cayce interpreted the dreams that the man had the night before. The dreamer listened closely, as a rule, because he had made a fortune buying and selling stocks with Cayce.

On March 5, 1929, the Wall Streeter had his first dream reflecting misgivings about the bull market. He jotted his dream down on a night-table pad and phoned it into Cayce. "Dreamed we should sell all our stocks including box stock [one considered very good]. I saw a bull following my wife, who was dressed in red."

Cayce took this bull right by the horns. "This is an impression of a condition which is to come about, a downward movement of long duration, not allowing latitude for those stocks considered very safe. Dispose of all, even box, great change to come."

The dreamer was apparently sensitizing his own subconscious channels for precognitive dreams by a conscious effort to remember them each morning. On April 6, a month after the first market dream, the broker had another provocative dream.

The dream was shorter, but considerably more complex than the first. "Dreamed a young man was blaming me for murder of a man. A gang asked, 'Is there anyone else in the world who knows this?' I answered, 'K. Cornell.' Saw dead man. Gang started to administer poisonous hypodermic which had been used on dead man. I felt needle and expected death."

The dreamer awoke, startled. And then fell back into a troubled sleep. By this time his dream apparatus was so linked up to his conscious that he dreamed his own interpretation of the dream. "This," he wrote, "represented fight going on in Reserve Board—stock stimulation."

That same day, Cayce prophetically clarified the dream: "There must surely come a break where there will be panic in the money centers, not only of Wall Street's activity, but a closing of the boards in many other centers and a readjustment of the actual specie—higher and lower quotations to continue for several moons while adjustments are being made—then break."

What followed is history. After the October crash, exchanges were closed in Wall Street and elsewhere. There was a major adjustment in the specie—the United States and a number of other countries going off the gold standard.

Cayce's interpretation of the symbolism involved in the first dream would now be generally accepted. The red dress was obviously a danger warning, the bull a bull market, on its way out. Ironically, the wife was on the way out, too, divorcing the dreamer shortly thereafter.

In the second dream, Cayce went along with the "gang" identified as the Federal Reserve. The hypodermic needle was construed as a "hypo" for a sinking market. The attack was on the dreamer's financial stability, and spelled his death financially. The apparent reference to the well-known actress, Katharine Cornell, went unexplained. But certainly, Cayce had scored a bull's-eye.

Dreams of death are particularly disturbing to many. But for Cayce this was often a hopeful symbol. On June 23, 1925, a subject was so shaken by a dream that he could only write: "Dreamed I died."

Cayce was reassuring. "This is the manifestation of the

birth of thought and mental development awakening in the individual. This, then, is the awakening of the subconscious, as manifested in death of physical forces."

I must admit I was not always satisfied with Cayce's interpretations. A Virginia woman, of Anglo-Saxon heritage, was having a physical reading for a condition of obesity, hemorrhoids, and a kidney disorder, when she threw in a request for a dream interpretation. It had come to her in 1932, before Hitler's rise, and when things were relatively quiet on the international scene. Looking back, it seemed rather evidential of the hard times Britain was soon to have.

The dream follows: "My husband and I seemed to be in a large dwelling, and looking out toward the sky we saw large black circles floating through the air. We thought this very strange, and soon discovered that the circles looked like black auto tires or large truck tires. Suddenly, out of the sky a big black machine, resembling the large caterpillar machines used during the World War, came down to earth. We said we had better get out of the place, for we realized it was the intention of this machine to crush people to death. Too, we realized that it meant troublous times, so we tried to get out of its way as quickly as possible. We walked down to the river front, and there saw a British ship tied up at the wharf. Someone said it had fired on the lone watchman while in his office on the wharf, but found out later that the watchman had fired on the British ship—which seemed to please us very much. We realized there were troublous times in the making, and I was very much afraid. We walked further down the long wharf, and saw many more British ships."

It seemed to me, looking back on what had happened up to and through World War II, that this was a plain warning of the division in England before the war, with Winston Churchill the lone watchman, giving and taking cross fire from his embattled British colleagues. Or could it be Britain standing alone, resisting the destruction from the sky, including clusters of rockets and massive bombers, until that lone ship, Britain, had become many British ships—many allies?

Cayce caught the difficulties Britain would be in, but his explanation was rather general. "This is a prophetic vision relating to those peoples that were mostly shown [the British], as to the straits to which those peoples would pass, are passing. The fear that was felt would be the natural tendency,

knowing and feeling the relationships of that land [Britain] to
the whole world, as related to the self's own associations.

"The conditions seen, as from whence the aid or power
came, as if from on high, in the form of circles that increased
as they ballooned in their action through the heavens, indicate
the way, character or manner this people would aid themselves, in the appeal to the spiritual than to the power of
force that was implied by the act of the lone watchman."

Certainly, on reflection, it could be said that Churchill and
Britain put their faith in God, but it seemed to me a prophecy about a war, dealing with a dream as detailed as this
one, should have been more specific as to what the upshot of
it all was going to be on earth.

I mentioned my dissatisfaction, or disappointment, to one
of the A. R. E.'s dream experts, Everett Irion. He looked at
me with obvious surprise.

"Don't you see? Cayce was looking at the broad side of it.
For in the last analysis, it was the spirit of the English that
made them hold out, when practically everybody else had
collapsed before the Germans."

"But why," I asked, "were these people of obvious English
background pleased in their dream to see a British ship fired
upon?"

Irion shrugged. "I would have to know more about their
own frame of reference, and what these symbols meant to
them. It could very well have been that the firing on the ship,
say by Churchill, the lone watchman, conveyed the feeling
that the British Navy, then downgraded by the appeasers, was
to be jolted by this 'attack' into some recognition of the reali-
ties of the situation. This would certainly have pleased any
Anglophile." He laughed. "I'm trying to reason this; Cayce of
course saw it intuitively, and certainly the intuitive should
have a better grasp of the subconscious."

If a dream was prophetic, was the foreseen event then
fixed? After a dream which was clearly precognitive, materializing a year later when she walked into a room and saw
the same people and furnishings she had envisioned in sleep,
Gladys Davis asked Cayce to explain how it was that dreams
came to fulfillment. "Are such conditions set at the time
dreamed of," she asked, "and why would one dream of any
given condition?"

Cayce replied that the law of cause and effect was immutable, that as "thought and purpose and aim and desire are set in motion by minds," the result is certain and fixed, and therefore foreseeable. "For its end, then, has been set in that He, the Giver of the heavens and the earth and those things therein, has set the end thereof."

The dreamer had tuned into a particular cycle of activity, Cayce suggested, because of her interest in the people involved. "Dream is but attuning an individual mind to those individual storehouses of experience that has been set in motion. At times, there may be a perfect connection, at others there may be the static of interference by inability of coordinating the own thought to the experience or actuality or fact set in motion." There were different reasons for different dreams. "Those experiences that are visioned are not only as has been given to some, to be interpreters of the unseen, but to others as prophecy, to others healing, to others exhortation, yet all are of the same spirit."

Considerable emphasis has been placed in the Cayce readings on the psychic content of our dreams. In fact, as Hugh Lynn Cayce observed from his own study, the dream state may be the safest, quickest way for most of us to become aware of extrasensory perception, an agency of our own subconscious. Telepathy, clairvoyance, precognition, all seem commonplace in the dream world; all they require is the proper interpretation. And Edgar Cayce was that interpreter.

In December 1926 a woman came to Cayce with a disturbing dream about a friend she had not seen in years. In her dream, her friend, Emmie, had committed suicide.

Cayce went into trance and explained that the dream was telepathic rather than prophetic or literal. "Such conditions had passed through this mind—or it had contemplated such conditions. They have passed."

A check was made of Emmie, and it developed that she had seriously contemplated suicide at one time. But the crisis had passed.

It was an odd dream, since the dreamer had apparently tuned into a thought that had been dismissed and buried away, and which was no longer in the conscious circuit of the other's mind. How then had the dreamer reached out and drawn in this information? It was real enigma, even granting that ESP was a reality. Cayce was asked to indicate how this telepathic message had originated. His explanation may well apply to all psychic dreams: "Other dreams there are, a correlation between mentalities or subconscious entities, wherein there has been attained, physically or mentally, a correlation of individual ideas or mental expressions, that bring from one subconscious to another actual existent conditions, either direct or indirect, to be acted upon or that are ever present." As Cayce pointed out, time was only an illusion at best. "Hence we find visions of the past, visions of the present, visions of the future. For the subconscious there is no past or future—all is present. This would be well to remember in much of the information as may be given through such forces as these."

In the normal frame of reference, it was difficult to gauge the source of some telepathic dreams. However, if Cayce was infallible, as some suggest, then certainly evidence can be adduced for the survival of not only life, but of life interested in what it has left behind of friends and family on this terrestrial plane.

One dreamer, back in September 1926, reported to the sleeping Cayce: "My mother appeared to me. She said, 'I am alive.' "

Cayce, still somnolent, cut in, "She is alive."

The dreamer appeared a little more shaken by the interruption than by the dream, but bravely continued on. His mother had then enjoined in the dream, "Something is wrong with your sister's leg or shoulder. She ought to see a doctor about it."

Psychic researchers, crediting the psychic quality of the dream, might accept it as a dramatization of the dreamer's subconscious, rejecting it as evidence of a surviving spirit. But not Cayce. In advising the dreamer to heed the dream warning, he stressed: "The mother, through the entity's own mind, is as the mother to all in the household. Warning, then, of conditions that may arise, and of conditions existent. Then, warn the sister as regarding same."

The brother knew nothing of any physical difficulties his sister was having. He checked, without telling her about the Cayce reading, and she mentioned, rather surprised, that her leg and shoulder were bothering her.

Mother—or perhaps the subconscious self, tuned to the sister's subconscious—had known what it was talking about. And so had Cayce.

The dream state, when body and mind are relatively quiescent, is apparently the best channel for psychic messages.

Some people, who have no apparent psychic ability, waking, become surprisingly attuned in the sleeping phase. At one point, the Cayce home in Virginia Beach was virtually a dream laboratory, establishing precognition for even the most dubious who followed the dream readings.

One young woman alone, in four years, had eight readings, analyzing more than three hundred dreams, a large number of these foreshadowing precognitive experiences with remarkable precision.

On June 6, 1925, this married twenty-one-year-old woman's dream record visualized a nameless girl friend (obviously self) at a dinner table making violent love to an old friend. Cayce warned of a return to an old admirer, and several years later, a checkup disclosed, the dreamer broke up her marriage to marry her admirer. The admirer then walked out on her, making the warning most apropos.

According to Cayce, virtually everything is dreamed before it happens, and so it was hardly a surprise to him that he was able to anticipate through her dreams practically everything of major account that was to happen to this woman in the next thirty years.

On June 7, 1925, she had a perfectly wretched dream. She dreamed of a weak-minded child, though she had no children at this time.

Cayce was never more prophetic, and tactful. "Any condition," he stated, "is first dreamed before becoming reality."

It took a while for this dream to materialize, and the woman may very well have forgotten it. Then one day, some twenty-five years later, one of her children, now an adult, became a mental case.

There was a method to her dreaming. She kept a pencil and pad at her bedside, and her dreams increasingly remained with her as she awakened. On July 18, 1925, she had a dream that her husband wasn't coming home any more. It hardly required a Cayce to sense trouble ahead on this one, though he did convey the warning. Five years later her husband stopped coming home—to her home, anyway. They were divorced.

More and more, as she kept a dream record, the woman's dreams seemed clearly to be prophetic. On December 27, 1925, for instance, she dreamed that she and her sister were at her mother's bedside. The mother was unconscious, and both the dreamer and her sister were sobbing, "Don't leave us."

It was again an almost literal warning, this time of her mother's death.

Although her marriage appeared tranquil on the surface, there was obviously considerable suppressed material for the subconscious to brood over. For on July 17, 1926, she dreamed explosively of her relationship with her husband. She saw herself traveling on a boat with him. It was raining, and a flash of lightning struck the boat. The boiler blew up.

To Cayce, this was again a clear warning of an impending marital blowup.

By this time, this young woman was becoming so clearly psychic in the dream state that admirers of Cayce wondered whether they had not found a potential disciple in the young matron. On November 17, 1926, for instance, she saw her cousin being married. It was literal as all that. Cayce read the dream as precognitive. The cousin was married several months later.

Cayce was for everybody dreaming. As a clue to people interested in evaluating their own dreams, he suggested that the dream could be typed by its very nature. He was asked once, by a subject, "Are my dreams ever significant of spiritual awakening?" and he replied in rhetoric a bit more diffuse than usual:

"As experienced by the entity, there are dreams and visions and experiences. When only dreams [without any spiritual message] these too are significant, but rather of the physical health. In visions where there are spiritual awakenings, these are seen most often in symbols or signs. In training yourself to interpret your visions, the expressions of eye, hand, mouth, posture, or the like must be understood in your own language. When these are then symbolic, know the awakening [of the spirit] is at hand."

The trouble with dream symbols, of course, was that they varied with the individual outlook. So as Hugh Lynn Cayce has so aptly pointed out, each individual to interpret his own dreams—in the absence of a Cayce—must realize that the symbol for one intellect is not always the symbol for another.

Out of the Cayce dreamology, though, certain common symbols appear to have almost standard reference:

Water—source of life, spirit, unconscious; boat—voyage of

life; fire—wrath, cleansing, destroying; dead leaves—body excrement or drosses; mud, mire, tangled weeds—needed purification or cleansing; naked image—exposed, open to criticism; and fish—an almost universal symbol of Christ, Christian, or spiritual food.

A person, identified or otherwise, often represents what the dreamer feels toward that person; clothing, the manner or way in which one person appears to another, usually the dreamer.

Different animals reflect some phase of self, as the individual dreamer feels about that animal. If he thinks about the fox as being tricky, and then dreams of a fox, he may regard himself deep down inside as being a rather shady person, and this may indicate great inner conflicts of which his conscious mind knows nothing. Different races, groups, associations influence or color the animal connotation. For the Hindu, or those steeped in Yoga or Oriental culture, the dreamed snake is both a symbol of wisdom and sex. The bull, for some, may symbolize the sex glands, and hence sexual activity.

The Cayce "dream book" flows on. Self-revealing dreams, stemming as they do from wish fulfillment, suppressed desires, and other worries and conflicts, are replete with symbolism. A gorilla may represent man's lower animal nature; a madman, unrestrained anger; a ship's captain, the steady helmsman—the higher self, sound principles; a house where one once lived, may relate to a traumatic experience there; a rough road, the experiencing of harsh travails.

Often we are not up to directly facing the ugly side of our natures, hence the protective symbolism that makes it possible for dreams to be unpleasant without startling us into blood-curdling nightmares.

The following dream, self-revealing in nature, was significantly obscure. The dreamer wrote it down carefully, not missing a single detail in the transfer from pillow to pad: "A policeman was leading a man who had his two hands tied up across his chest. The policeman led him up to the gallows, about which a great crowd of people were gathered. Just as they were about to slip the noose over his head he slipped down a long slide, the policeman clinging to him. The man crawled desperately and speedily on his stomach, through the milling crowd, thus escaping the policeman."

The dreamer elaborated on the prisoner: "I could see his black nude form as he crawled very quickly along the ground. Finally, he came into a yard of a brickhouse, still crawling on his stomach very fast. He continued in this manner until he bumped his head on the brick wall of the house. This threw him backwards and stunned him. As he lay there on his back, an old woman came out of the house and regarded him. She started toward him and as she did so, the man stood up and the back of him suddenly appeared to me as a nude Negro, with an animal tail attached. He resembled both a Negro and an animal."

The dreamer was a forty-eight-year-old woman, whose son was about to marry a Southern girl. She felt she had no strong prejudices against Negroes, but had dwelt consciously, in view of the impending marriage, on the lynching problem in the South, some thirty years ago.

The Cayce dream reading made the dark figure, the Negro who at the same time seemed an animal, a symbol which was turned inward for an examination of the self—actually, the center of nearly every remembered dream. What the Negro represented to the woman was symbolic only in reflecting her own hidden attitudes, dramatically revealing the prejudices she was concealing from herself as well as others.

"In taking on the animal form," Cayce explained, "the entity sees in itself a still more dreaded condition. In the opening part of the dream the entity sees the dark figure as someone bringing trouble to itself by its own doing. This truth escapes as it were from the mass criticism, and then is halted by the wall. As it stands up, the entity recognized the self—or the lower nature of self. The woman is admonished [in the dream] to study 'all the elements of truth': even those about self which become 'troublesome' and 'obnoxious.' "

As it developed, the woman admitted she was strongly disturbed within herself by the thought of sexual relations between blacks and whites and yet this feeling made her darkly ashamed of herself, so that she herself, dream-wise, became the Negro she secretly deplored. Once acknowledging the truth, she seemed more at ease about the problem, to the point, anyway, where she no longer dreamed about it.

The Cayce readings revealed a certain consistency in the inherent symbolism of dreams since, in the dominant white Anglo-Saxon culture, the average person in the mainstream of society—at work, school, or play—is exposed to pretty much the same attitudes and outlooks, whether or not he accepts them.

The symbolism of the dark animal figure, conveying an impression of sinister, unbridled power, cropped up with striking frequency in dreams analyzed by Cayce, and as Cayce saw them—correctly, the psychoanalysts now tell us—the figures revealed an unfavorable side of the individual, which the conscious blocked, and the unconscious obscured.

This might be an apparent prejudice, as with the woman who dreamed of the Negro, or suppressed animalistic sex urges, or greed, bad temper, envy, anything obviously negative impairing the individual's own regard for himself. A middle-aged woman brought a typically nightmarish dream to Cayce. She was considerably agitated, for the dream had been violent, and perhaps prophetic: "My husband, his mother, and I were living together in a house in New Jersey. I heard much shooting and excitement. All of the windows of our house were open and it was raining and storming outside. We rushed to close and lock them. Some terrible wild man seemed to be running through the town shooting and causing great trouble, and the police were chasing him."

Cayce was able to reassure the woman. She had no storm to worry about, no fireworks, no explosive shooting. All the excitement, all the pent-up storm was in her. She had a rotten disposition, and unless she learned to curb it, was headed for trouble. Or as Cayce put it: "The large man, the bugaboo, that comes to the entity in these emblematical [symbolic] conditions here presented, and as seen in others, is in self and self's temper. See?"

She saw.

Because the symbols must be seen in the dreamer's own perspective, he may interpret them better than anybody else if he understands the symbology. Some symbology, of course, is general. As the house was the body in a Cayce dream reading, a burning house could be anger, or it could be the end of a marriage, if the house burned down, as it would then be all-consuming. One dream can express many different things. A Norfolk housewife, interested in the work of the A. R. E., dreamed that her home was burning. All she saw left was the number, 912. She had had other precognitive dreams before that had materialized—a girl friend's divorce, a relative's getting in trouble with the police.

The day after her dream, she walked into a shop to pick

up a dress and puzzled by the significance of the numerals, she related what she had dreamed.

The number caught the proprietor's ear. "What did you say those numerals were?"

"Nine-twelve," she repeated.

He checked through some papers, and then his eyes widened. "Why didn't you tell me about this yesterday?" he said in an angry voice.

The girl shrugged, "What difference would it make?"

"What difference? I would have won two thousand dollars, it's the winning number."

She explained that she didn't know about such things.

"You were supposed to come in for that dress yesterday," he said accusingly.

He threw the suit across the counter at her. "Next time you dream of three numerals, tell somebody about it."

Weeks later, studying up on dreams, the girl wondered whether the rest of it was prophetic, too. Her own marriage had just gone up with the flaming house.

As interpreted by Cayce, many symbols were of an obvious nature, easy to adapt to dreams, generally. Missing a train or bus—hurry up to get life in order; barbed wire entanglement or rough highway—difficulties along the way; one shoe, a poor foundation; right turn, the correct course; left turn, the wrong; beaver, an industrious person or job; mud, scandal or dirty linen; rabbit, timidity or sex; a wall a barrier to new ideas, lack of open-mindedness. In the same vein, repairing an old house indicated changing concepts, crossing a stream or river the beginning of a new venture.

A baby or child, generally, meant a new start, or if associated in the dreamer's conscious mind with problems, it could signify small problems. In Norfolk, in a tavern known as Gigi's, the proprietress, Mrs. Sally Coty, had been dreaming precognitively ever since she could remember. But when she saw children in her dreams, it didn't mean anything creative, it meant problems, small problems, because her children had always represented small problems to her.

"I dream of a child, and the next day, I know I'm going to have trouble, a little trouble—like the health authorities or the liquor authorities coming in to complain about something."

She tried to close off her dreams, but it wouldn't work.

She, too, had had a dream about a number once, but it was in New York City, when she had a store on Mulberry Street, and she knew what to do about it. She was in a state of emotional strain when the dream came. She was going into a hospital for major surgery, and had been told that her hospitalization insurance did not apply. She needed more than a thousand dollars, and had nowhere to turn for the money. On this particular night she had dreamed of a number—4-11-66—and was musing about it, when she looked out through the window of her store onto the street. There, standing idly, where she had never seen him before, was a man named Charlie, a runner for the Italian lottery, which was big in the neighborhood.

She went to the door. "What are you doing out there, Charlie?"

"I have the day off," he said.

She took out three one-dollar bills. "Here," she said, "are three numbers, will you play them in the lottery for me?" She considered his appearance a "sign."

The lottery was decided at the end of the week, and this was a Monday.

"I'll be back Thursday," Charlie said.

She didn't care to explain she was going into the hospital. "Take it now," she insisted.

He finally agreed.

"That weekend," the dreamer recalled, "my brother phoned me at the hospital, and said, 'Charlie's looking for you—he's got $1,500 for you.'" The numbers had come through.

While Cayce is gone, dreams live on at the A. R. E. After attending a dream seminar at Virginia Beach, a young man kept a record of his dreams, interpreting them according to his own frame of reference and standard symbols mentioned by Cayce. What he did with one dream, apparently anyone can do with his own dreams, perhaps opening up a new realm of insight into one's life. The following dream was analyzed months after the study project. The young man, in his early twenties, saw himself standing at the ocean, fishing. The water was clear but turbulent. Standing next to him on the sand was a small figure, a replica of himself, weeping. His larger self caught a fish, an orange-hued flounder, and gave it to the smaller self, who promptly stopped crying. But the flounder flopped out of the smaller figure's hands, landing in a clump of bushes, and the small self began to cry again. The dream's larger self poked through the bushes for the fish, but as he parted the foliage, discovered the fish being eaten by two animals, a white rabbit and a beaver. The beaver ran off, vanishing; the rabbit leaped into the ocean, swam about for a while, then returned tired and bedraggled.

After writing down the dream, the young man studied each symbol separately, passing over some whose meaning was not readily clear, then coming back to them in a day or two. After two days of intermittent study, he had compiled a list of symbols, relating each symbol to his own feeling about it, hoping in this way to find out what was stirring in his unconscious mind.

He began with ocean. "I have read that water means spirit or source of life, or the unconscious." Then:

> Fishing—act of seeking in the spiritual realm.
> A fish—something out of the spiritual realm.
> The self (larger)—myself as I am now in the physical.
> Smaller self—could this be my childhood? was I starved or hungry in childhood? (sobbing over not getting the fish).
> Crying—wanting something, stopped crying with fish.
> Fish got away—lost something which started smaller self crying again.
> Beaver—work like a beaver.
> Rabbit—timid.

This was the first listing. Reworking his dream, the young man began to form a discernible pattern:

> Ocean—whatever the ocean stood for—spiritual source of life or the unconscious—it was beautifully clear, but turbulent.
> A fish—a fish was the symbol used by early Christians; could this mean Christ, or spiritual food?
> The self (larger)—I seem to be seeking, or fishing, as I am now doing in real life, for direction for my life and solutions to my problems.
> The self (smaller)—this isn't a child. It is an exact duplicate of me. Can this be the part of me which needs spiritual food, small, undeveloped, a part of me that is crying out and is satisfied when

> given the fish? Maybe this is not my childhood
> (as first thought), but rather part of me as I am
> now, which needs help.
>
> Fish got away—somehow my spiritual food is getting
> away.
>
> Beaver—when I think of a beaver, I think of work.
> Maybe this is my job.

The dream could not be properly analyzed without knowing more of the young man's situation. He was working in a factory at the time, making parts for missiles, was troubled about making munitions that might be destructive one day, and had taken to hanging out with bad company, using profanity carelessly and drinking at bars after work. Consequently, a bickering relationship had developed at home with a young wife.

In a very real sense, it then became apparent to the non-psychic dream interpreters, that the beaver (his work) was actually eating up his spiritual food.

Like many essentially idealistic, puritanically schooled young Americans, he blocked out sex symbolism—and the symbolism was rather obvious in the white rabbit. He had written subsequently that he had raised them as a boy. "Sometimes I liked them. A lot of times it was hard work taking care of them."

What he apparently meant, it developed from questioning, was that he was intrigued by the rabbit's sex habits, and he had apparently learned something from watching them. His sex attitude—the rabbit—could be consuming his spiritual food—the fish.

Reviewing the dream, and the thought process connected with its interpretation, it would seem, offhand, a great deal of bother for one dream. However, the dream, with its interpretation, did have something to do with reshaping the young man's life. It got him thinking about himself, about the warning he had apparently received, and he acted on it. He quit his job (the beaver ran away), and got another he considered more constructive.

He took stock of his marriage, the sex habits that endangered that marriage (the rabbit swam around for a while) and attempted to reform. Dreaming had awakened him, and perhaps saved his marriage.

Only recently—1965—the A. R. E. held its first seminar

on dreams. It was supervised by Dr. W. Lindsay Jacob, a Pittsburgh psychiatrist, who has helped patients by analyzing their dreams; and Dr. Herbert B. Puryear, a clinical psychologist at Trinity University in San Antonio. Both had studied the Cayce dream readings, both found dreams an invaluable channel for resolving the inner conflicts of the emotionally torn. Just as Cayce had pointed out the relevance of all dreams, Dr. Puryear, too, observed, "No dream comes from nowhere." The emotionally disturbed dreamed recurringly of being engulfed by water, or of violent accidents, or even atomic attack; the last often characteristic of a brooding depression bordering on the suicidal.

What Cayce had said about dreams forty or fifty years before, science—and advanced science, at that—was now postulating. "The physical, psychical, and spiritual are reflected in different kinds of dreams," Dr. Jacob pointed out. Flying saucers, for instance, could mean something beyond our comprehension, a wheel an expression of spirituality, a camel the subconscious, an automobile the dreamer's own body; his higher-self, a clergyman, judge, law officer, or an old man with a white beard. They all had significance for the students of dreams.

About thirty persons of various ages joined in the dream seminar. The young and eager seemed particularly with it. Some college students, who had hitchhiked across the country to participate, lyrically reported a series of dreams within dreams. This was a device, expert Everett Irion passed on, to apprise the subconscious of a psychic message, usually precognitive. Other dreams revealed the students involved in ego-releasing conflicts to better understand themselves. This was the new generation that accepted the psychic as readily as travel to the moon, and their enthusiastic openness apparently induced significant dreaming.

Much was learned in the seminar about dreaming. When the dream was unpleasant, the subconscious would often block off all dreaming. A youthful-appearing grandmother, who ordinarily dreamed regularly, suddenly could not remember her dreams, no matter how many conscious suggestions she gave herself, or how diligently she put pad and pencil at her side. While others in the dream class cheerfully sat around and recalled their dreams, she had nothing to report. Nevertheless, during the night, when each sleeping member of the seminar was under personal observation, her eyeballs were seen moving under closed lids, a telltale sign of dreaming. Just as the eyelids stopped quivering, she was awakened, so that her dreams would be fresh in her memory, but she could only shake her head. She could remember nothing. The class good-naturedly accused her of blocking. Everett Irion, conducting the class, tried to get her to recall the last dreams she had, thinking they might provide a clue. Searching her mind, she finally recalled a fragmentary dream she had shortly before the seminar began, a week previously. And then she remembered still another dream. Obviously, she had begun blocking, as soon as the seminar opened, not wanting to discuss her dreams with anybody, nor touch on a situation that might have been stirring her subconscious. Only recently, she disclosed under group questioning, she had been going through a bit of an emotional crisis. Her granddaughter, who had been living with her for some time, had just been taken back by the mother, and the grandmother was heartsick and lonely. She was yearning for the child, so much so that she broke into sobs just talking about it.

The dreamer was a Mrs. Belva Hardy, a youngish middle-aged type, and a well-known teacher of music. She was interested in dreams, generally, and quite willing to explore her own with me. She remembered both dreams well now. The most significant vision came the night she checked into A. R. E. headquarters for the dream seminar. She called it the Porpoise Dream. Two porpoises were playing in the water, in a setting similar to the Marine Land of the Pacific. They were leaping and gamboling about and talking together; they were extremely happy. Meanwhile, Belva was standing on the bank, watching. Suddenly somebody came by with a straw hat turned upside down—passed the hat in front of her and asked her to give some food to the porpoise. She dropped three kernels of corn into the hat and said, "Be sure to bring it back because I don't have much."

Even to a neophyte, the meaning seemed apparent. Evidently, Belva's dream subconscious had been triggered by the approaching dream conference, and her subconscious had dredged up the problem. It was obvious who the porpoises were, and she, Belva, was on the sidelines.

Next, Belva dredged up her fragmentary dream: "A young couple is silhouetted some distance from me. The young lady is dressed in blue. The dream said, 'Don't bother to write this one down—there is more coming.'" She was already blocking.

After this fragment, Belva went dreamless four straight nights. Everett Irion pointed out that if dream material is ignored or suppressed, the individual does not dream for a while.

In some detail, Irion had clarified the symbology of the Porpoise Dream. The Pacific signified peace; corn was the highest spiritual food, the three kernels representing Father, Son, Holy Ghost, and when Belva said, "Be sure to bring it back," this very clearly meant that she wanted the child back.

The obvious interpretation had also struck her. The two porpoises were her daughter and granddaughter. Their reunion was an extremely happy one, and they were enjoying each other. She should cut her own ties, and bless the situation. This would free her mind, including the distracted subconscious, and prepare her for whatever was best for her.

Belva got the message. She sat down and prayed, and her prayers were for what was best for the child. Permeating good will, she subsequently visited her daughter and the child in California. The daughter reacted with similar warmth and understanding. When the conversation got around to the child's schooling, the daughter suggested, surprisingly, that the girl might do better in an Eastern school. "I had broken my hold on the child," Belva observed, "and now I found her coming back to me—this time for her own good and not to fill my own little needs." At last report, the child was with the grandmother again, and Belva was dreaming good solid dreams every night. She had nothing to keep from herself.

Chapter Thirteen

AT LAST, ATLANTIS

Just as man has gazed fascinated into the sea, atavistically peering into his past, so has he engaged in a restless quest for Atlantis. In the ocean, said naturalist Rachel Carson, he found from whence he had sprung, and in Atlantis, a dream of a superior culture, prefacing the brief few thousand years of recorded history with which he measures his meager progress.

Since Plato first described the Lost Continent of the Atlantic twenty-five hundred years ago, more than two thousand books have been written about a legendary land that nobody has seen. There have been books to prove Atlantis, books to disprove it. Some have been by erudite scientists, others by dreamers in search of a Shangri-La.

While oceanographers, geologists, and ordinary sea-divers have been fanning out over the Atlantic for centuries in the underwater quest, Edgar Cayce merely went to sleep, and saw visions of a magic continent which went through three periods of breakup, the last some eleven or twelve thousand years ago.

Waking, Cayce didn't know anything about lost continents and when his first mention of Atlantis was called to his attention, he rubbed his eyes and said in that gentle way of his, "Now I wonder where that came from, and if there's anything to it?"

At various times, Cayce's Atlantis, just like Plato's Atlantis, boasted a technical culture, which eventually deteriorated to a point where the last denizens were victims of their own destructiveness.

Cayce's readings on Atlantis, continuing for a span of twenty years, were given before the first atom bomb was touched off, before it was known that man finally did have the power to blast himself back to the Dark Ages, or turn the clock back to the Stone Age and life in a cave by bleak campfire. Could it be that it had all happened before?

"If we believe in evolution," the Geologist pointed out, "then we must believe in some sort of superior society existing before our skimpy recorded history, since obviously we haven't come very far since the time of Moses, Plato, Aristotle, or Christ."

There was an anthropological gap, from about seven thousand to thirty thousand years ago, when anything could have been possible for all we know. Whole cities and successions of cities had been buried before, as many different layers of Troy revealed—so why not a whole country or continent? From magnetic grains, from fossil remains, from layers of earth crust, we know the earth goes back millions of years, and yet we have no certain knowledge of what happened only yesterday, geologically. Had some cataclysm, destroying most or nearly all of humanity, also destroyed the records of that humanity? And could it not happen again, at presumably any time, now that man had the weapons of his own destruction at hand? Or perhaps the tilt of the global axis, sending billions of tons of melting glacial ice down on us from the Pole, would suffice?

Cayce's and Plato's Atlantis corresponded in many details, though Cayce had never read the two dialogues, in which the greatest mind of antiquity passed on the story of the island empire beyond the Pillars of Hercules.

Cayce had seen three periods of destruction, the first two about 15,600 B.C., when the mainland was divided into islands, and the last about 10,000 B.C., when a group of three large islands, along with some lesser, were swallowed up overnight, as Plato had suggested.

Though the precise outlines of Atlantis, before its breakup into the islands mentioned by Plato, were never given in a Cayce reading, he indicated that it extended from what is now the Sargasso Sea area in the west to the Azores in the east, and compared its size to "that of Europe, including Asia in Europe; not Asia, but Asia in Europe."

Before the last holocaust, waves of Atlanteans had, according to Cayce, dispersed in all directions, accounting for the superior, and often strangely familiar cultures, in such diverse areas as Egypt, Peru, Mexico, Central America, and in our New Mexico and Colorado, where they presumably became a colony of mound-dwellers.

Before the final breakup, which centered near the Bahamas, the culture of this superior people, eroded by greed and lust, had disintegrated to a point, Cayce said, where their destruction, like that of Sodom and Gomorrah after them, was inevitable.

Cayce even gives us a picture of the destruction, which Plato doesn't. "With the continued disregard of those that were keeping all those laws as applicable to the Sons of God, man brought in the destructive forces that combined with those natural resources of the gases, of the electrical forces, that made the first of the eruptions that awoke from the depth of the slow-cooling earth, and that portion now near what would be termed the Sargasso Sea first went into the depths."

Cayce says cryptically that archives dealing with the existence of Atlantis, concealed in three areas of the world, will eventually be revealed: one of these areas is Egypt, where the ancient Egyptian priests assured the Greek lawmaker Solon, the source of the Plato tale, that they had the account fully preserved.

Of course, since Plato's story has been discounted through the centuries, even his reference to a continent—clearly North America—beyond the Atlantean islands being disregarded as part of an allegorical myth, it is hardly likely that the same breed of historians and scientists would heed an unlettered clairvoyant dipping into his subconscious to elaborate on one of the most engrossing tales ever told.

Even the Geologist, gradually committed to Cayce and his wonders, found it hard to swallow Atlantis at first. But after delving into the scientific research of others, he began his own research, taking him at one point to the waters around Bimini, where Cayce forecast that the first of the sunken remnants of Atlantis would dramatically reappear. As the Geologist investigated, the scientific evidence began piling up.

If Cayce was right in his clairvoyant medical cures, why shouldn't he be right about other things? The information was certainly coming out of the same bottle, so to speak.

Cayce had observed that the lowlands of the Continent of Atlantis, before this presumed breakup into islands, paralleled the present Atlantic seaboard, and the Geologist pointed out that ocean troughs parallel to New England, seventy to a hundred miles at sea, showed from their ancient sedimentation that they had once been above surface. And what of the mid-Atlantic submarine ridge, spectacularly rising in spots, as it may once have dropped? "Sedimentary material from a depth of two miles on the ridge, revealed the exclusive presence of fresh water plants," the Geologist noted, "evidence that this section of the ridge was once above sea level."

Curiously, as recently as 1966, there was some confirmation of a gently sloping plane extending into the North Atlantic, and scientists at the Oceanographic Institute at Woods Hole, Massachusetts, theorized it was a likely abode of the earliest humans in this continental area some twenty thousand years ago. However, oriented as they were, they visualized this slope as easternmost North America, not westernmost Atlantis.

To some, the Azores, eight hundred miles due west of Portugal, represent the eastern marches of the last of the Atlantean islands. And they have been acting up lately, just as their counterparts may have once before.

Recent activity in the nine islands of the Azores is a striking reflection of the instability that may have dropped Atlantis in the Atlantic thousands of years ago. Quiet for centuries, the Azores began erupting in 1957, curiously close to the year 1958, which Cayce saw as the forty-year beginning of large-scale breakups around the globe.

As perhaps with Atlantis, the 1957 quakes and volcanic eruptions created migratory waves, as they broke up islands and destroyed thousands of homes. In February of 1964, there was another four days of nightmare quakes, and thousands of refugees fled the isle of São Jorge, hard hit by a thousand tremors.

The '57 quake recalled early scenes described by Cayce. The Geologist picked up a report by one of the refugees, Bernadette Vieira, who with her family fled São Jorge and settled in Santa Clara, California.

Bernadette's experience was most graphic: "She ran screaming down the village street as a volcanic island arose from the sea between São Jorge and nearby Fayal Island.

"On that day the earth shook, and stone-walled houses toppled. Hundreds of persons were killed. Hot ashes fell like rain. Crops were ruined, and livestock was killed.

"The volcanic island sank back into the sea as quickly as it had risen."

In the '64 quake, panicky residents feared the tremors might activate two dormant volcanoes on either tip of São Jorge. "The ground is trembling almost continuously," a Portuguese news agency reported, "the people of São Jorge feel like shipwrecks on a raft." In one community of thousands, only three houses were left standing. Telephone and telegraph communications were cut. The air smoldered with sulphur fumes. A hastily assembled flotilla carried doctors, ambulances and blood plasma to the stricken island in response to the SOS:

"Important damages. Many ruins. Request all navigation available in proximity proceed southern coast this island render assistance."

There was more: "If the volcanoes erupt," the Geologist read aloud, "they could split the island and cause it to crumple into the sea." The Geologist brought out a map, showing how the Azores archipelago, strangely scattered in midocean, stretched for four hundred miles, with its chain of craggy coastlines, volcanic mountains, crystal-clear crater lakes and lush subtropical vegetation.

Whatever a mainland had in fresh water, fauna and flora, these islands surrounded by seawater, also had, plus a legacy of volcanic instability.

"Could it really be," I asked, dubiously pointing to the loop of rocky isles, "that this was once Atlantis?"

The Geologist shrugged. "Why not? What's left is due west of the Pillars of Hercules, where Plato fixed the original islands. Geologically, where any phenomenon occurs in the present, it also occurred in the past, as part of normal evolutionary change. All that had to vary was the degree of change. Instability is an obvious feature of that area."

The Azores have caught the fancy of even the Russians. "In 1963," the Geologist pointed out, "a leading Russian geologist, Dr. Maria Klionova, reported to the Academy of Science of the USSR that rocks had been dredged up from depths of 6600 feet, sixty miles north of the Azores, which gave evidence of having been exposed to the atmosphere at approximately 15,000 B.C.—just about the time Cayce fixed for the breakup of the Atlantean mainland."

Similar evidence had turned up long before. "In 1898," the Geologist said solemnly, "the crew of a ship laying underwater cable near the Azores was grappling for a line in water two miles deep. As the grappling hooks scraped the ocean bottom, they turned up unfamiliar particles of lava, which from its peculiar glassy structure could only have solidified in the open air."

Reflecting the instability of the ocean bed in this area, a British freighter reported sighting a steaming volcanic island just south of the Azores before the turn of the century, but the island had disappeared before geologists could get back to it. On a smaller scale than Atlantis, land has dramatically vanished in various parts of the world. "In 1883," the Geologist noted, "the island of Krakatoa, near Sumatra, blew up with a loss of thousands of lives. In 1916, Falcon Island, east of Australia, disappeared without a trace, reappeared in 1923, then disappeared in 1949."

The floor of the ocean often rears up violently. "After a 1960 earthquake had leveled the Moroccan town of Agadir," the Geologist noted, "soundings revealed that nine miles offshore the sea bottom had buckled up 3300 feet in one great convulsive thrust." In August 1923 the Western Union Company, searching for a displaced cable, discovered that the Atlantic floor had risen two miles at one point since the last soundings twenty-five years before.

Cayce's Atlantis broke up into five islands, the three largest being Poseidia, Aryan, and Og. His most striking prediction concerned Poseidia. For in June 1940, as noted by the Geologist, he made a forecast that should soon materialize, if he was clairvoyantly on the beam.

"And Poseidia," he said, "will be among the first portions of Atlantis to rise again. Expect it in sixty-eight and sixty-nine ['68 and '69]. Not so far away."

And where to expect it? The Geologist had the clue in still another Cayce reading. "There are some protruding portions that must have at one time or another been a portion of this great Atlantean continent. The British West Indies or the Bahamas, and a portion of the same that may be seen in the present, if a geological survey would be made, notably in the

Gulf Stream through this vicinity, these [portions] may yet be determined."

Eagerly the Geologist combed through scientific literature on the geology beneath the Gulf Stream. Rather wide-eyed, he read of a submerged stream valley 2400 feet below the waves between Florida and the Bahamas, of giant sinkholes submerged six hundred to nine hundred feet off the tip of Florida, of mysterious bumps picked up by depth sounders in the Straits of Florida. The bumps appeared about the size of homes; only these "houses," if they may be called that, are two thousand feet below on the ocean floor. Geology appeared to be getting ready for Atlantis. "Before Cayce's death in 1945," the Geologist said, "the scientific assumption was that the ocean basins were huge bathtubs into which detritus [debris from disintegrating rock] was sluiced for many eons. However, through a new instrument, a sub-bottom depth profiler, it has been discovered that in great areas, the accumulation of sediment is remarkably small, especially on portions of the ridges, as would happen if there had been continents very recently where the ocean floor is now."

Current research confirms relatively recent sinkings of large land areas near Florida and the Bahamas. The *National Fisherman* featured an article, "Huge Sunken Piece of Florida Identified South of the Keys," referring to a 1300 square mile plateau submerged south of the Florida Keys. Geologist L. S. Kornicker described a submerged chain of islands and lagoonal basin ten miles south of Bimini in the Bahamas, at depths of forty to fifty feet. Whatever happened occurred at the approximate time of the Atlantis debacle. "Kornicker suggests," the Geologist said in a bemused voice, "that the features of the submerged area were formed eight thousand or more years ago when sea-level was about forty-eight feet below its present level."

With some excitement the Geologist stumbled upon an obscure Cayce reading discussing how the Atlanteans constructed giant laser-like crystals for power plants. "The records of the manners of the construction of same," he read, "are in the sunken portions of Atlantis, where a portion of the temples may yet be discovered, under the slime of ages of seawater, near what is known as Bimini, off the coast of Florida."

Columbus reading about the continent beyond the Pillars of Hercules could not have been more excited than the Geologist reading about Bimini, presumably a residual of the western perimeter of Atlantis. There was no rest now, until the Geologist could organize an underwater party to make soundings off Bimini. After extensive preparation, he found himself flying sixty miles due east from Miami to Bimini. The pilot of his seaplane, learning of the mission, excitedly told him of large clumps of rock visible on his daily run at a certain angle. From the pilot, the expedition got the general location of two of the more conspicuous clumps. Scuba-diving in the crystal, azure-blue waters north of Bimini they came upon a scattered pile of lime-encrusted granite boulders, each about five to fifteen tons. Their spirits soared, but they fell again. The rocks were rough-hewn and looked as though they had come from a quarry. And they had. A ship carrying granite ballast had been driven on the shoals and wrecked thirty years before.

But our scientists weren't that easily discouraged. They changed course, tacking in thirty-five-foot depths southeast of Bimini, and after two fruitless days, they saw on its side in the coral sea a beautiful round white pillar about sixteen feet long. Could this be one of the pillars of the sunken temples of Atlantis, suddenly exposed in relatively shallow water by an upward thrust of the sea-floor? Examination of a pillar fragment revealed that it was of purest marble. But it still could have been washed off the hulk of a battered freighter. The Geologist realized—reluctantly—that it would take another expedition, armed with heavy salvage equipment, to raise the column and determine its origin. Still, the party made a number of depth-borings, which the Geologist tantalizingly refuses to discuss until their message can be clarified, perhaps in the very near future, when Poseidia, or some part of it, would rise again—Cayceites hoped.

Meanwhile, what evidence was there that a highly civilized man lived from 7500 to 30,000 years ago, dispersing over wide areas from a central base? In the Pueblo Valley, southeast of Mexico City, the Mexican anthropologist Juan Armenia Camacho turned up pieces of bone decorated with carved figures, estimated at thirty thousand years. "These bits of bone," the Geologist stressed, "indicate that civilized man was in the New World much before anybody believed, except for Cayce, who put the flesh where Camacho put the bones."

Mexico is alive with a tradition of age-old visitations by a gifted people from the East; this led the pyramid-building

Aztecs to be on the lookout for a returning White God, and made them vulnerable to the blandishments of Spanish Conquistador Hernando Cortez and his rapacious horde.

Almost every native group in Central and North America have inherited stories of ancient floods, with formidable landing parties arriving from the East. In Mexican lore, the Geologist pointed out, "there is a record of an early landing from a land called Aztlan, apparently an ancient variation of Atlantis. The Mayan Book of Chilan Balam, a record of this advanced culture, gives a detailed account of a great catastrophe to the East. The Delaware, Sioux, and Iroquois tribes have a legacy of a great flood, and the almost extinct Mandan Indian of Missouri held special memorial services about a great war canoe, symbolizing the ark which traditionally brought their forebears from the East during a Great Flood."

The press was always from the East. "Curiously," the Geologist said, "none of these visitors or invaders were from the West, always the East, always the Atlantic." He looked over at me innocently. "Have you heard of the Welsh legend in which a small bird rides on the back of a larger one as it attains great height, and then flies higher when the larger bird becomes tired?"

I shook my head.

"Well, the Iroquois have exactly the same folk tale."

The Geologist had assembled many indications of a central source of civilization on both sides of the Atlantic—and Atlantis. "We all know about the great pyramids of Egypt," he said, "but how many know that the archeologists have been digging up even more extensive pyramids of similar design in Mexico?"

He plucked from his bulging files a commentary of ancient civilizations in the Americas, from the *New York Times* in December 1961, author William Luce noting: "Thirty-two miles from Mexico City is an archeological site so old that even the Aztecs knew virtually nothing about it. This is Teotihuacan, the site of the Pyramid of the Sun. A ruin five hundred years before the arrival of Cortez, the pyramid has been reconstructed into a structure as tall as a twenty-story skyscraper. The 216-foot climb to its top is a fine way to end a tour of ancient Mexico. . . . Never excelled in Mexico as architects and engineers, the Teotihuacans also were master sculptors and painters."

The author posed the great enigma. "The ruins raise as

many questions as they answer. Who the people were who
built them, where they came from, why they built them and
what happened to them are questions that will be luring
scholars and tourists for some time."

The Geologist had marshaled his evidence. On both sides
of the Atlantic were almost identical calendars more accurate
than those developed in Europe for hundreds of years. "The
accuracy of the mathematical calculations, as reflected in
both the architecture and astronomy," the Geologist pointed
out, "was equally remarkable in both Egypt and the early
Mayan civilizations."

In the Yucatán, in southern Mexico, in Peru, were land-
marks of a culture that was old when the conquering Spaniards arrived. "Pizarro and his men found two thousand miles
of well-paved road in Peru, along which were dotted remains
of many fine hotels. Where did they come from?"

There was an amazing similarity of place names; for example, names of five cities in Asia Minor about the time of
Christ, and five cities in Central America:

Asia Minor	Central America
Chol	Chol-ula
Colua	Colua-can
Zuivana	Zuivan
Cholima	Colima
Zalissa	Xalisco

The Geologist frowned as I compared the brief lists. "The
important thing to remember, is that the New World communities were already named when the first European explorers
arrived."

In studying the Cayce readings, the Geologist saw nothing
about Atlantis inconsistent with what had been adduced from
the ocean floor, common artifacts on both sides of the Atlantic, and the Plato account. "According to Cayce, Atlantis was
one of the oldest land areas, also one of the places where
man first made his appearance. The early continent occupied
the greater part of what is now the North Atlantic, and our
present Eastern seaboard was then the Coastal region, as
were parts of Europe. At the time when the poles shifted,
and Lemuria in the Pacific was submerged, the Atlanteans
were achieving great technological advances. Several thousand years later, misuse of the laws of natural power caused a

stupendous upheaval that split the continent into five islands. The major Atlantean mass plunged into the Sargasso Sea in this first cataclysm. The remaining populace continued to deteriorate until, finally, eleven thousand years ago or so, Nature seemed to rebel at the iniquity, and the remaining islands were swallowed up in the last of the giant cataclysms."

Cayce mentioned Atlantis originally in November 1923, in an early life reading originally dealing with a previous incarnation. "Before this," he said, "the entity was in that fair country of Alta, or Poseidia proper, then this entity [the subject] was in that force that brought the highest civilization and knowledge that has been known to the earth's plane. This, we find, was nearly ten thousand years before the Prince of Peace came." Cayce's description of the last breakup differed from Plato's in the implication of what the large-scale mass movements were all about. Plato's source saw the Atlantean migration as part of a great invasion, repulsed by an Athenean military that could hardly have coped with a major power. More plausibly, the Cayce version implies that the Greeks drove off a group of stragglers, just one of the many homeless contingents island-hopping their way to new homes.

The first wave of migration, in the second breakup, may explain the Basques, a hardy race of unknown origin, and unrelated language, living in the mountain fastnesses of northern Spain. "With this," said Cayce, "came the first egress of peoples to that of the Pyrénées." It was so long ago that all connections with a motherland were gradually eradicated. "Later, we find the peoples who enter into the black, or the mixed peoples, in what later became the Egyptian dynasty, also those peoples that later became the beginning of the Inca, that built the wall across the mountains, and with the same those of the mound-dwellers."

Into agrarian Egypt, the newcomers may have carried the arts of medicine, embalming and architecture, and fanning out in the opposite direction, carried the fruits of their culture to Central America and Peru, where the early natives, like the first known Egyptians, mummified their dead.

The first Atlantean disturbances or upheavals came twenty-eight thousand years ago, but not till 17,600 B.P. (Before Present) was the continent actually broken up. "What would be considered one large continent," Cayce said, "until the first eruptions brought those changes, producing more of the nature of large islands, with the intervening canals or ravines, gulfs, bays, or streams."

Structurally speaking, it wouldn't have taken much to change the face of the Atlantic. Only a slight warping of the earth's crust—barely one-eight thousandth of its diameter—could have caused large portions of the ocean floor to rock to the surface, while larger portions sank.

The upheaval affecting the continental land mass was visualized as the unhappy result of a merger of destructive man-made forces with those of nature, as might happen if a powerful nuclear bomb were to upset the equilibrium of the earth in the area of a major fault. By current standards, it must have been indeed an advanced civilization that could blow itself up. If one is to believe Cayce, the misuse of solar energy brought about the debacle. And there is evidence, the Geologist reported, to support the idea that man was sufficiently advanced technically to utilize the etheric or cosmic rays of the sun as a primary source of power. "Very ancient maps of Greenland and Antarctica have been found, showing these areas in an unglaciated state," the Geologist pointed out, "and the experts think that ancient cartographers, from the subtle rise and fall of its mountain topography, might have mapped the area from the air."

As a factor in harnessing the power of the sun, Cayce mentioned a firestone whose magical power apparently resembles the laser beam, which was not produced for some thirty years after the Cayce reference. The sleeping Cayce's description of the stone reminded the Geologist of the power generated by filtering the rays of the sun through the ruby. The concept would have been dismissed as fanciful until recently. "The activity of the stone was received from the sun's rays," Cayce said. "The concentration through the prisms or glass acted upon the instruments that were connected with the various modes of travel [trains, ships, etc.], as the remote control through radio vibrations or directions would in the present day."

The firestone, or ruby of its time, was housed in a dome-covered building with a sliding top. Its powerful rays could penetrate anywhere; just as the laser beam, it could be either a death ray or a constructive energy source. It was hard to conceive that which Cayce put into words: "The influences of the radiation that arose in the form of the rays were invisible to the eye but acted upon the stones themselves as set in the motivating forces, whether aircraft lifted by gases or guiding pleasure vehicles that might pass along close to earth, or the crafts on or under the water."

All over Atlantis, stations were set up to produce this power, then something inadvertently went wrong and the breakup followed. "These, not intentionally, were tuned too high and brought the second period of destructive forces, and broke up the land into the isles where later there were further destructive forces." Cayce gave a detailed description of the stone source of all this energy: "A large cylindrical glass, cut with facets in such a manner that the capstone made for the centralizing of the power that concentrated between the end of the cylinder and the capstone itself."

As Plato suggested, the collapse came with a disintegration of moral values. Cayce describes the last days: "As cities were built, more and more rare became those abilities to call upon the forces in nature to supply the needs of bodily adornment, or to supply the replenishing of physical beings as hunger arose. There was a 'wasting-away' in the mountains, the valleys, then the sea itself, and the fast disintegration of the lands, as well as of the peoples, save those that had escaped into those distant lands."

It seemed incredible that so advanced a people could go hungry and lack for clothes.

The Geologist smiled wryly. "Think of the millions starving today all over the world—India, China, Russia." He mused a moment. "And if our population keeps up at the present rate, we may have our own food problems in another fifty years. As it is, our big deal, domestically, is the anti-poverty program, and we're the richest country in the world."

In one of Cayce's trance recalls, the Geologist saw not only indications of Atlantis, but of Cayce's gift of prophecy. Cayce had picturesquely described a meeting in 50,000 B.C. of many nations on Atlantis to deal with hordes of huge beasts then overrunning the earth. These beasts, said Cayce, were ultimately coped with by "sending out super-cosmic rays from various central plants."

It sounded like the sheerest fantasy. But Cayce had made one tangible statement subject to scrutiny, in 1932: "These rays will be discovered within the next twenty-five years."

Marking time, in 1958 the Geologist turned to the Encyclopædia Brittanica and found two references to recent discoveries of potential death rays. Only the year before, experi-

mental physicists at the University of California had reported
a successful effort to produce antineutrons. "With the discovery of the antineutron," the Encyclopædia reported, "also
came the theoretical possibility of a source of energy hundreds of times more compact than any previously existing.
Antineutrons could in principle be combined with antipro-
tons to build up 'antimatter.' When antimatter came into contact with ordinary matter all of its mass would be converted
into energy rather than only a fraction of it, as is the case
with nuclear fission and fusion reactions."

It seemed extremely complicated.

"Not at all," said the Geologist with a smile. "The antineutron beam passes over you, and you become a mass of invisible energy." The process was not reversible.

But there was another ray, more in keeping with the firestone described by Cayce. The radiating force was "achieved
by storing up energy in a small insulating crystal of special
magnetic properties, so that the crystal passes on more energy
than it receives." In other words, the laser. And already, as
suggested by Cayce, the ruby has been used as the crystal to
convert matter into boundless energy, by amplifying light
waves from the sun.

Despite the "evidence," the Atlantis material appeared too
fanciful to be true. Since Cayce tuned in on the collective unconscious, perhaps he had somehow tuned in on some delightful fable concocted by some inventive or capricious
mind.

"It was real in somebody's mind, and so it became equally
real in Cayce's subconscious," I suggested.

The Geologist shook his head. "That won't wash. Otherwise, Cayce would have been guilty of producing every false
medical diagnosis ever made by some confused practitioner;
diagnosis, whatever it was, was certainly real to that mind
projecting it."

Even climatically, Cayce apparently knew what he was
talking about when he looked back those "10,600 years before the Prince of Peace came into the land of promise."
Yucatán, a haven for the fleeing Atlanteans, had a different
climate then. "For rather than being a tropical area, it was
more of the temperate, and quite varied in the conditions and
positions of the face of the areas themselves." It was this sort
of thing that reassured the Geologist about Cayce's unconscious insight. "The major climatic change that led from the

cold glacial climate to the present earth climate occurred close to 11,000 years ago," he observed complacently. "A study of pollen from cores taken from the Mexico City region more southerly than the Yucatán, establishes that the area was once cooler and dryer than now."

He turned to Cayce's description of the physical changes in the area. "In the final upheaval of Atlantis, much of the contour of the land in Central America and Mexico was changed to that similar in outline to that which may be seen in the present."

The Geologist had an explanation for this, too. "This means that since migration took place before the final upheaval altered the Gulf of Mexico to its present outline, these migrations must have been to points at present subsided in the Gulf." He turned back to Cayce again. "The first temples erected by Altar and his followers were destroyed at the period of change in the contours of the land, those of the first civilization following have been discovered in Yucatán but have not been opened."

This hardly seemed likely. But the Geologist wasn't so sure. Almost casually, he said, "We might have this evidence of Atlantis if we could only understand the significance of unique stones discovered in Yucatán back in 1933."

Cayce had apparently foreseen the archeological activity that would turn up some relic of the gigantic firestones that the Atlanteans had used for a seemingly unlimited power source. "In Yucatán there is the emblem of same," the sleeping Cayce had said. And as if to guide archeologists to the stones, he cautioned, "Let's clarify this, for the pattern may be the more easily found. For these pattern stones will be brought to the United States. A portion is to be carried to the Pennsylvania state museum. A portion to be carried to the Washington museum or to Chicago."

It may only be coincidence, but in November 1962, *Fate* magazine reported, "Three elaborate, sealed Mayan tombs over two thousand years old have been discovered by University of Pennsylvania museum archeologists on the Yucatán Peninsula of Guatemala."

Atlantis was obviously not legendary to the man who put it on the map—Plato. "The brilliant, sophisticated mind that conceived The Dialogues and The Republic," the Geologist observed, "was the same that referred plainly in the Timaeus to the mighty power which was aggressing against the whole of Europe and Asia." Writing four centuries before Christ, Plato was dealing with a reality that was anything but obscure, the nameless fear of the Atlantic beyond the protective Strait of Gibraltar. He referred to an impenetrable Atlantic which not even the hardiest mariners dared brave, for fear of being mired, until a series of intrepid navigators set out for India two thousand years later.

Not only Solon told the story of Atlantis. Socrates, too, had given a similar account, Plato recalls, "by some coincidence not to be explained."

Obviously, Plato thought it more than coincidence.

In the Timaeus, Plato mentioned the repulse of the invading Atlanteans. In the Critias, named for his grandfather, to whom Solon reported, he describes the legendary Atlas, as the first king of Atlantis. The Atlantean story, the Egyptian priests said, had been set down "in our sacred registers as eight thousand years old." As Solon lived about 600 B.C., that would put the final destruction between ten and eleven thousand years ago. Like other peoples, the ancient Greeks had a legend of a cataclysmic Noah-like flood. From their archives, safely sealed in some pyramid perhaps, the Egyptians remembered many such disasters.

The Atlantic itself indicates Greek influence, Atlanticus being the Latin for the Greek, Atlas. Plato again casually picked out something which confirmed his reliability, the reference to the "continent" beyond the Atlantean Islands. "Obviously," the Geologist pointed out, "he was referring to a continent we all know well—North America."

Perhaps, reading his Plato, Columbus got the idea that beyond the Pillars of Hercules, beyond the Atlantis of Plato, he would find the true continent, which could only be India, for what other continent was there?

It might be pertinent to briefly review the Plato story, beginning with the Egyptian priest advising Solon: "As for those genealogies which you have recounted to us, Solon, they are the tales of children. You remember one deluge only, whereas there were many of them. You do not know that there dwelt in your land the noblest race of men which ever lived, of whom you and your whole city are but a remnant. This was unknown to you, because for many generations the survivors of that destruction died and made no sign. For there was a time, Solon, before the greatest deluge of all, when the city which now is Athens, was first in war and was preëminent for her laws, and is said to have performed the noblest deeds and had the fairest constitution of any.

"Many wonderful deeds are recorded of your State in our histories. But one exceeds all the rest. For these histories tell of a mighty power which was aggressing against the whole of Europe and Asia. This power came forth out of the Atlantic Ocean, for in those days the Atlantic was navigable; and there was an island in front of the straits which you call the Pillars of Heracles. The island was larger than Libya and Asia [Asia Minor] put together, and was the way to other islands, and from the islands you might pass to the whole of the opposite continent [America] which surrounded the true ocean. For this sea [Mediterranean] which is within the Straits of Heracles is only a harbor, having a narrow entrance, but that other is a real sea, and the surrounding land [America] may be most truly called a continent.

"Now in Atlantis there was a great empire which ruled over the whole island and several others, as well as over parts of the continent [America], and, besides these, they subjected parts of Libya as far as Egypt, and of Europe as far as Tyrrhenia. The vast power gathered into one endeavored to subdue our country and yours and the whole of the land which was within the straits; and then, Solon, your country shone forth magnificently, for she was first in courage and military skill, and was the leader of the Hellenes. And when the rest fell away from her, forced to stand alone, after having undergone the extremity of danger, she triumphed over the invaders, and preserved from slavery those not yet subjected, and liberated all the others dwelling within the limits of Heracles. But afterwards there occurred violent earthquakes and floods. And in a single day and night of rain all your warlike men sank into the earth, and the island of Atlantis in like manner disappeared beneath the sea. And that is why the sea in those parts is impenetrable, because there is a quantity of shallow mud in the way, caused by the subsidence of the island."

In still another dialogue, Plato gives a colorful description of Atlantis: "And there were temples built and dedicated to many gods, also gardens and places of exercise, some for men, and some for horses. There was a race-course a stadium in width, and in length extending all round the island for horses to race in. Also there were guardhouses at intervals for the body-guard, while the most trusted had houses within the citadel, and about the persons of the kings. The docks were full of triremes and naval stores, and all things were quite ready for use.

"For many generations, as long as the divine nature lasted in them, the people were obedient to the laws, practising gentleness and wisdom in their intercourse with one another. They despised everything but virtue, thinking lightly of gold and other property, which appeared only a burden to them. Neither were they intoxicated by luxury, nor did riches deprive them of self-control. They saw clearly that worldly goods are increased through friendship with one another, and that by excessive zeal for them, the good is lost and friendship perishes. By such reflections of a divine nature, all that we have described increased in them. But then this divine portion began to fade away, and they, unable to bear their good fortune, became unseemly, and began to appear base. Yet to those who had no eye for true happiness, they still seemed blessed at the very time they were bursting with unrighteous avarice and power."

With the statement that this wickedness had apparently angered the Gods, the Plato fragment broke off, presumably lost in the shuffle of the years. Undoubtedly, the greatest philosopher of his time had little idea of what he was stirring up with his tale of a Lost Continent, but Cayce was another matter. After portions of Atlantis rise, said Cayce, then comes a period of upheavals that "must in the next generation come to other lands." That reading was in December 1943, and Webster defines a generation as the period when "father is succeeded by child, usually taken to be about thirty-three years." And so in another ten years, in 1976, Atlantis may no longer be a mystery. And the Geologist? He wants to be around Bimini when fresh land surfaces, or will it be the Azores? Time—and Cayce—may yet resolve one of the more intriguing riddles of man's past.

Chapter Fourteen

REINCARNATION

The expression "down-to-earth" was coined for Eula Allen. She came from the State of Washington, where she once bred and raised horses. She had married and raised a family, and was a grandmother several times over. She lived in a big comfortable house with her husband, retired Naval Commander Harold Allen, farmed the fields around her house, counseled friends far and wide, and wrote about the things that Edgar Cayce had once planted in her consciousness.

I had an immediate sense of ease with her, the feeling of relaxation that comes with knowing, intuitively perhaps, that one is meeting an honest human being. Her blue eyes twinkled brightly through clear panes of glass, a friendly smile formed on her lips, she gave me her hand, and the clasp was as dry and firm as a man's.

I stole a look around the room as she guided me to a comfortably upholstered chair. It was oversized, yet warm, with a warmth that came together from many sources—the jars and bottles of every color and description, glinting in the sun that slanted through the windows, the burnished woodwork whose merging grains seemed vitally alive, the books and magazines sprawled colorfully across tables and chairs. It was the living room of people who obviously enjoyed living.

Eula, I presumed, was in her sixties, but she was the ageless type, who would be as sprightly in mind and spirit ten years from now as she had been ten years before. She was tall, with a straight back, and a direct demeanor. It seemed hard to believe that anybody so down to earth could believe in the esoteric.

"Was it Edgar Cayce who convinced you of reincarnation?" I asked.

She laughed out loud. "Edgar Cayce saved my life," she said with emphasis.

"Is that why you accepted reincarnation?"

"Not at all," she said easily, "Mr. Cayce never forced his beliefs on anybody."

I wondered how she had met Cayce.

She smiled. "Like so many other people, I imagine. I was tired, rundown, a bag of bones, I could hardly get around. I was forty-two at the time, had recently had a baby, my husband was at sea, and I came down with an acute kidney infection. The doctors at the Norfolk naval hospital told me the kidney would have to be removed, and when I refused surgery they said they wouldn't take responsibility for what happened."

She was living in a furnished room at the time, and a friendly landlady had introduced her to a woman who had regained her health through a Cayce reading. That woman, Mignon Helms of Virginia Beach, had never been ill a day since.

Eula had an adventurous mind, and the thought of healing force operating through the unconscious mind of a stranger intrigued her. "I knew enough of life to know that there was no limit to the power of the mind, and for that reason perhaps I had refused surgery, feeling that it wouldn't get at the real difficulty, and yet would leave me maimed."

She had had an experience of her own with her son Bruce, that made her ready for any form of mental healing. Fifteen years before, Bruce, then twelve, had been critically ill with rheumatic fever. The pulsing of the heart could be heard across the room. Eula had never considered herself religious. Her family was among the first white settlers between Walla Walla (Washington) and Lewiston (Idaho), and there had been no church background. But as the boy lay on the table, she prayed. She visualized God, and she visualized a perfect heart, keeping the picture of that perfect heart in her mind all through the ordeal. The crisis came, as the doctor watched grimly, and then the boy's breathing suddenly grew less labored, his temperature dropped, and he relaxed into normal slumber. The doctor stood up with a tired sigh. "I don't know how," he said, "but he'll make it."

Eula hesitated. "I prayed, Doctor, do you think it helped?"

He looked at her curiously. "I can't think of anything else that helped," he said. "You saved that boy's life."

And so what Cayce did made sense to Eula Allen.

After Mrs. Helms got through her description of how Cayce had helped where the doctors had failed, Eula asked, "When can I see this man?"

"You must ask for an appointment," Mrs. Helms replied, "but you don't have to see him. Just say where you will be at the appointed time."

Eula Allen blinked. "But I would like to be there," she said, finally.

The reading was fixed for the 18th of February, 1941, with Mrs. Helms present, along with Gertrude Cayce and the inevitable Gladys Davis.

The sleeping Cayce never once mentioned the infected kidney. He said that Eula was anemic, running on nervous energy, and described a strain and heaviness in the lumbar and sacral areas, the region of the kidney, an aching that extended up to the mid-back. "In these areas of the nervous system, there are engorged or enlarged ganglia [nerve centers from which impulses are transmitted], and these, rather sore to the touch, spread into the muscular areas of the body."

The organs themselves were sound, except as they were lacking stimulation from a blood deficiency due to impeded central nervous impulses. "Hence, the organs are not diseased but at times dis-eased."

He recommended small quantities internally of olive oil, three pellets of Adiron daily, one with each meal, and the use of an electric vibrator before bedtime for a half hour, along the spine, especially over the areas of the neck and head, between the shoulders, and across the ninth dorsal vertebra, through the lower lumbar and sacral areas.

Even though the treatment seemed sketchy, Eula Allen found a strange confidence in the man who let her out the door with a kindly smile and warm handshake. "I've known you before," he said, squeezing her hand gently.

Back in her room, Eula reviewed her last medical report. The kidney was swollen to the size of a small cantaloupe, and her general health depleted. The condition had been chronic for fifteen years, periodically recurring, but acute now for six weeks. Pain in the back intense, temperature high. Surgery recommended.

But she put her faith in Cayce, and the electric vibrator. In three days, the kidney swelling was reduced to normal, and she was out of pain. She continued the treatments, and in six months gained forty pounds. She hadn't felt this well since she was twenty-five. And she kept remembering, oddly, what Cayce had said, "I've known you before."

In time, her curiosity got the better of her, and she wanted to know what he meant. It was strange, but she had had the same feeling about him. And so for the first time, really, sitting down, chatting with Cayce, she heard about reincarnation. "Does that mean," she asked with a worried frown, "that I may come back as an animal?"

Cayce laughed. "Certainly not, that's transmigration, and you may not even have to come back at all, if you become perfectly developed in this life." Even with the confidence she had in the amazing healer, it was hard for her to get used to the idea of reincarnation. Cayce didn't press her. She attended his Bible classes and listened. "The soul is eternal," he said, "and God's arm isn't short. You go out and you come in again." Reincarnation involved only highly developed human souls, not animals.

For more than a year she thought it over, then decided to have one of Cayce's life readings. These were designed to delineate past lives, which had most influenced this one, revealing attitudes, inclinations, and personalities presumably carried over from earlier existences in different bodies. Although the Cayce health reading had convinced her of his subconscious link to the Universal Mind, reincarnation was still a difficult thought, even for one believing in survival, and Eula wasn't sure of that, either.

Eula discovered, as Cayce spoke, that she had had previous sojourns in Ireland, Rome, Syria, Peru, Atlantis, (where so many sojourned) and in our own Wild West before the Civil War. But what interested her most at this time, she being of a practical turn, was the insight into her own temperament as seen through these so-called incarnations.

"The material appearances have been quite varied," Cayce said, "yet very sincere, very stern in most activities. Thus, the entity is qualified to interpret almost any phase of the individual experience, and others will listen."

With a secret smile, I recognized that I had chosen Eula as

an interpreter of the Cayce record, and had listened avidly, if somewhat confused, for hours. I had been much impressed at the same time by her openness and candor, amused by her two-fisted characterizations of some of the trustees of the Cayce legacy. They would not have been so amused.

Cayce, even more amusingly, had warned Eula. "The entity should be guarded not as to what it would say or as to whether it would say, but as to what and how and when it says. Just remember that others listen and recall, 'Ye shall give an account of every word that is spoken.' For in speaking thy words are given power."

I could vouch for Eula's eloquence, but obviously this was no reflection of reincarnation. But she had still other distinctions. "The entity may be expected to be associated with many who have had, or will have much to do with the changing of policies, local, state, national and international."

That seemed quite an order for a grandmother, even one as articulate as Eula.

I looked up from the life reading which Eula had put before me. "I see where you're running your own State Department."

She regarded me rather sharply, but said nothing.

"Are you actually advising the Great Powers on the problems of the day?" I smiled.

"People from all over the world come to my home—India, China, Washington, but who they are and what is a private matter."

A thought struck me. "Why, if people have lived other lives, don't they remember anything from them?"

"But they do," she said. "It's just sometimes that they don't remember that they are remembering. Jesus said, 'I'll bring all things to thine remembrance,' but he didn't say how." Despite the subject matter, she still gave the impression of being down to earth.

"What do you remember?" I asked.

"Well, Mr. Cayce mentioned that in an Irish incarnation I was a Rosa O'Deshea, who came to the New World at an early period." She looked at me calmly. "Though I have no Irish strain in me genetically, I have always felt terribly sentimental about Irish music, poetry, and folk tales. Also, the privations I went through in coming to this country stood me as good experience in the rough ranch life in Washington State in this life."

I like Irish music, too, particularly "When Irish Eyes Are Smiling," without any tangible link to the Ould Sod.

"You'll have to do better," I said.

Eula's eyes flashed, and she said with some asperity, "I don't have to convince you of anything."

I peered into the reading. "It says here that the 'entity should be guarded, not as to what it would say or as to whether it would say, but as to what and how and when it says.' "

"That's right," Eula said.

"But what good is it all, the life reading or a belief in reincarnation, except for the pleasant euphemism that death is not the end?"

Again an expression of exasperation crossed Eula's normally benign countenance. "Remembering, even subconsciously, teaches us; it provides opportunities for us to go on and learn."

Speaking of a sojourn which carried the entity—so both Cayce and I thought of Eula—from Palestine, where she studied at the feet of the Apostles to bondage in Persia, the mystic had related: "From that sojourn there are great latent talents as a teacher, a leader, an instructor, a director. All of these abilities are a part of the entity's present experience. Yet, there was so little of the home life in that sojourn. It was for that the entity returned in the present experience."

Certainly, Eula had been a good homemaker, married twice comfortably, four children, the last born to her when she was forty years old. The children were grown, the two girls marrying well, one son a lawyer, the other an engineer. As a housewife, her cup runneth over.

Had she done any teaching?

She hadn't stopped teaching, in class and out, even with all her household functions.

It still seemed a most trivial basis for proving out reincarnation. "Weren't you ready to accept reincarnation when Edgar Cayce's health reading led to your cure?"

"It certainly made me more amenable. If his subconscious was right, where the professional medicos' conscious was so wrong, why shouldn't this selfsame subconscious be equally accurate and the professional theologians equally wrong?"

But this had only predisposed her, she insisted, to giving the whole subject an honest, open appraisal. "What sense does anything make," she said, "unless we are here to learn?"

I shrugged. "Many would argue that it makes no sense."

"Everything else does," she shot back, "all life has a rhythm and plan, the seasons, vegetation, the movement of the tides and the planets. There is an order about everything, so why not man? And certainly the integral part of man is not his body, but his spirit."

I again invoked the anatomist, who had opened up a cadaver, and asked his students to pick out the soul.

Eula sniffed. "That man was a fool. I could point at the same body, and ask, 'Is this the man we knew?' Without spirit and mind, he is only a slab of meat, and even the doctor would admit man is more than that."

Yes, Eula was sure she remembered, and remembering, made progress. In her life reading, she had asked, "What is the meaning of the pulling sensation in my fingers and hands?"

"These," Cayce replied, "should come more from the tendencies that are a part of the experience, the writing, see?"

Ah, Eula was to be a writer.

"I always felt an inclination that way, and Cayce told me that I should get myself published."

Even for an established writer, this was often more easily said than done.

But Cayce was determined.

"How can I best apply my understanding for the benefit of others?" she had asked.

"Put it on paper, and publish it."

And what had been published?

Two books had already come out of Eula, based on the knowledge of the universe she had gained from the Cayce readings. One was *Before the Beginning*, a summation of the spiritual creation; the other, *The River of Time*, of physical creation as visualized by Cayce.

The books had been received only perfunctorily by the Cayce press. But, surprisingly, they were now so popular they could hardly be kept in stock.

It made some things clear about herself that she had never understood before. As a child, upset by the gambling of ranchhands on her grandfather's spread, she had boldly broken up the games, barging in on the players and destroying every pack of cards she could get her hands on. Now, she understood why. She was reacting from having once been a dance hall shill. Subconsciously, at least, she was remembering, and trying to do something about it.

Still, I wondered how deep this belief in reincarnation cut. "Are you afraid to die?" I asked.

She shook her head. "Death is like stepping out of an old car, into a new one."

"Then why were you so concerned about your son's possible death of rheumatic fever?"

"I didn't believe in reincarnation then, and besides, even now, I would be deeply affected by the suffering of anybody I loved, not necessarily by their death, if I thought they had learned something in this life before they went."

"How about all the innocents—children—that Stalin and Hitler exterminated? Why should they have suffered?"

"It makes no sense unless you do accept reincarnation, for then one accepts the law of compensation, karma, carrying over from one life to another. Edgar Cayce frequently spoke of people paying in one life for that done in another, profiting equally from the good they had done. In one of my previous lives, as a Roman, Cayce said that I commanded a fleet manned by galley slaves. Even before my reading, everytime I saw a picture of slaves, my stomach would turn over. It stirred up all kinds of unconscious memories. Now it makes sense."

"I still don't understand all this suffering as being part of God's will."

She looked at me sharply. "God sets up certain laws defining the order of the universe, and these can't be changed."

"But certainly God is more merciful than a mere sinner, who would not want anyone to suffer."

"God's law cannot be changed," she said.

"Then why pray for your son?"

"We have access to God's law, and the way things shape out depends on our own attitudes in accordance with this law."

Ironically, for a reincarnationist like Eula, God's law represented virtually the same thing to detached scientists, an endless cycle of matter and energy, capable of entering into an endless variety of physical combinations in perpetuity. "We are all part of God," she said, "and God is part of us. There is no conflict, no punishment, merely opportunities to develop." She looked up at me with a disarming smile. "Why should everything we have had so much trouble experiencing be taken from us, when nature is so economical in other respects?"

There was no questioning Eula's sincerity, and if her belief in reincarnation helped her be a better, more productive person, that was a plus sign indeed for reincarnation.

"Why do you now find it so important to believe in reincarnation—wouldn't being just a good Christian, believing in the message of God through Christ be sufficient to get you into Heaven?"

She gave me an almost pitying glance. "Don't you know that Christianity embraced reincarnation for three hundred years, until the Roman influence expunged it after the Emperor Constantine recognized the Church? What do you think the early Christians were thinking of when they asked Christ whether he was Elijah, who had come before? They were thinking of reincarnation, that's what."

Her mood changed suddenly, and she regarded me with a concerned air. "If you thought of reincarnation as rebirth, I think you could understand it better. Just as the earth has a constant rebirth so does the spirit. Don't you remember Christ saying that 'Unless man is reborn again, he cannot enter the Kingdom of Heaven'?"

"Wasn't that a reference to baptism?"

Eula threw up her hands. "Christ was not interested in show but substance, that is at the heart of everything he said or did."

It seemed time to get back to earth. "In one life," I said, "you lived in the good old U.S.A., and rather recently, which is quite a shift from all these glamorous lives in Persia, India, Palestine, Rome, Greece, Egypt, and Atlantis, lives with no possible way of being checked out."

"First of all," Eula said, "let's get things straight. As a soul develops, the chances are that development will be faster in advanced cultures, and since Cayce only dealt with meaningful past lives, he drew on lives in growth-making civilizations."

"So what did you learn in the Wild West?" I asked.

She snorted. "See for yourself." She pointed to a well-worn copy of the life reading spread out before us. "Back in the Gold Rush days, on the Barbary Coast, I was a dance hall girl, even a prostitute, I guess."

Cayce had put it quite picturesquely. "The entity was in the earth when there were those journeyings from the East to the West—Gold! In '49 the entity, with its companions, journeyed to the Western lands. Hardships were experienced on the way, yet the entity was among those associated in those acts with those in their relationships to such conditions—rowdiness, drink, spending. Yet the entity was one to whom many, many came for counsel."

As in her Irish life experience, Eula had a specific identity. "The name then was Etta Tetlow. Records of these may be found in some of the questioned places in portions of California, even in the present." Then came the provocative conclusion, "In activities, with all types of that early land did the entity have connection."

I had seen no specific reference to a dance hall experience, prostitution, or the Barbary Coast for that matter.

Eula smiled. "Well, that last remark would appear to speak for itself. What kind of woman deals with every kind of man?"

"How about Etta Tetlow—dance hall girl?"

Eula gave me a sly smile.

"Three years ago, in 1963, I was in California doing some lecturing on Cayce—Pacific Grove, I believe—when a woman sauntered up and said, 'Hello, Etta.' "

Eula winced. She had never been able to stand that name, Etta.

Somehow, in a book on reincarnation, Eula's incarnation as Etta Tetlow had been brought to the woman's attention. Browsing one day through colorful old posters, she found some dating back to the boisterous days of the Barbary Coast in San Francisco. The posters listed the entertainment at one of the local dance halls. One name stood out—Tetlow.

Eula did not take this incarnation lightly. Even before this report of an Etta Tetlow in California, she was concerned by the shadiness of her past-life past. Troubled, she sought out the waking Cayce. "If I was a prostitute," she said, "how could I ever hope to touch the hem of the Master's robe?"

It occurred to me that the Master, so generous to sinners, could hardly have minded. But Eula apparently thought he might.

Cayce received her gently. "Why so concerned? You know better now, don't you?" He pressed her hand. "Make it a steppingstone, instead of a stumbling block. We come back to learn."

Eula's main purpose in this life, Cayce had said, was to

build a family, and she looked proudly on her thirteen grand-children scattered around the country. One was top man in his Air Force group, another had won rare distinction scholastically as a naval architect, still another was a champion swimmer. The son with the pulsing heart had taken his heart through World War II. He, too, had been skeptical about reincarnation, and still might be, for all Eula knew. When he was twenty-two, before going off to war, his skepticism had driven him to a life reading. Cayce correctly forecast he would be a lawyer, but said his job in this life, because of his karmic past, was to prevent people from getting into trouble, not sitting in judgment on them. He had gone against this precept, becoming a county prosecutor in northern California, and then things had started to go wrong in his life.

Eula was a bit vague on what had gone wrong. "It's his life," she said, "and I don't like to get too personal with it."

"Didn't the public like him as prosecutor?" I asked.

"Oh, yes, they even wanted to put him up as judge."

"Then what went wrong and how did it relate to his becoming a prosecutor?" I looked at her rather curiously. "After all, somebody has to be a prosecutor, so it can't be all that wrong."

She laughed. "Yes, but somebody else may have reached a different point of advancement from past experiences."

At any rate, she had recalled the Cayce reading to her son while he was debating the judgeship. "You know," she said darkly, "you were told never to sit in judgment."

He looked thoughtful for a moment. "I know," he said.

"Then you know what to do."

He turned down the post.

And what had happened to his life since?

"Both personally and professionally it started to get back where it had been. He was now heeding the law, the Divine law, which Cayce had interpreted for him."

Just as she and Cayce shared the feeling they had known each other in the hazy past, Eula felt she had been acquainted with me. "I was in some sort of supervisory capacity with you then."

"You still are, at this point," I said.

She smiled. "Haven't you felt at ease, as though we've been through some experience together?"

As a matter of fact, I had been drawn to her instantly, but

put it down to the curious empathy we do seem to have for some people at sight.

"But what is that," she said, "but a vaguely remembered past?"

Again I saw no evidence. "Don't you think the life we live now is the one that counts, even if there is reincarnation?" I had chanced across a sentence in *Life is for Living* by Eric Butterworth: " 'The life you once lived can only be found in the life you now express.' "

"Naturally," Eula agreed, "but if there is a Cayce around to show you the twist in the road, that is all the better."

At first glimpse, reincarnation had seemed wishful thinking on the part of those shrinking from the apparent oblivion of death. Before the glory of the Resurrection, the concept of reincarnation was not a difficult turn in the spiritual road to everlasting life. My own faith in the moral lesson of Christ was implicit; yet, like others, I found myself shying from the implicit message of rebirth. Yet, had not St. John quoted Him, in a statement parenthetically absolving all on earth of guilt in the Crucifixion? "Therefore doth my Father love me, because I lay down my life, that I might take it again. No man taketh it from me, but I lay it down of myself. I have power to lay it down, and I have power to take it again. This commandment have I received of my Father."

He had power to take it up again. And what He did, others could do with the Father's help. Was that not the message of Christ—that, and a cry for universal love, mocked through the ages?

Had Edgar Cayce, as his readings suggested, trod the bitter road with the Master, absorbing a message that made his own gift possible, as all gifts were made possible, with God's acquiescence?

Was Cayce's unique gift, scorned as Another's had been scorned, a steppingstone in the ultimate revelation of what life was all about? Were the truths in his miraculous healing manifested to bring credence to the broader spiritual truth of purposeful life? Did Cayce's subconscious, merging with the Universal Consciousness that was the Father, Creator, and Creation, come along at a time when a troubled world, stifling in the limited horizons of materiality, was ready, even eager, for some sign of its place in a universal plan?

There was nothing accidental, nothing left to chance in the Creator's grand design; so Cayce believed as he pictured reincarnation as an instrument, not an end in itself. "Each and every individual," he said once, "follows out that line of development in the present earth plane as it has received from the preceding conditions, and each grain of thought or condition is a consequence of other conditions created by self."

It was difficult for me, as for others, to conceive of a spirit with a volition of its own. How did the spirit find its way to another body, where did it rest and restore itself, why did it keep coming back? "Must each soul continue to be reincarnated in the earth until it reaches perfection, or are some souls lost?" That was the puzzler put to Cayce.

Cayce had a ready answer. "The soul is not lost; the individuality of the soul that separates itself is lost. The reincarnation or the opportunities are continuous until the soul has of itself become an entity in its whole or has submerged itself."

"If a soul fails to improve itself, what becomes of it?"

"That's why the reincarnation, why it reincarnates; that it may have the opportunity. Can the will of man continue to defy its Maker?"

Constantly, Cayce minimized the ego, aware that many cultists mistakenly became enveloped in grandiose past lives at the expense of this one. Like Butterworth, he felt the past could only be expressed in the life lived now, otherwise no life became important.

"The real purpose, as should be for each soul, is the message of love of the Savior for the children of men. That phase of Christian experience [reincarnation] is questioned by many, yet there is this period when the fact needs stressing to answer many questions. But that this is to be the primary fact—reincarnation—no. That is merely the plan as He demonstrated."

Believing in Cayce—and reincarnation—Cayce's followers were constantly inquiring whether he would come back, in what guise and how soon. One corporate lawyer, who had made a fortune astutely following the Cayce readings dealing with real estate and finance, had tried to establish some arrangement whereby Cayce, on his slated return in another body, could profit through the clairvoyant gains he had achieved for the lawyer in this life. The slumbering Cayce seemed cool to collusion of this sort. Others queried Cayce about his next sojourn, after reading a newspaper article describing how a reincarnationist had attempted to leave his money to himself after death. The article revealed the utter frustration of the reincarnationist's plan, oddly reminiscent of a scene from the Broadway musical, *On a Clear Day You Can See Forever:* "Arthur M. Hanks, who made a fortune peddling flowers in the Los Angeles financial district, left no will because he believed he would return through reincarnation, and claim his life's savings. He has been dead seven months now, and today Judge Joseph P. Sproul opened the way for relatives to divide the flower peddler's $100,000 estate."

With this springboard, intimates of Cayce put the question to his Universal Consciousness: "You will give at this time information which will help us to understand the laws governing the selection by an entity of time, place, race, color, sex, and the parents at any rebirth into the earth plane, especially the possibility of Edgar Cayce, present in this room, bringing through in his next incarnation memory of this life." Then came the stickler. "If possible we would like to be advised as to how proof of such memory can be established by leaving a record or money now that may be called for during the next appearance."

Cayce examined each phase of the question. The times of reincarnation—or rebirth—varied, according to the development of the entity, and "as to the manner or the character of the removal from the material experience. As to race, color, or sex, this depends upon that experience necessary for the completion, for the building up of the purposes for which each and every soul manifests in the material experience. One incarnation naturally merges into another. 'As the tree falls, so does it lie,' saith the Maker and Giver of life. So does the light, so does the nature of an individual. For the beginning in the next experiences are ever tempered by how sincere the purpose was of the entity in the experience before. For indeed, as has been given, whatsoever ye sow, so shall ye reap."

Just as a leaf fell prematurely, so could human life be cut off. "They who have done error suddenly, they who are advanced, they who have not met a whole expression, may go suddenly, as you count time."

I was rather disappointed, as Cayce's following may have been, in his failure to program a future of his own. If he could see for others, why not for himself? "As for the entity Edgar Cayce," I read finally, "this depends then as to when

that experience has been reached in which the union of purposes of entities in materiality has created that expression,
that phase, to which the entity's development may reach to
find expression through same." As for the time of his return,
Cayce was vague. "It may be perhaps a hundred, two hundred, three hundred, a thousand years, as you may count
time in the present. For how gave He? The day no man
knoweth, only the Father in heaven knoweth, and it is provided you so live, as He gave, that 'I may sit upon the right
hand and my brother upon the left.'"

Ostensibly, the session had produced little of practicality. I
could almost sense the disappointment of Cayce's audience in
the next question. "Would you suggest any way that a record
may be left by an entity?"

Cayce got to the heart of the matter, playing on a word to
discard one point and make another. "By living the *record*,"
he stressed. For as one lived deeply, developing spiritually, so
he developed the faculty of remembering. "For when the purposes of an entity are the more in accord with that for which
the entity has entered, then the soul-entity may take hold
upon that which may bring to its remembrance what it was,
where, when, and how. Thinkest thou that the grain of corn
has forgotten what manner of expression it has given? Think
thou that any of the influences in nature that you see about
you—the acorn, the oak, the elm, or the vine, or anything—had forgotten what manner of expression? Only man
forgets."

And why just man?

"Only in His mercy such was brought about. As in Adam
they forgot what manner of men they were. For 'God's Book
of Remembrance' may be read only by those in the shadows
of his love."

As he did in the conscious, Cayce showed no interest subconsciously in the prospect of money in this life or another,
and coolly disregarded this as incentive to remembrance. "It
was almost," a witness said, "as though he were refusing to
participate in any little game of clairvoyance, as he had once
refused to submit to the tests of psychic researchers intent on
reducing his gift to their own meager measurements."

Cayce's own remembrance was remarkable. His references
to Atlantis, Lemuria and other lost civilizations could be dismissed as speculative, but other phenomena could not be so
easily scouted. He frequently lapsed into languages that were

clearly recognizable—French, Italian, Spanish, German, and others that were unrecognizable. These ventures into tongues he had no knowledge of in the waking state were triggered by the subject matter or subjects. Once he read for a man in Italy, who had deputized a friend here to sit in on the reading. The friend, of Italian extraction, asked a question, and the answer came back in fluent Italian. Another time, reading for a German, Cayce branched off into idiomatic German, bespeaking intimate knowledge of the Teutonic.

Cayce clearly had not responded to the satisfaction of his friends as to the nature of his next return. However, in a dream a short time before, he had visualized himself as being born again, and gave time and place. As happened so often in his life, a significant dream came during a great emotional crisis. He had been arrested in Detroit for "practising medicine without a license," and had been subjected to the ignominy of public trial as a charlatan. On the train back to Virginia Beach, he had one of his most singular dreams. He had been born again in A.D. 2100 in Nebraska. "The sea," he recalled, "apparently covered all of the western part of the country, as the city where I lived on was on the coast. The family name was a strange one. At an early age, as a child, I declared myself to be Edgar Cayce who had lived two hundred years before. Scientists, men with long beards, little hair and thick glasses, were called in to observe me. They decided to visit the places where I said I had been born, lived and worked, in Kentucky, Alabama, New York, Michigan, and Virginia. Taking me with them the group of scientists visited these places in a long, cigar-shaped metal flying ship which moved at high speed.

"Water covered part of Alabama; Norfolk had become an immense seaport. New York had been destroyed either by war or an earthquake and was being rebuilt. Industries were scattered over the countryside. Most of the houses were of glass. Many records of my work as Edgar Cayce were discovered and collected. The group returned to Nebraska taking the records with them to study."

There were other dream details. In one city, virtually completely destroyed, Cayce stopped to ask the workmen where he was. They looked at him in surprise, and to his surprise, replied, "New York."

From this dream many have fashioned a dreary prophecy of ultimate doom, pointing out that Cayce's prediction of gathering destruction from 1958 to 1998 implied that this was only the "beginning" of holocausts that were to continue indeterminately.

However, Cayce was not quite so pessimistic. Interpreting his own dream, he likened his period of personal trial to the tests that others would face, rocked with doubts of the ultimate purpose of the Creator. "And the vision was that there might be strength, there might be an understanding, though the moment may appear as dark, though there may be periods of misinterpreting of purposes." And there could well be, he indicated, challenging times for mankind. But in the end, was a promise given in the Bible. "Though the very heavens fall," Cayce paraphrased, "though the earth shall be changed, the promises in Him are sure and will stand—as in that coming day—as the proof of thy activity in the lives and hearts of thy fellow man."

Cayce himself, in the conscious state, found support for reincarnation in the Bible, though modern theology spurned it. "Reincarnation has so long been considered a part of the eastern religion," he said once, "that we have cause to consider it foreign to Christianity. However, I doubt if anyone who has really studied the Bible could say that it was not contained in that Book. Throughout the ages, the question has been asked, 'If a man die, will he live again?' "

The unschooled psychic, who loved to intersperse his Bible reading with homely poetry, observed, "One of the poets gave, 'Dust thou art, to dust returneth was not spoken of the soul.' It has been generally considered that if a man live again, it is his soul that lives." Cayce pointed out that the Bible was replete with references to rebirth. "There are many instances when the Master said, 'Ye must be born again.' " Again, He said to Nicodemus, "The wind bloweth where it listeth, and thou hearest the sound thereof, but cans't not tell whence it cometh, and whither it goeth. So is everyone that is born of the Spirit."

His own readings helped Cayce to understand much that he could not understand before. "We may read much in, or we may read much out, but did He mean what He said when He said to Nicodemus that 'Ye must be born again?' Did He mean it when He said to the Scribes and Pharisees, 'Before Abraham was, I am.' Did He mean it when He said that John the Baptist was the incarnation spiritually of Elias? He said so."

Cayce turned to where the disciples asked Jesus, "Who did sin, this man or his parents, that he was born blind?" And Jesus answered, 'Neither hath this man sinned, nor his parents; but that the works of God should be made manifest in him.'"

To Cayce, this clearly reflected a prevailing belief in reincarnation. "Now it wouldn't have been possible for the man to have sinned in this world, as we know the world, just in being born blind. They must have believed that the man lived before, else they wouldn't have asked such a question." Another time, as Cayce recalled, as they came down from the Mount, Peter and John asked the Master, "Why then say the scribes that Elias must come first?" And Jesus answered, "Elias is come already, and they knew him not, but have done unto him whatsoever they listed. Likewise shall also the Son of Man suffer of them." Then the disciples understood that He spake unto them of John the Baptist.

Again, as Cayce quoted, "For all the prophets and the law prophesied until John. And if ye will receive it, this is Elias, which was for to come."

Cayce turned to Paul. "'The first Adam brought sin into the world, but the last Adam brought life.'" He did not push his own interpretation. "Whether that's figuratively speaking or not, is for us to determine within our own experience."

Even after his first life readings, Cayce did not immediately accept reincarnation; he considered it alien to Christianity. "I was taught the Christian way of thinking, that a man only has one life, and as a man dieth so is he."

But as he began to look at the Bible with new eyes, so did he look around him, and into himself. "Always there was within me a feeling that did not find answer in what was ordinarily given as the answer for such feelings. How is it that some people we meet we immediately feel as if we had known all our lives, and others we have known for years in this life and still do not feel close to them or understand them? I don't believe anyone can answer that unless there is more than just this life. Nothing lives again unless it dies, even the grain of wheat in bringing forth that which will propagate its own self."

His own readings often proved out reincarnation for Cayce. In one reading, he told a woman that she had lived ten thousand years ago in what is now New Mexico, and had made certain hieroglyphics still to be found in that location.

"Later," Cayce said, "the woman wrote me that she had gone there with friends, and had found the marks just as indicated." Cayce had never been to New Mexico and neither had she—in this life. "When she saw those indications, something answered within her so that she knew she had lived there and had made those marks."

Just as some felt they had known one another before, so did the pattern of relationships in this life often reflect a previous association. "If the information [in the reading] tells us that we were associated with certain individuals during certain periods in the earth's plane, and we see in the present an exact replica of the description of former associations, we are bound to see the consistency of it."

At a church forum, Cayce once submitted to questioning on reincarnation. "Do you think," someone asked, "that when a soul enters the earth plane it knows what sort of environment it is coming into, and the conditions it will have to face?"

Cayce drew on his subconscious knowledge. "It must know that it is entering the environment which is necessary for its own development. It knows that this is its opportunity to pass through that experience necessary for this development."

Weren't these past-life readings keyed more to the ego than anything else?

It was something Cayce had thought often about. "We hear the question, 'What good will it do me to know that I lived as John Smith during the Revolution, or was a first settler, or that I was among those in the French Revolution, or a wine seller in such and such a period?' Well, our soul, our entity is what it is today from how it has reacted to various experiences in the earth's sphere."

"How does the spirit find the body?" another asked.

"I do not believe that a soul enters until the breath of life is drawn. The soul doesn't enter at conception."

For reincarnationists, the following colloquy was enlightening:

"Is the soul sent here, or does it come of its own desire?"

"Comes of its own desire," Cayce said, "for desire remains throughout all development of man, or of the soul, whether we speak of material, mental, or the soul portion. Desire goes right through, and is possibly the motive force behind the soul, for without a desire to do a thing we can't get very far."

"If the soul knows so much, why does it have to do all these things over again?"

"It's very much like we have in a school. We go over and over a lesson in mathematics until we know not only that it is rote, but that we can get an answer by doing that. We have to know the principle of the thing, or the basis of it. Man goes over and over his lessons, and necessarily under such different environment that it builds that which is lacking, that has kept it from understanding its relationship to its Maker."

"Do you believe that every human being has a soul?"

Cayce then advanced a unique concept of man's relationship with God. "I believe that every human being has a soul, that which makes it akin to the Creator, that which is given an individual that he may become a companion to the Creator. As we see in the forces all about us, Nature herself desires companionship. So does God. He gives us the opportunity to be his companion, by giving us a soul, which we may make a companion with Him, but we have to do the making."

Chapter Fifteen

THE CAYCE BABIES

The pretty blonde was browsing through the Book Room occasionally picking up a volume and thumbing its pages. She was pretty and supple enough to be in the chorus line of a Broadway show, and she had a demure, yet sensuous way of moving, showing her trim tailored slacks to advantage.

The A. R. E. receptionist caught my look of enquiry.

"She is a Cayce baby," she said, "Rae Denny Horton."

The girl looked over and smiled.

"Cayce baby?"

"Yes, she had a reading from Edgar Cayce when she was a child."

The girl's smile broadened. "Two readings," she said, "the first when I was two years old."

"Did you toddle in for it?" I asked.

Her good-natured smile seemed part of her personality. "I wasn't even there. My mother sent in for it. She believed in Edgar Cayce because he had helped her healthwise, when the doctors had failed, and so she got life readings for both myself and my sister."

"You believe then in reincarnation?" I asked.

The girl looked surprised. "Of course," she said, "it explains practically everything that has happened to me, as Edgar Cayce made so clear." When she was two, he had said she would have a talent for dancing, music, the theatre. She had turned to ballet when she was three years old, before she could possibly know about the readings, and, discounting maternal influence, had gone on to win a dance scholarship in her hometown of Norfolk, enabling her to study in New York. Her mother's suggestive force hardly gave the daughter her flair.

At twelve, her dancing won unusual recognition. After classes at a New York ballet school, she was recommended for a professional start in New York. Her family explained that she was only twelve. "We thought she was older," was the disappointed rejoinder. "There would be too much red-tape with child authorities unless she was fourteen."

How had Cayce picked out her special dancing ability?

Mrs. Horton plucked her readings out of a library file. Her eye ran down a mimeographed page. "The inclination to ever be the actress at all times will necessitate judgments as to the training of the activities, especially in the vocal direction as well as in the ability to dance."

She had not studied any musical instrument, and only after marriage had she sought voice training. She was divorced now, with three children, and thought she might sing professionally. She was still young enough, in her late twenties, to pursue a career, vocally, since she did have professional experience, having studied at the Pasadena (California) Playhouse and worked at a big club in Brooklyn.

Scanning the readings, a sentence caught my eye. "After the twelfth to the fourteenth year, she will take care of all the rest of the family, if needs be."

Had Rae taken the job at fourteen?

She shook her head. "Odd, that sentence never struck me before." Her family had been well off, and there had been no need to work, though a job, rejected at twelve, was available at fourteen.

How much had she been influenced by the readings?

"I never thought of them until recently, yet looking back, I see how the whole pattern of my life, including my marriage, was anticipated."

"Personality has a lot to do with shaping our lives," I said, recalling the Greek axiom that character is fate.

She smiled. "Edgar Cayce certainly caught my personality." My eye turned back to the reading. "A very demure, meek entity; and then one almost *wild* at times in its determination for its own way." The stress on *wild* had been underlined in Cayce's voice even in trance.

I appraised the slim, cool-looking figure, with the sunny face. "True?"

She nodded. "I'm afraid so, at times."

Her finger picked out a paragraph in the life record. "As to the appearances in the earth, as indicated even from the temperamental abilities of the entity, *many* have been the appearances. These that are given here, though, are those indicating the greater urge in the early development of this entity in the present sojourn."

She looked over at me. "Do you know what that means?"

I shrugged noncommittally.

As her life developed, Rae felt somewhat confused as a teen-ager. She was a pretty girl, and quite comfortable about being a girl, she thought, but the feeling came over her at times that she would be much happier as a boy.

Was this the "greater urge" mentioned by Cayce? It seemed hardly likely. I regarded her lithe, sinuous figure with detached appreciation. "You make a strange-looking boy," I said.

"I seem to have a lot of masculine traits. I was less emotional than my husband, for instance, and I realize now that I resented his trying to run things."

"That's the new breed woman—aggressive, dominant, omniscient."

"I also have a practical masculine turn of mind. In school, I just didn't learn anything, even a geometrical problem, by rote. I had to know why."

And what had all this to do with reincarnation?

"There," she said, picking out a well-thumbed passage in her reading, "there, I was a Frenchman in that incarnation, and entertained the king and his court." In that life, I read, her name was Cheveaux, and she was a man, of course.

That was one of the things that intrigued me: the way the entities kept changing sex. Conceivably, it could lead to homosexuality, if there was a karmic overload from the opposite sex. However, that was obviously not Rae Horton's problem. But Cayce did say something about masculine influence. "And in the present life those experiences and expressions will be seen as a part of the entity's development, in that masculine thought will be a manifestation in the early portion of its experiences, the desire to know the whys of life."

I looked over at Rae. "You saw this reading by the time you were eight, and you've read it a hundred times."

"You will notice," she said determinedly, "that I had a Greek life, and was a singer and dancer in that experience." Because of this experience, Cayce had noted, "And through the present life, in the early portion, the entity will find the desire for the activities which keep the body in perfect form and activity."

From the looks of her, Rae hadn't passed out of the "early portion" yet.

"I've always loved to drape myself in flowing Grecian costumes, just as I love French perfume."

"That's a common failing," I said.

"Perhaps because these are common backgrounds."

But Atlantis was her major preoccupation. "I feel a strong affinity for Atlantis at all times. I've read about everything I can on it, both in the Cayce readings and in articles and books."

"I suppose," I said rather drily, "that you had an Atlantis experience, too."

No, but her ancestors came from there. "The entity was in the Egyptian land, of the Atlanteans and the extremists," Cayce said. "Yet in those periods of perfecting the body for special service, the entity—among associates and companions even in the present—aided many in bringing greater interpretations of body and mind as related to the spiritual aspects of life. The name then was Is-So-El."

"Well, Is-So-El," I said, "what do you think that meant, 'associates and companions even in the present'?"

Is-So-El laughed. "Haven't you felt an immediate rapport with some people, as though you had special reason for feeling close, or just the opposite, for that matter, raising the hackles on your neck?"

"I always blamed an overactive thyroid."

"The fact remains," she smiled, "that Cayce was right about practically everything else about me."

She had a health reading at the age of five. She was pale and sickly, and her hair was falling out. Cayce prescribed Calcios, a substance taken with bread or crackers, and in a couple of weeks the girl's hair had started coming back. She certainly had no problem now, the blond tresses falling thickly over her shoulders.

She regarded me pleasantly. "Cayce was so right about my

health. So why would he be right about one thing, and not the other, since it was all from the same unknown source?"

I could only shrug. "Perhaps Cayce was infallible only when the motivation was right, when people needed help desperately, and couldn't get it elsewhere."

"But the life readings were as helpful as the physical, in underlining people's personality weaknesses, and setting up guides for future behavior."

"These life readings are downright suggestive. They could have made a dancer out of almost anybody, or a girl who always had to know why."

As she flipped the pages of the readings, her eye fell on a follow-up in the back. She had never seen it before. It had just been taken out of the A. R. E. research file. When she was ten, a dancing teacher had reported she was the only one in the dancing school to do acrobatic work on her toes. At the same time she had won a prize for her dancing on a television show, and at eleven, just after her scholarship award, a teacher observed, "It is very seldom that a good ballet dancer can also be a good acrobat."

Rae finished the report with a smile. "I wonder if dancing in ancient Greece was more fun than Brooklyn," she said. "It couldn't have been any worse."

Rae Denny Horton's reading had not appeared to chart her life with any great detail. Still, other readings told subjects they would become architects, tailors, and doctors, because of influences carried over from past lives, and they had become architects, tailors, and doctors. The architect had been a builder, a carpenter, an architect in previous incarnations, according to Cayce, and the aptitudes had been brought over into this one as a sidelight; the main purpose of course always being development. Cayce had said that the best way of getting to heaven was on the arm of somebody you were helping.

It was intriguing to consider the possibility that people were mechanically inclined, writers, musicians, healers, as they subconsciously remembered what they knew of these fields. In doing something perhaps subconsciously familiar, they often touched off a chord stirring around uneasily in the back of their consciousness. The World War II soldier, stopping off in Bavaria, suddenly saw himself a Crusader in the very spot he was now enjoying a beer, remembering with a start that Cayce had once put him in the Crusades.

It was certainly a complex pattern, however you looked at it, for it visualized a broad master plan that embraced each and every body and mind in the universe, each with its own little niche. Only God in his omnipotence could handle such a program. Yet, as even the atheistic Einstein recognized, there was a definite order in the world, call it what you will, and man, like the rest of nature—the planets, comets, the seasons—had a place in this order. Life was orderly, even if man's life wasn't. As the Hindus had noted, life sometimes seemed like a tree. Buds died, prematurely whisked away by the wind or rain, before they could leaf. Others became leaves, and fell off at varying stages. Still others lived through their season, then inevitably dropped off, as the experience ended—only to begin again in the spring, the same tree having different leaves, with perhaps different impulses, and all again inevitably dying.

Still, what did trees have to do with people, except to form a provocative analogy? How was it that Mozart at five produced the music of mature genius; or Josef Hoffman played the piano at two and a half? Commenting on child prodigies, the talented Alan Jay Lerner, author of *Brigadoon, My Fair Lady, Camelot,* expressed the view these prodigies must have surely lived before to have been so gifted. "They remembered through the subconscious," he felt, "the source of all inspiration."

My attention was drawn to a newspaper article describing a six-year-old Turkish boy whose paintings had been the rage of European art galleries for four years. "Bedri [Baykam] started painting when he was only two years old," the *Christian Science Monitor* reported. "He has turned out more than one thousand water colors and over five thousand drawings, but he has never had a painting lesson in his life."

And what did Bedri paint? Turkish scenes, Saracen, pastels of the Middle East and the Holy Land? Bedri, untraveled and unlettered, unable to read or write, daubed his colors into delightful representations of the American Wild West. "One of Bedri's favorite subjects," the article went on, "is cowboys. In a sequence of a few sketches, which have tremendous movement, he is able to tell a whole story."

It would have been interesting to have known what an Edgar Cayce would have said about Bedri. For another, Cayce had said once, "There is the natural interest toward things of the artistic nature and temperament. There are the abilities to use the voice, as well as playing almost any musical instrument."

The subject, growing up, had displayed ability, but had not done very much with it, though in a previous life, said Cayce, he had been a better than middling composer named Franz Liszt.

Success didn't necessarily follow; musical progress was subordinated to the broader need of learning humility and service. It was a most comforting concept, reincarnation.

Very few who received a Cayce life reading ever argued with the aptitudes he saw as part of the personality pattern, but not all accepted the underlying concept. One housewife told Cayce after a life reading for her husband, "Most of the things you said about my husband I know to be true, character, abilities, and practically everything about his physical condition as we know it, but I have wondered what the catch is, and I find it, reincarnation!"

There were many "Cayce babies," and it was interesting to follow-up some, in view of Cayce's prognoses. I sat across the luncheon table one day from a young man who had a life reading when he was but four hours old. Just after birth, the suggestion was planted with the sleeping mystic: "You will give the relation of this entity and the universe, and the universal forces, giving the conditions which are as personalities, latent and exhibited in the present life; also the former appearances in the earth plane, giving time, place and the name, and that in each life which built or retarded the development for the entity; giving the abilities of the present entity, that to which it may attain, and how."

That was twenty-three years ago, and the parents had carefully kept the reading from the boy, so that it would not influence him. It was not until his sophomore year in college that he had taken a look at it. He was now taking graduate work in a Western university, and planning to be a physician. He was a young man of even disposition, but obvious determination. He came from a family of moderate circumstances, but had already showed a remarkable facility for making money in the stock market, through using information gained by chance or from friends. He was in more than a dozen stocks, was constantly buying and selling through two brokerage houses, and had established credit with a couple of banks. Some of his stocks had multiplied a dozenfold. As a sidelight, too, he kept a patch of land near his college, which he worked as a garden. In all, he appeared to be an unusually productive, versatile young man. I would have said offhand that he was bound to succeed.

Still, what could Cayce have said of an infant but four hours old? Together, the young man and I went through his reading. "A very determined individual," Cayce had said, "yet not high-tempered, but having his way."

That had been my impression.

"In the experience before this," the reading continued, "a farmer, a wide-awake, high-minded individual."

The young man smiled. "I found that odd, because originally I wanted to be a farmer before I wanted to be a doctor, and used to love working on my uncle's farm, not to mention the little farming I do now."

It was just as well that he switched, for Cayce had put it firmly, "In this experience the entity should be a doctor, and should, and will be, a very betraveled individual." He envisioned an "unusual career" as a doctor.

The youth had made up his mind to be a doctor, before he knew about the reading; he had already been to Europe. Cayce was checking out.

"He will be an observer of little things," Cayce had said. "He will be wealthy, which will come from listening, taking advantage of the opportunities." As a boy of thirteen, with a newspaper route, he had overheard one of his customers on the telephone telling a friend to buy into the stock of a fertilizer firm. It sounded good to him and he received permission from his father to put $250 of his savings into the company. In a few years, this investment was worth more than three thousand dollars, and the boy's aggregate stock holdings added up to more than ten thousand dollars, after paying his own way through four years of college.

I was sure he would be wealthy, if that was what he wanted.

"Teaching also is indicated in the experience. Thus the unusual opportunity of education, by travel as well as by that of association and of pedagogy." He was already teaching, while working for his doctorate in psychology, and had received a full scholarship, financing study for both his Master's Degree, which he had already obtained, and the doctorate.

Here was a prediction not yet subject to validation, since only time would tell: "Entering at this particular period (born October 1942), there will be in the affairs of the earth those activities similar to those as the King of Sweden, in keeping peace in the earth."

I asked the young man if he knew what this meant. He shrugged pleasantly, maintaining the "even-temper" of the reading. "It's very flattering," he said modestly, "but I will have to wait and see, I guess."

I couldn't remember what the King of Sweden had been like, but as a perennial neutral he had quietly interested himself in discussions aimed at ending the conflict raging in 1942.

There was more. "The entity will be one of strong body, and should be allowed to engage in all characters of sports, not as an activity for pay but as developing of body, of mind."

The young man smiled. He had been too busy to participate much in sports, but had been on the college wrestling squad. "I've never been in a hospital," he said quietly, "never had a real illness in my life."

I looked down the page. "Beware of activities that have to do with the digestion, and the throat. These are weaknesses in the karmic forces influencing this body."

He seemed to be enjoying his lunch, and his throat was clear. "It may yet happen," I said.

He gave his even-tempered smile. "I'll just have to watch for that."

There was a word for the parents who had requested the reading. "Educate, put then in the way of the entity those things that may have to do with every form of those activities, spiritual, mental, and material, that may be helpful in bringing to those in the material plane the consciousness of health-giving force in the experience of those that suffer."

Had the parents thrown subtle suggestions of a career his way in the green formative years? "They never did advise me, one way or the other," he said, "and I understand it now; they wanted to see how it would turn out."

There was little of counsel in the reading except, born under Libra [October] he was told when choosing a companion, presumably a wife, to pick one born in January or October. He had not yet been confronted by a decision, and being a rather level-headed young man didn't go around asking girls their birthdays.

There was one last word of advice. "Beware of politics for this entity: though there will be opportunities for same."

The young man shrugged and looked away. "I'm not sure I know what that means."

He had a number of previous lives, one in his own family, another as a physician at the time of Christ, again as a farmer. Lives in Sweden, China, Egypt, had given meaningful experiences.

And that was it.

The young man smiled evenly. "The reading seems to have worked out well, as far as analyzing my life goes, but I haven't made up my mind on reincarnation. It's almost too pat a way of explaining everything we don't understand. The need is there, and the concept supports it."

"You haven't been influenced then by previous incarnations as a doctor and farmer?"

"I just don't know. Some day, the message may come as it did to my father. But I'll have to find out for myself."

"Then how did Cayce pinpoint your strong and weak points?"

He frowned. "That I don't know, either, except that clairvoyantly, he may have been able to look into the future."

We shook hands, and I knew, without a Cayce, that here was a young man destined for success. He had an inner calm and resolve beyond his years.

The next day, the father called. "How did it go?" he asked.

"You know," I said, "he doesn't believe in reincarnation."

"We've never imposed our beliefs on him. He's a most determined young man." He laughed. "When he was a boy, eleven or twelve, another boy his age borrowed his bicycle without permission, bringing it back without the chain. I happened to look out the window, and saw him standing over the boy, with the chain in his hand, forcing him through sheer will to put it back. He never got flustered or upset, but the other boy obeyed without a word."

I recalled the boy hesitating over the warning on political activity.

The father chuckled. "I don't blame him," he said. "You know, he was always politicking in school. In high school, he was elected president of the student body, campaigning all over town, and it stirred a certain amount of criticism. In college, he was president of his class, but his campaigning again stirred opposition, and even friends ganged up on him. He was a disillusioned young man before it was over, brooding over the frailty of human friendship. He's never run for any student office since."

But what had it to do with reincarnation?

"There is some aptitude remembrance, in his flair for farming, in his ambition to be a doctor, and in other qualities from the past; the ability to listen and evaluate, have certainly stood him in good stead. He's been self-supporting since he was a teen-ager."

It still seemed nebulous grounds for reincarnation.

"In one of the previous lives mentioned by Cayce," the father said, "as a four-year-old boy he saw his grandfather killed by a horse. The horse caught his foot and fell, and the rider, tossing the boy to safety, was crushed under the animal. It was an unforgettable experience."

He had been born again to the same family, apparently permissible in reincarnation. And there was remembrance, remembrance that he consciously knew nothing about. "When my boy was four, we had been out for a walk, when we saw a horse rear up with a girl on it. There was nothing to get alarmed about, but my son, normally stolid, stood trembling, his whole body in a sweat, as though having a nightmare. The horse soon quieted, but the boy kept staring, rigid with fear. Then taking hold of himself, he advanced determinedly and put his hand on the horse's forehead, stroking the animal as though he was trying to overcome his obsession." The father had never seen fear in the youngster before or since. "There is no doubt in my mind that the old memory came surging in, and then he determinedly tried to rid himself of his fear."

Granted reincarnation, signs were apparently all an independent researcher could hope to find, unless he had a pipeline to Universal Knowledge. Remembrance was one of these signs, of course, but again a Cayce was needed. A young woman, morbidly fascinated by circuses, left in a panic every time they trundled out the lions and tigers in their steel-barred cages. Without knowing of this idiosyncrasy, the sleeping Cayce told her that she had been a Christian in an earlier life in Rome, and had been fed to the lions. No wonder she was scared. For another girl born lame, just as the Biblical child was born blind, Cayce explained that during the reign of Nero she often sat and laughed in the Col-

osseum, as the Christian martyrs were killed or maimed by the
wild beasts. I read elsewhere in Cayce of people who had used
the sword cruelly in one life being plagued in this by unexplained fear of all cutting instruments, including an inoffen-
sive bread knife. And I recalled Eula Allen saying that the
millions who had perished in war must have killed others in
earlier wars. From Revelation, I suddenly remembered: "He
that leadeth into captivity shall go into captivity: he that kill-
eth with the sword must be killed with the sword." I had always considered this in the framework of one life, but it certainly didn't work out that way; wickedness so often went unnoticed, even rewarded. It was that kind of a world.

But karma, the reincarnationist's debit and credit ledger,
changed all this. It was the load we carried from one life into
another. "Karma," said Cayce, "is the lack of living to that
which ye know ye should do. As ye would be forgiven, so
forgive in others. That is the manner to meet karma." A positive attitude could also help. For a woman lamed by
rheumatic fever in childhood: "The attitudes that have been
held by the body have been and are helpful, yet these conditions being karmic, must be met by the body, in adding to
the being and the soul of the body, patience, kindness, brotherly love, long-suffering, and the like."

Again, even with the opportunity to work off karma, it
seemed a paradox that a merciful God should subject his
creatures to an apparently endless cycle of punishment. "We
are taught to turn the other cheek and forgive," I told one
reincarnationist, "and this in God's name. Am I to assume
that we have learned this lesson better than our Maker?"

The reincarnationist smiled. "If you don't accept reincarnation, does injustice and bloodshed then disappear? At least,
with reincarnation, there is a purpose, an aim, a hope for
development. The life snuffed out today has a chance in the
endless tomorrow." He eyed me rather sardonically. "It seems
to me that the Maker who gives his creatures another chance
is more merciful than one who lets the world spin around
like a top."

With it all, I neither accepted nor rejected reincarnation.
Thinking of all the inexplicable phenomena I had witnessed
over the years, of people somehow predicting the future, of
clairvoyance, of telepathy, it would have been absurd to have
closed myself off through either the inadequacy of my understanding or of the evidence. I didn't understand how

electricity worked, nor did anybody, and yet it worked. The Cayce readings could hardly be taken as proof of reincarnation, since they were valueless as evidence, unless they could be proved out with something tangible. For instance, Cayce had advised a young man of twenty-three, obsessed with wanderlust, that this expression was a carryover from a previous life in Peru, before the Incas. "In that land now known as Peru, the entity was then among those that ruled in the land and was subjugated by the Incas that took possession of the land from those that ruled." There was a little more, tracing the wandering spirit. "The entity lost through this experience, for in that of bringing the wreck of the peoples from the desire to rule brought destructive forces to others and to self. In the urge seen from this experience, the entity finds that self becomes wandering in body, mind, and in desire." In other words, he was a sort of Ulysses. That was all very nice, but when Cayce predated the Incan civilization he was again off in a subconscious dream world of his own. "How," I asked Gladys Davis, who was busily inventorying the Cayce readings, "how can anything so esoteric as reincarnation be indicated out of anything so apocryphal as a civilization we have not even an indication of?"

Edgar Cayce's secretary, rummaging on her desk, came up with a copy of *Science News* for April 9, 1966, billed as The Weekly Summary of Current Science. On the front cover were two shadowy figures, captioned "Undersea Pillars." I turned curiously to the article, as Gladys said casually, "There's something there about the Incas that might be pertinent."

The article dealt with information that seemed right out of a Cayce reading: "Strange carved rock columns, shown on this week's front cover, some with writing on them, have been sighted by cameras six thousand feet under the sea off the coast of Peru. (Photo credit: Duke University)

"This unknown Atlantis of the Pacific lies too deep for exploration from a surface ship, said Dr. Robert J. Menzies, director of ocean research at the Duke University Marine Laboratory, Beaufort, North Carolina. A mobile deep-diving vehicle is needed for precise observation. Two upright columns, about two feet or more in diameter, were sighted extending five feet out of the mud. Two more had fallen down and were partially buried, and another angular squarish block was seen, said Dr. Menzies. The pieces were sighted from a

surface ship carrying apparatus for lowering cameras to within a few feet of the ocean floor. The oceanographic cruise of
the research vessel *Anton Brunn* lasted for six weeks off the
coasts of Peru and Ecuador in the waters of the Milne-
Edward Deep, a deep trench that drops off to almost 19,000
feet in places. The cruise was sponsored by the National Science Foundation."

There was more, indicating that just as Cayce had said,
there may have been a counterpart of Atlantis named Lemuria in the Pacific. "The sunken columns," the article continued, "are located about fifty-five miles off the city of Cal-
lao, the port of Lima, capital of Peru. This is near the Ring
of Fire, the zone of earthquakes and active volcanoes that
encircles the Pacific Ocean. The area had once been covered
by at least six hundred feet less of seawater, about eleven
thousand years ago at the time of the great glaciers of the Ice
Age, said Dr. Menzies. The area is now slowly sinking."

So Lemuria, or whatever, was still subsiding. The
oceanographer had come across the mysterious sea pillars accidentally, while foraging around for specimens of a small
mollusk. His expedition had found sixty thousand specimens
of sea animals and taken a thousand underwater photographs
before it stumbled across the sunken ruins. "We did not find
structures like these anywhere else," he reported. "I have
never seen anything like this before."

But what of our friend who had lived before the Incas in
Peru? Near the pillars there had been other discoveries. "Old
Inca ruins have been found around that area, and civilizations predating the Incas by many years are now believed
to have existed nearby." That was not Cayce, but the *Science
News*. And still, this reference to a pre-Incan civilization was
but a sign. Yet perhaps, this was all that was needed. For was
it not written in the Book, in Job, clearly the story of mankind and its tribulations, was it not said: "For we are but of
yesterday, and know nothing, because our days upon earth
are a shadow."

Chapter Sixteen

THE RECKONING

Edgar Cayce gave his last reading on September 17, 1944, and it was for himself. He was tired, frazzled, worn out. As Gladys Davis said, there was no place to put another patch. His own readings had repeatedly warned that if he "read" more than twice a day, he would disintegrate. But with the war on, and thousands appealing for help, he could not resist doing as much as time—and his waning strength—would allow. In the months before his death, thousands of requests for readings had piled up, arriving at the rate of fifteen hundred a day. People were concerned not only for their own health but for the welfare of loved ones in the far corners of the earth. Cayce's own two sons—Hugh Lynn and Edgar Evans—were on the battlefronts, and the compassionate Cayce could not turn from anybody. As his fame spread through books and articles, he undertook seven or eight readings a day, but, even so, the most desperate appeals had to take their place, and this generally meant a five or six month delay. Often the sick worsened and died before Cayce could get to them, and this knowledge, as well as the work, wore on him. He felt weak and inadequate. Working around the clock, he couldn't catch up with his backlog in three or four years. As he helplessly looked at the huge mailbag, crammed every day with fresh appeals, he would lie down with a sigh, and pray that something would come through. In time, the man who seemed to know everything when asleep, could no longer go to sleep. His weary body and mind would no longer respond to his suggestion, and so he had to put the readings away for a while, and hope for a renewal of strength. Just before his last reading, he visited biographer Tom Sugrue at Clearwater Beach in Florida, which the readings had picked out as ideal for convalescence. Sugrue had asked for help on an article on the human aura, and Cayce, though his own aura was dimming rapidly, could not refuse. He also hoped that he would rest up enough to get on with the work. "He had no more power to refuse me anything," Sugrue commented later, "than he had to refuse anyone else."

As it turned out, he was too restless to relax, even with Sugrue, whom he loved. He had taken his correspondence with him, responding with counsels of patience and good cheer, compensating in this way for not giving the readings. It struck Sugrue that Cayce was hastening his own end. "I suggested that he spend his time fishing and gardening, except for when the readings were given, but in the letters he received were stories of misfortune and suffering. Each was a cry for help, and had it gone unanswered, he would have heard it among his flowers or on the pier, fishing. His heart was heavy and his mind numb with the burden of his helplessness. Though at first, he stayed asleep longer than ever, pushing himself, he could not even dent the pile of requests. It was this more than anything that broke him."

The night before he said goodbye to Sugrue, he had a dream that was manifestly prophetic. "I was on a train going to Florida," he told the writer. "I had retired, and I was going to live there." Only the evening before, looking out at the sea, he had remarked what a beautiful place it would be to rest. But as both Cayce and Sugrue knew, only death could retire the man who had said in sleep: "Mind is the builder. Knowledge not lived becomes sin."

Even without the last reading, he knew what the answer was. The end was near, but he felt only regret that this life experience was to be interrupted when he was needed so badly. He called on his friend, Dr. Woodhouse, in Virginia Beach, and the doctor said, "You know as well as I what is wrong with you." He was clearly disintegrating, as that reading had warned.

Mrs. Cayce had framed the questions for that final reading. "How can the body best free himself of worry and anxiety concerning the office routine?"

"Get out of the office," came Cayce's reply.

In the hills near Roanoke, Virginia, there was a nursing home where the readings sometimes sent patients. "This would be preferable to anyplace where there would be anxieties from others outside. Commence soon." "How long should I stay?" the next question was put.

The answer was to the point. "Until you are well or dead."

Like more orthodox therapists, he had never followed his own advice, and it was rather late in the day to begin. But restless, at home, with each day's bag of mail staring at him accusingly, he went to Roanoke anyway. He now neither could sleep to read by, nor to rest. The vital energies were slipping away. In April of 1926, nearly twenty years before, he had had a dream which symbolized the way he would die. In this dream, he visualized himself immersed in a tub of hot water, and scalding to death. He interpreted this dream in a subsequent reading. In resisting physical pain one day, his body would become protectively immersed in water, and death would follow. When he died, the cause was diagnosed as pulmonary edema. Two weeks before the end, a physician had warned, "The danger lies in his strangling to death."

In late November, as thin as a wraith, but still wearing a smile, he returned home to spend his last days, looking across the lake where he had fished so often. On New Year's Day, 1945, he told visitors cheerfully, "It is all arranged. I am to be healed on Friday, the fifth of January." His friends understood what he meant, when they arrived on Friday for his funeral. He would be elsewhere, wherever this healing would occur. The night before his death, as his wife reached across to kiss him goodnight, the man, whose gift had always been his obsession, looked at her reflectively, and said with tenderness, "You know I love you, don't you?"

A lump came to the throat of the woman who had made him her whole world through forty years of marriage. She nodded silently, unable to trust her voice.

He smiled gently. "How do you know?"

"Oh, I just know," she managed.

"I don't see how you can tell—but I do." His mind traveled down the years when his work had been the consuming passion of his life. "You know," he said, "when you love someone you sacrifice for them, and what have I ever sacrificed because I love you?"

She hushed him as though he were a child, closed his eyes,

and, kissing him lightly, stole from the room. He died the next night, January 3. He was sixty-seven.

Gertrude began to fade rapidly. She told her friend, Lydia J. Schrader Gray, that she felt as though one of her vital organs had been bodily removed. She had two sons at war to live for, but she felt that Cayce was gently pulling her to his side. Three months after Cayce's death, on April 1, 1945, on a beautiful Easter Sunday morning, Gertrude Evans Cayce followed her husband hopefully beyond the divide. The Cayce family lived, as it believed. On March 30, the day before his mother's death, Hugh Lynn had written from his Army post in Germany: "It makes me deeply happy to know how ready you are to pass through that other door. There is so much beauty in your living, that I cannot be sad at the possibility of your joining Dad. You held up his right hand—sometimes both hands—here, so it does not surprise me that he may need you now." And the son designated to spread the Work showed his readiness for the task. "We have come, Mother," he saluted, "to an understanding of karma in a way that we have for a long time been explaining to others, and I find that your life represents so much that is fine and beautiful that I cannot allow my selfish desires to mar this period of waiting and wondering. My prayers are that you will not suffer. I know that you must realize how much love has been, is, and always will be yours."

In death, there has been no deification of Edgar Cayce at Virginia Beach. Long before Stalin's successors, Cayce had de-emphasized the cult of the personality. The supreme law was: "Thou must love the Lord thy God with all thy strength, and love thy neighbor as thyself." But the A. R. E., Cayce's Association for Research and Enlightenment, is still run by a voice from the dead—Cayce's. More than forty years ago, when there was no widespread acknowledgment of extrasensory perception in any form, the sleeping Cayce plotted the growth of the Work. "For such work must of necessity first appeal to the individual and through individuals, groups, classes and then the masses, as it gains credence necessary for recognition by the general public."

Just as Cayce foresaw, the A. R. E.'s work after his death began with an inventorying of his readings, branched out to a library offering help to researchers. "The institution," Cayce blueprinted, "should be built around a place where the records of that accomplished through these sources [Cayce's clairvoyance] are kept." The chief aim, he stressed, was not the revelation of psychic phenomena, but of "better understanding of the purpose of life." He was most specific. "First, put the information in an orderly manner, so that any phase of human experience may be had from that already given." In suggesting how the Information should be siphoned to the outside world, he mentioned a number of persons who should one day be received. On three occasions, I noted with interest, my own surname cropped up. "Choose from among those," Cayce directed, "that are gifted in the putting together of data so obtained into scientific matters, in those of story, verse or fiction, and let the same then be given to the hundreds of channels or outlets."

As he had once advised Tom Sugrue how to plot his bestseller, *Starling of the White House*, he now counseled others, "Let it be known that that being dispensed comes from such sources, as is verified by those who found in their lives the answer to their problem—and such then becomes then more worthwhile to readers, whether of Snappy Stories or of Sunday School lessons."

In 1956, through an unexpected gift, of the sort that the sleeping Cayce would have understood, the A. R. E. was able to buy back Cayce's old hospital in Virginia Beach—known as the White Elephant—reopen the vaults and begin the analysis of some fifteen thousand readings which apply more than ever today in their broad understanding of the nature of the universe. Today, at A. R. E., the files have been laboriously classified by categories—cancer, arthritis, homosexuality, reincarnation, Atlantis, etc., as recommended by the sleeping psychic. Doctors, archeologists, scientists, oceanographers, and cultists have all found their tasks easier—for Cayce stressed simplicity. "Be able at a glance, from whatever phase of human experience, to have the information in the setting it was presented to that individual. Whether it pertain to marital relations, separating the silt from the gold, or adding to a body that vibration necessary to alter the very fires of nature within the individual itself." It was difficult, perhaps impossible, however, to help those whose intellectuality would not permit them to grasp that which was intellectually inconceivable. "Do not attempt to cast pearls before swine," said the Scripture-minded mystic, "nor give to those who read such as of the fiction of the day."

Many of course did consider reincarnation a pleasant fiction. It was an interesting Cayce concept, though I wasn't at all sure it made life easier to consider still another life on this plane. Reincarnation presupposed some sort of order in a world apparently predisposed to disorder. Still, it was difficult to accept God and believe with the hedonists that there was nothing but the everlasting present and sensual gratification in that present. Theirs was a world without plan, organization, a schemata of any kind. And yet the lowliest bureaucrat, in the pettiest assignment, governed his minuscule activity with some table of organization. Were we to suppose God less capable?

Despite myself, I was intrigued by the small boy who climbed on the Cayce lap, and mentioned their being together on the Ohio during an Indian massacre. That boy, grown to manhood, was serenely unaware of what he had said that day. If regressed, under hypnosis, would his subconscious dredge up a previous life, coinciding with Cayce's own life reading for himself? And would this be evidence for reincarnation? I didn't know, but I supposed some would think so.

Inherently, the value of Cayce seemed to rest in the recognition that his glimpse into the divine purpose of the universe could be shared by all ready to count themselves an infinite part of that infinite universe. Cayce dealt with the mundane and the bizarre, the trivial, and the universal. In his prophecies, he stressed a lesson of courage and resolution in adversity, so that to man at one with Nature even disaster was a manifestation of God's superior, if often unrevealed, purpose. Predicting widespread destruction in New York and California, he still did not take a dark view of the forecast destruction, nor did he think it would help to move around to avoid it. As anybody might, in the circumstances, a concerned religious had asked, "Should California or Virginia Beach be considered at all, or where is the right place that God has already provided for me to live?"

Cayce suggested that his questioner look inside himself for the well-being he was rightly concerned about. "As indicated, these choices should be made rather in self. Virginia Beach or the area is much safer as a definite place. But the work of the entity should embrace most all of the areas from the east to the west coast, in its persuading not as a preacher, nor as one bringing a message of doom—but as a loving warning to all groups, clubs, art groups, those of every form of club, that there needs be, in their activities, definite work toward the knowledge of the power of the Son of God's activity in the affairs of men."

Essentially, as was especially evident in his healing, the Cayce message was one of faith, in self and God. God was not some vague, remote indescribable entity. He was a friend, a companion. He worked through God, and God worked through him. His will was implicit in every wonder that Cayce performed. The sleeping Cayce saw body, mind, and spirit not only as a flowing, electrically vibrant current of blood, lymph, and nerve impulses, but as an entity of faith, hope and charity. The mind, become negative, reacted in dis-ease, which, neglected, became disease.

He did not push anything at anybody. Reincarnation, Atlantis, Lemuria, these were no stranger than his traveling through space to pick out a jar on a drugstore shelf hundreds of miles away, or his description of how a rabbit serum should be prepared against cancer years before medical researchers turned up a similar concept. Not dissimilar from one who had trod the earth two thousand years before, he applied the wisdom of a connected universe to virtually every facet of human thought and behavior. During the war, as so many had, a worried mother consulted him, psychically, because of her concern that her only son, in the Army, might be killed or injured in battle. The mother, already helped by a Cayce health reading, expressed her anxiety over the safety of her son, then stationed in the U.S. "Please give advice, guidance, and help to this confused mind, and answer the questions, as I ask them."

Cayce put the problem on a spiritual plateau, indicating that the over-all cause had to be considered in weighing the mother's private concern. "To be sure, there is built within the consciousness of the entity [the mother] an aversion to strife, to war, and to all phases of military activity. But in an hour of trial, when there are influences abroad that would change or take away that freedom which is the gift of the creative forces to man, that man might by his own innate desire be at-one with God, there should be the willingness to pattern the life, the emergencies, the exigency as may arise, much in the way and manner as the Master indicated to each and every soul. According to the pattern of the life as He gave, one should ever be able and willing, even to lay down the life, that the principles may live as he indicated, that of freedom not only from the fear of servitude, but that the whole earth may indeed be a better place for an individual, for those that are to come to reside in."

In the Christ story, Cayce saw clearly the tribulations of every son of man on the terrestrial plane, climaxed on earth with the Crucifixion. "When He withheld not His own son, how can ye ask Him to withhold thine." There was practical advice. He suggested the mother revise her attitude so that her courage and resolution, her faith, would be transmitted to her son, encouraging rather than depressing him. "So live then, so think, so act in thy conversation, in thy convocation with thy fellow man, that others may know, too, that the Lord walks with thee. Instill that hope, that encouragement in the mind and in the heart of thy son, that he, too, may look to the Lord for strength, for purpose, for sureness; and that in the peace which is to come there will be the needs for his activity among the children of men, that the way of the Lord may be sure in the earth." The earth was the house of the Lord, and Christ, too, had showed anger when it became "a den of those who took advantage of their fellow man." He stressed how Christ's travail could reinforce the woman's own strength. "He, too, brought that knowledge to those that seek His face, that He knows the heartache of disappointment, the heartache of fear, even as He prayed: If it be possible, let this cup pass from me—not my will, oh God, but Thine be done."

After listening to the message she had requested, the mother, apparently missing the prophetic reference to her son's postwar activity, very humanly asked, "Is there any other branch of the service where my son could serve, that would be less dangerous?"

The sleeping Cayce recognized that she had not got the message. "No portion of the service is dangerous," he stressed, "if he is put in the hands of God. Look upon that condition which disturbs—not from a material angle—but from the standpoint of a mental and spiritual blessing to others in the opportunity offered."

There is probably nobody more concerned than a mother about her only son. "Could he be transferred to some post closer to his home?"

"This may be, but is it best? Rather than making the environ by doubts and fears, isn't it better to put it all into the hands and upon the heart of thy Elder Brother, in the hands of thy God?"

"Is it best for him where he is?" she persisted.

"Consider well the Master's answer, No man is in this or that position save by the grace of God."

"Could he better serve in some defense work outside the military service?"

For a brief moment, the sleeping Cayce appeared to lose patience. "If it had been, would not this have been the place? If what has been given is studied, these questions will be answered." And then came the sharp enjoinder. "Fill the place better *where ye are,* and the Lord will open the way." The stressed words were Cayce's. "Only as we are able to realize consciously that we live and move and have our being in *Him,* can we put it all into His hands, and leave it there, doing our duty as we see it from day to day."

The son eventually went overseas, and saw battle service without harm. However, there was a family loss. The father, for whom similar concern had not been shown, died suddenly a year later, at the height of the war. Perhaps Cayce had foreseen this event when he counseled, "Fill the place better where ye are."

The greatest of the American psychics conveniently left a guide on psychic development for those with some of this ability, or for researchers interested in its development. In trance once, he pointed out that the psychic force, traveling through the subconscious, functioned through certain glands. "In the body we find that which connects the pineal, the pituitary, the Leydig, these may be truly called the silver cord." The force was more active in women, whose conscious powers were not as highly developed perhaps, permitting greater development of the subconscious. The higher levels subconsciously would be attained only through a spiritual outlook, an avoidance of the material—a lesson that psychics who have striven for notoriety might well heed. "One fed upon the purely material will become a Frankenstein that is without any influence other than material or mental," he warned.

He saw nothing unusual in the psychic force, pointing out that it was as much a part of the natural talent, as the powers that man drew on to create the ability to fly; it was similar to the inspiration for great works of art, poetry and mathematics, as in the Einstein theory of relativity, that came to the great mathematician "mystically."

Not everybody should develop as a psychic channel, only those capable of providing more understanding of the individual's relationship with the creative forces. The potentiality of a gift like Cayce's was endless. Cayce pointed out many times that Christ, performing his wonders, had said that with the aid of God others could do the same. Cayce, in humility, felt that he himself was merely a reflection of the unlimited scope of human potential, in the continuous struggle to get in tune with the universe he lived in—boundless man trying to find himself in a boundless universe.

In his own apparent boundlessness, there seemed no limit to Cayce's ultimate service, in practical and spiritual areas. As more and more doctors poked into the Information, as researchers worked out of his legacy of readings, it appeared probable that the Cayce fight against infection and disease would mount through the years. In a small way, I had a dramatic experience myself with the wonders of Cayce's therapy. I had developed an irritating hardening of the rim of the outer ear, an excrescence the size of a small pea. It interfered with sleep at night, and became increasingly annoying to the point where I consulted a doctor. He scanned the offending area under the magnifying lens, and said, "Actinic keratosis, a prelude to skin cancer. Nothing very serious, as it's usually localized and can be removed. However, you might check with a dermatologist." The condition had resulted from too much sun.

Instead, I checked with Gladys Davis. "What would Cayce have prescribed?" I asked.

There was no hesitation. "Castor oil. Rub on a little morning and night, alternating with camphorated oil, if you want."

In a spirit of experiment, I did as suggested, while keeping the name of a skin man in the back of my mind.

I put it down to imagination at first, but after twenty-four hours there was a comforting sense of relief. At the end of three days, applying the oil, my probing fingers told me that the thickening of the skin was greatly reduced. At the end of a week, the crustiness was distintegrating and there was no pain. The actinic keratosis, soothed by the camphorated oil mornings, and the castor oil at night, had vanished in six weeks.

What Cayce had done as a mystic might be repeated by another one day, though there was only one Shakespeare, Nostradamus, Da Vinci and Plato, as though to show what man was capable of. Nonetheless, Cayce pointed up the potential of the psychic in more than one way. Once, for instance, he gave a demonstration before the psychology class of a Kentucky school. One of the students, taking advantage of this priceless opportunity, asked the Universal Mind about funds being mysteriously drained away from her father's business in Mississippi. Cayce described the thief, and how the thefts were being managed. Soon, he heard from the student's father. On the basis of Cayce's information, they had grabbed the thief and saved the business. It was trivial, but then life was made up of trivia, and it appeared easier to accept the psychic on this level.

Whenever there was an unusual earthquake, particularly in California, I thought of Cayce. On June 27, 1966, a moderate tremor—5.6 on the Richter scale—hit the Paso Robles area, 175 miles south of San Francisco, and left visible fractures in the earth along a twenty-mile section of the San Andreas fault. The western side of the fault had moved north several inches. And the unusual feature—for California quakes—was that even after the quake the surface cracks seemed to be growing. "I must emphasize," said Louis Pakiser of the National Center for Earthquake Research, "that this is a very rapid movement."

For many, including the Geologist who had a specialized interest, Cayce's upcoming earth changes were perhaps his greatest revelation. However, only the future will tell how accurate the prophet was in his X-ray-like probing of the center of the earth, and its forecast axis tilt. Even now, little is known of the axis on which the earth turns. But, provocatively, bolstering Cayce, some geologists profess that the polar points have wandered through millions of years of time, continually altering the topography and climate of the small speck of the universe known as Earth. From earth borings, from cores and sedimentations, the scientists have established the ages of mountains, lakes, deserts and other areas of the globe. Striking discoveries by recent deep-sea and paleo-magnetic research have made possible recreation of periods millions of years ago, in which it has been surmised life was somewhat similar to our own. More strikingly, most of Cayce's readings on prehistorical life were given in the 1920s and '30s. And all these, available before his death, preceded the scientific finds that have confirmed major aspects of the prehistorical portrait of the changing earth as he gave it. The

Geologist was principally impressed that where recent research often modified, or repudiated, long standardized concepts of geology, it tended rather to strengthen Cayce's psychic readings, a trend that seems to be intensifying with time.

The Cayce key year 1958 has passed, prefacing some earthly fireworks as he suggested, and now 1968, or '69, will soon arrive to test Atlantis rising, though Cayce explained elsewhere that the rise would be gradual, and might not break the surface immediately. After that, who knows? Perhaps the break-ups could be prayed away, as Cayce so often suggested, without such ever materializing. And yet even as a source of destruction was possibly gathering momentum in the crust of the earth, under his very feet, man could still look overhead hopefully for eternal salvation. For as Cayce read so often from Matthew: "Immediately after the tribulation of those days shall the sun be darkened, and the moon shall not give her light, and the stars shall fall from heaven, and the powers of the heavens shall be shaken. And then shall appear the sign of the Son of Man in heaven, and then shall all the tribes of the earth mourn, and they shall see the Son of Man coming in the clouds of heaven with power and great glory."

All one needed was faith—a faith that Cayce had come along to bolster in a time of need.

SPECIAL OFFER: If you enjoyed this book and would like to have our catalog of over 1,400 other Bantam titles, just send your name and address and 50¢ (to help defray postage and handling costs) to: Catalog Department, Bantam Books, Inc., 414 East Golf Rd., Des Plaines, Ill. 60016.

ABOUT THE AUTHOR

Popular author and researcher JESS STEARN has covered a wide range of subjects—from a revolutionary study of male homosexuality in the best-selling *The Sixth Man*, to a fascinating report on prophecy and precognition in the equally best-selling *The Door to the Future*. He is also the author of *The Search for the Girl with the Blue Eyes*, *Edgar Cayce—The Sleeping Prophet*, *Yoga, Youth, and Reincarnation* and *Soulmates*. Mr. Stearn was for many years a prize-winning feature writer for the NEW YORK DAILY NEWS and later an associate editor of NEWSWEEK.

The Association for Research and Enlightenment is a non-profit organization interested generally in parapsychology and its spiritual dimensions—and interested specifically in making practical use of the Edgar Cayce readings. The organization has an open-membership policy and welcomes those of all ages, from all walks of life, from all faiths.

The A.R.E. Library/Conference center is located in Virginia Beach, Virginia, Atlantic Avenue at 67th Street.

If you would like to receive further information, please write to:

A.R.E.
P.O. Box 595
Virginia Beach, Virginia 23451

The Edgar Cayce story is one of the most compelling in inspirational literature. Over the course of forty years, "The Sleeping Prophet" would close his eyes, enter an altered state of consciousness, and then speak to the very heart and spirit of mankind on subjects such as health, healing, dreams, meditation, and reincarnation. His more than 14,000 readings are preserved at the Association for Research and Enlightenment.

Bantam has an entire library of books on Edgar Cayce. See if your bookshelf isn't missing one.

- ☐ 25635 SEX AND THE SPIRITUAL PATH $3.50
- ☐ 25659 REFLECTIONS ON THE PATH,
  Puryear $3.50
- ☐ 25278 EDGAR CAYCE PRIMER,
  Puryear $3.95
- ☐ 23441 EDGAR CAYCE REMEDIES,
  McGarey $3.95
- ☐ 26085 EDGAR CAYCE: SLEEPING PROPHET,
  Stern $4.50

Bantam Books, Inc., Dept. PW3, 414 East Golf Road, Des Plaines, Ill. 60016

Please send me the books I have checked above. I am enclosing $_____ (Please add $1.50 to cover postage and handling.) Send check or money order—no cash or C.O.D.'s please.

Mr/Ms _____

Address _____

City/State _____ Zip _____

PW3—4/87

Please allow four to six weeks for delivery. This offer expires 10/87. Prices and availability subject to change without notice.

EXPLORE THE SPIRITUAL WORLD WITH
SHIRLEY MACLAINE AND JESS STERN

Check to see which of these fine titles are missing from your bookshelf:

Titles by Jess Stern:

☐	26085 EDGAR CAYCE: SLEEPING PROPHET	$4.50
☐	25150 SOULMATES	$3.95
☐	05075 SOULMATES, a Bantam hardcover	$14.95
☐	26057 YOGA, YOUTH, AND REINCARNATION	$3.95

Titles by Shirley MacLaine:

☐	05094 DANCING IN THE LIGHT, a Bantam hardcover	$17.95
☐	25045 OUT ON A LIMB	$4.50
☐	25234 "DON'T FALL OFF THE MOUNTAIN"	$4.50
☐	26173 YOU CAN GET THERE FROM HERE	$4.50

Look for them in your bookstore or use the coupon below:

Bantam Books, Inc., Dept. PW4, 414 East Golf Road, Des Plaines, Ill. 60016

Please send me the books I have checked above. I am enclosing $_____. (Please add $1.50 to cover postage and handling.) Send check or money order—no cash or C.O.D.'s please.

Mr/Ms _____

Address _____

City/State _____ Zip _____

PW4—4/87

Please allow four to six weeks for delivery. This offer expires 10/87. Prices and availability subject to change without notice.